FIFTY
PLAYWRIGHTS
ON THEIR
CRAFT

FIFTY PLAYWRIGHTS ON THEIR CRAFT

CAROLINE JESTER AND CARIDAD SVICH

Edited by Caroline Jester

Bloomsbury Methuen Drama
An imprint of Bloomsbury Publishing Plc

B L O O M S B U R Y
LONDON • OXFORD • NEW YORK • NEW DELHI • SYDNEY

Bloomsbury Methuen Drama

An imprint of Bloomsbury Publishing Plc

Imprint previously known as Methuen Drama

50 Bedford Square	1385 Broadway
London	New York
WC1B 3DP	NY 10018
UK	USA

www.bloomsbury.com

BLOOMSBURY, METHUEN DRAMA and the Diana logo are trademarks of Bloomsbury Publishing Plc

First published 2018

© Caroline Jester and Caridad Svich, 2018

Caroline Jester and Caridad Svich have asserted their right under the Copyright, Designs and Patents Act, 1988, to be identified as authors of this work.

British Library Cataloguing-in-Publication Data
A catalogue record for this book is available from the British Library.

ISBN:	HB:	978-1-4742-5088-7
	PB:	978-1-4742-3902-8
	ePDF:	978-1-4742-3903-5
	eBook:	978-1-4742-3904-2

Library of Congress Cataloging-in-Publication Data
A catalog record for this book is available from the Library of Congress.

Cover design: Louise Dugdale

Typeset by RefineCatch Limited, Bungay, Suffolk
Printed and bound in Great Britain

To find out more about our authors and books visit www.bloomsbury.com. Here you will find extracts, author interviews, details of forthcoming events and the option to sign up for our newsletters.

CONTENTS

ACKNOWLEDGMENTS

We would like to thank all of the playwrights who have been so generous with their time and wisdom in order to make this book possible. We are also grateful to Anna Brewer for her vision to connect both sides of the Atlantic and everyone at Bloomsbury Methuen Drama. Caridad would like to thank Zac Kline and R. Alex Davis for their invaluable work recording and transcribing some of the interviews, and Rachel Dart who has been super with everything; her special thanks go to Christopher Shinn. Caroline would like to thank Micheline Steinberg for continued support.

INTRODUCTION

Caroline Jester

What do you get when you put twenty-five British and twenty-five American playwrights together? Or should that be twenty-five American and twenty-five British playwrights? Not everyone calls themselves a playwright so how can we collect all of these people together in just one book? Shouldn't the theater makers be somewhere else? And how has a poet found her way in here? I think I've just spotted a painter as well, and even some who call themselves "artists who write for live performance." And don't forget the musicians and the screenwriters. That one has moved into the gaming industry; she clearly needs to be removed. You can't be called a "playwright" if you enter the digital world.

But the aim of this book isn't to create chaos and confusion. What all of these "playwrights" have in common is that they write "plays" and need a live audience to experience them.

Caridad Svich and I interviewed fifty playwrights on both sides of the Atlantic over the course of one year that has seen what could be described as a paradigm shift. The United Kingdom is leaving the European Union and the man nobody thought would become the Republican Party's Presidential Candidate is now the President of the United States. Each day brings more talk of division, whether that is debate around how to come out of a single market or building walls around countries. What we hope is that this book will celebrate the diversity that exists in both countries within the craft of playwriting. "Craft" in this book means the skill and understanding the playwrights have in turning their ideas into plays.

There are many divisions within the theater industry and labels that are put on plays and artists that create them. We want to move away from this and put playwrights together who wouldn't usually be found next to each other in one collection.

If theater, as described in this book, has one foot in the past and one in the present with an eye on the future, then an intergenerational dialogue between playwrights could unpick some of the divisions and labels that are created. Given that theater is a dialectical form, don't we need to listen to all perspectives? If this is what playwrights do in their plays, can't we learn from the artform and apply this to the wider conversations around the industry?

All fifty playwrights were asked three core questions:

1 What is a playwright?

2 Does the audience influence your work?

3 How do playwriting and the playwright fit into the digital age of storytelling?

What you won't discover is a definitive answer to any of these questions but "fool" might be one of my favourite answers to question 1. And "the audience" isn't a homogenous group of people either. The relationship each playwright has with their audience differs as greatly as the people who share the finished play. But it is one of the most important relationships because the playwright needs the audience, even if they don't always think about them when they are writing. Can the playwright and their work continue to find a relevance in an age of digital media? It could be argued that, given the events noted above, there has never been a greater need in our very recent history to come together and explore multiple points of view.

Finding a way to structure this book has been difficult. The very act of structuring could be seen as trying to label and categorize the playwrights. Most of the playwrights in this book could easily cross over into other chapters but we had to find a way to focus the conversations. Going back to the craft of playwriting became our starting point and each chapter has a central question.

Chapter 1 tries to find out if the ideas that eventually become the plays start from the same place. How does a playwright know which thought, image, or feeling to follow? Chapter 2 is concerned with how those ideas are structured to become the play, and the extent to which where these are staged influences how they are told. Chapter 3 attempts to gain an insight into the playwright who crosses into other artforms. Do such shifts help or hinder the craft of playwriting, and why is there an assumption that being a playwright comes before any other form of storytelling, that you have to be a playwright before you can be a screenwriter or a poet or a painter? Crossing national borders and the increasing difficulty involved in doing so concerns the next ten playwrights in Chapter 4, not from the perspective of whether they need a visa to see productions of their own work but whether there's something within stories that helps them move more easily through borders than humans? And we end by asking in Chapter 5 whether the playwright should be responsible for anything else other than writing the play.

As you will discover, playwrights like to break rules. Edward Bond was interviewed for the final chapter but didn't follow the structure we were creating for the book of questions and answers. It feels more appropriate therefore to put this interview at the beginning. His play *Saved* was instrumental in the abolition of theater censorship in the United Kingdom and without it, who knows if all of the plays from the playwrights in this book would have ever found an audience? It also feels appropriate to have a playwright lead the conversation. Our roles as "curators" perhaps are now over. And as there are many forms of censorship, Edward Bond's introduction feels almost a call to arms with an eye to what the future could be if we fail to connect with the past, in the present.

There is a short biography at the beginning of each interview to enable you to discover more about each playwright. US spelling and style has been chosen for ease of reading and is broadly reflective of general cultural trends where US English is more widely recognized and utilized. Our vision for this book is to cross as many borders as we can.

I hope you enjoy the conversations as much as Caridad and I have enjoyed the privilege of talking with all of the playwrights. Caridad sums up my feelings about the artform:

There are many kinds of theater, they can all co-exist.
        It's a plural form.
        It is a bastard form, magpie already, hybrid by nature, in a good way, between the church and the whorehouse.
        Anything is possible.

And I hope this book gives you an insight into the plurality of approaches that exist from the fifty playwrights that appear in this one book and who are making theater across the world.

A PLAYWRIGHT'S INTRODUCTION

Edward Bond

Edward Bond is internationally regarded as the UK's greatest and most influential playwright. He is the author of some seventy plays, among them *Saved* (1965), the production of which was instrumental in the abolition of theater censorship in the United Kingdom. His other plays include: *The Pope's Wedding* (Royal Court, 1962); *Early Morning* (Royal Court, 1968); *Lear* (Royal Court, 1971); *The Sea* (Royal Court, 1973); *The Fool* (Royal Court, 1975); *The Woman* (National Theatre, 1978); *Restoration* (Royal Court, 1981); and *The War Plays* (RSC at the Barbican Pit, 1985). His plays have been produced in more than sixty countries. Bond has formed particular relationships with French theater (which led to *The Paris Pentad*) and the Birmingham theater company Big Brum, for whom he has written ten plays.

What is the playwright's role? To create the just society.

Most questions about playwriting can't be answered usefully until it is known what a play is. We are the dramatic species. The human self creates itself by dramatizing itself and society collectively creates a culture by dramatizing its way of living. We live in two systems: the mechanical and the creative. The first is necessary to bare existence, the second to humanness. Nature is mechanical and follows mechanical laws. This is true even of evolution. Animals evolve to care for their own young but not for their species. Only humans do that; it's our morality. Humanness isn't imposed on us by genes. Each of us has to create it. Humans create their self only by creating their species.

Since Reagan and Thatcher there has been a fundamental change. You have to have been adult before the change to know how drastic it is. Thatcher said there is no such thing as society—so there is no community and, it follows, we cease to jointly create our humanity. For the last 400 years we have developed, through wars and peace, a democracy. That is what changed! Now everything is made for a quick sale to create maximum profit. Everything is consumption and entertainment. Without noticing it we have reverted to the "mechanical laws of nature." The market and the banking system operate through these laws, it is a matter of accountancy not morality, and the process is astonishingly mechanical. It lies outside human judgment, which is why there are such enormous unforeseen economic disasters. We try to cling onto our failing humanness. But now we don't live in a democracy, we live in a market.

As a result politics—which is part of the human culture of society—degenerate. The degeneration begins almost as a joke, another form of entertainment—Donald Trump in America and in the UK Boris Johnson. But because politics is part of the way society creates its shared human culture the joke sours and becomes sordid, debased and dangerous. Then what is "bad" becomes "good" and you are lost—you are in the paradoxes of drama. Creativity by definition seeks the "good." But who defines "what" is good? That is the "what" question. It is the easy part and the answer is mainly prudential. But "why" should we do something just because it is good? If the "why" and the "what" were the same, drama would not be possible. Why shouldn't we lynch people or gas Jews? The "why question" makes us human. The mechanical can't answer it; the flood doesn't mind who it drowns. So there is a wholly different sort of question. Why should we do the good? Only drama can sort this out. This produces the difference between theater and drama.

Theater is a market product and produces "acting"; drama doesn't just ask the "why questions" that make us human, but it also "enacts" the answer—because by identifying the right question we create the means of creating the answer we seek. That is unique to humanness—it makes us the dramatic species, as noted above. The "why" question is profound but you can seek it only when you know the answer. The answer is in every human being but it is buried under the subterfuges of survival and the corruptions of living in unjust societies. Drama's one subject is justice. I don't expect Donald Trump to understand this, but the playwright who doesn't has turned his or her back on not only the responsibility but even the craft of playwriting and on humanity in its present crisis. The "why" question comes from the logic of drama—is the logic that makes us human.

Usually drama isn't understood in this way. Instead it's based on remnants of obsolete, mostly nineteenth-century, ideas and performance practices that have become skills. I've written on this at length. I can't repeat it here (and for simplicity I must ignore the historical complications) but I must at least point at it, otherwise everything I say is wasted—I would even dare to say everything in this book would be wasted. Drama comes from the way the infant human mind enters reality before it can speak or have concepts *but is nonetheless already human*. The playwright has to imagine being in this situation, otherwise it is unreachable. The infant identifies itself with reality, it takes itself to be the world. What else could it do? This isn't a matter of self-inflation; it has to do with what later becomes the absolute implacable certainty of great dramatic figures in their moment of decision—and with minor figures when they are confronted by the "why" question, which they answer or fail to answer. The infant is the source of the drama concealed in all forms of play. The infant makes its own self at the same time as it makes human reality. It is the union of self-morality and social morality. The infant judges reality by its experience of pleasure and pain. This judgment is a stage in development unique to humans. The infant is already asking the "why questions," questions asked by Lear, Antigone, Medea, Hamlet. If these characters failed to answer the question, we wouldn't be here now; there would be no civilization. So humanness is the logic of drama, and in its own smaller world the infant must face the profoundest "why" question if it is to be human. It is not a question of the survival of the fittest but the creation of sanity: a characteristic only of humans.

So yes, we are the dramatic species. In the performances of a play, three brains become one: the brain of the audience and the actors respectively, but also of the stage, which thus is the third brain. It is the "site" we, as a society, re-create to represent the reality the infant entered into in order to create humanness. It is the site of the question of what is right and why should we do it. It is a moral arena. It can take place only on the triple stage. Theater has no triple stage. That has gone with the other changes. The most urgent thing playwrights can now do is understand the difference between drama and theater and why they are different. It is also a question for the whole "Institution" of playmaking but because of the market, the "Institution" can't ask it. But playwrights must ask it.

This has nothing to do with the difference between comic and tragic. Drama uses both. Molière's *Don Juan* is a farce that poses questions that even Hamlet wasn't able to ask. Yet Molière finds a fierce answer. The "why questions" produce answers that society bases its culture on. The answers set a way of life. It enables it to use, but be in control of, the mechanical. But when society becomes too complex and contradictory it must create new answers, and they must be in the logic of drama, of humanness. It must create a new drama. The Greeks did this and they became the basis of Western society. The Elizabethans, Shakespeare and his colleagues, did it, and this made the Enlightenment a practical daily activity, turned it into both the cement and the emollient of the modern world. The change is so total we notice it no more than fish notice the sea. The first two great crises in the human species, when humanness had to be re-created if we were to live as a community, were the Greek and the Elizabethan (Renaissance–Reformation), and this is why the Greek and Jacobean dramas still dominate our stage. We are living through the Third Crisis, and the danger is that we have abandoned creativity for the mechanical, and that society is becoming a ghost that wispily haunts the market. By the logic of drama—which is also the logic of human reality—that must fail. It is not that we are lesser people than the creators of the past but rather that we have forgotten the questions and how to dramatize them. In the last forty years, audiences have stopped going to theaters to find their humanity.

In passing I should say that this has nothing to do with the use of modern media. They are still new and their use must be created. Our ancestors did not invent the hammer in order to break glass windows or smash their thumbs. The theater companies that now do the most important work are small and under-funded. In desperate efforts to communicate, some of them turn to documentary about the scandal of our times. But history itself is a documentary, and the subject of documentary remains "what?" Drama must confront the non-mechanical "why?" Both Beckett and Brecht ignore "why?" and become false-market face-savers.

Much of what I've described about the "self" is supported to an astonishing degree by independent scientific and academic research. But the research is not yet used to draw the conclusions of drama. This is because our economy and politics are structurally mechanical. The market is not interested in what is in the bottle; it is interested only in what is *on the label*. The label sells the product. The danger is that theater becomes the label. A few years ago, there were seven or so musicals in the London West End; now there are some twenty. If you recall a brilliant piece of theater you saw years ago, you will have happy memories. You could even hum the tunes as you committed evil. The images of drama are more profound and less pliable. They change you and your life, and wait for you at every crossroads and every corner. Any stranger's face in the street may suddenly confront you with them. Our subservience to the market does not mean that this dramatic power is lost, reduced to the macabre or the sentimental. It remains the human birth right, the human responsibility, because, as I've described, it is the way all infants enter reality and create their self.

I found this again some months ago when I directed a production of *Dea*. What Antigone was for the last century, Medea is for us. Her questions are more radical and almost they are asked even by her children! Most of the cast in *Dea* were young. They were freed from the mechanical directions of authoritarian directors who make theater but not drama because they have become mechanics of the soul. It's how they survive. The actors discovered—or, I should say, created—their own creativity. They owned the triple stage. They were tumultuous but controlled. A critic said they were life-changing. At about this time the UK voted to leave the European Union ("Brexit"—part of the present right-wing slippage). The leader of the main UK party championing Brexit was an admirer of Donald Trump. He even went to America to tell him so. You see how these things hang together: However well you write you cannot escape from the fate of your society, its politics, and culture. Everywhere there are young actors such as those in *Dea*. And the new generations of playwrights are potentially the best there have ever been. These actors and playwrights could turn the Third Crisis into a human glory even greater than the Greeks and Jacobeans did. It is possible. They could save our species. But perhaps the actors and playwrights will never meet, never work together, because the market has easier ways of making profit. If that is so, the change will be as rapid as the other recent changes in society. Plays will not be about their supposed content but about the label on the bottle. Then it will no longer be possible to write plays. The playwright will be extinct.

It doesn't have to happen. We should take responsibility for our craft.

1

WHERE DO IDEAS COME FROM AND HOW DO THEY BEGIN THEIR TRANSFORMATION INTO PLAYS?

Surely playwrights know what they are going to write about before they put pen to paper, or fingertip to keypad? This chapter investigates where they find their ideas and how they follow them on the journey as they become plays. Each writer was asked whether their ideas come from a sudden conceit or if they are more planned. There really doesn't appear to be one clear route to follow.

José Rivera finds it hard to separate inspiration from craft when writing for theater but feels playwrights are always looking for that "riveting metaphor" to help a deepening understanding of our times. He writes plays not to understand himself but rather to understand an idea. It is through the craft of playwriting and the toolkit of conflict, spectacle, language, and story that he carves an idea, or "maps an obsession."

Steve Waters can look back on his body of work and notice the aspects of himself that keep popping in. He believes playwrights carry around instincts and experiences that make them alert to particular stories they want to write about. But he has to wait for those instincts and experiences to come into view. Once he senses character or a scene, everything starts to fall away. But once he imagines place, he can write the play.

Charlene James usually gets an idea from hearing a conversation, watching a documentary, or seeing a headline. It is an impulse, a reaction to something, but the idea needs to sit there and "marinade" before it starts to talk through her characters.

Quiara Alegría Hudes is interested in the inward battles we face and is open to inspiration from anywhere, waiting for the seed that has been planted to take root. She responds to the work of her predecessors as well as witnessing the changing landscape around her. It might be "feng shui," but what are the truths that have been hidden underneath?

Alecky Blythe uses the words of real people to create her plays and seems to follow their lead once an idea has struck. Casting her net as wide as possible before crafting the play ensures an authenticity to the story that doesn't come from a desire to write about an issue. And her dictaphone gives her a license to go to areas she hasn't been before.

Steven Sapp's ideas come from where he is in his life at that time. But he is part of an ensemble, and how ideas develop always begins in collaboration with others. He started in the poetry and open mic scenes in New York City, where there were no rules, and that organic process did not stop when the ensemble "arrived" in the theater scene.

Chris Goode is suspicious of an idea that seems to be complete. He will carry it around with him until something largely unconnected finds a space to lodge inside his head as well. When the differing strands entangle, a traction occurs and an idea begins its journey into a play.

Sylvan Oswald lets ideas stew inside for a long time. And the ingredients that make up the stew are disparate elements that have been chopped, with spices added, sealed in a jar, and buried in a hole. It is ready when it is ready, and thoroughly ingested before giving fuel to the play.

Naylah Ahmed can have a desire to address something that is unpindownable and it can be with her for many years before the writing begins. But how do you unravel what is unpindownable into a play that others can share?

Paula Vogel writes to share her concerns about the world we inhabit and her plays are written with a sense that she is trying to understand what disturbs her. And as a dialectical artform, the responsibility of playwriting is to "explore the gray areas and eschew the black and white."

As you enter the chapter, be ready to be taken on a journey. But there isn't one path to follow. Be open to many twists and turns along the way as ideas emerge and the creative processes begin. As with any creative process, it is usually best to acknowledge that it is a trip into the unknown.

José Rivera

José Rivera won the Obie Award for playwriting for *Marisol* and *References to Salvador Dali Make Me Hot* respectively, both of which were produced by The Public Theater in New York. His other plays include *Another Word for Beauty, Cloud Tectonics, Boleros for the Disenchanted, Massacre (Sing to Your Children), Adoration of the Old Woman*, and *The House of Ramon Iglesia*. Rivera's screenplay for *The Motorcycle Diaries* was nominated for the Academy Award for Best Adapted Screenplay in 2005. His screenplay based on Jack Kerouac's *On the Road* premiered at the 2012 Cannes Film Festival and was distributed nationally in the winter of 2013. His film *Trade* was the first movie to premiere at the United Nations.

Caridad Svich   *What is a playwright?*

José Rivera   Well, the word "fool" is probably a good word. Or as Kerouac would say, "holy fool." A playwright is partly magician, storyteller, plumber, surgeon, and carpenter. In writing theater, it's hard to separate inspiration from craft, and craft is so essential to writing a good play. There's a line from the movie about Steve Jobs—he's asked, "What do you do?" and he says, "I play the orchestra."

Playwrights play the orchestra. And we play the costume department and the lighting department. As we craft plays on the page, we are designing the elements, and we are, in a way, acting coaches as well. We're the ones that have the largest vision of the playmaking activity. In a larger social and political sense, we're called upon to be the canaries in the coalmine—to be several steps ahead of the zeitgeist and the headlines—and to have a sense of the larger movements of the culture, in any one direction or the other. Are we about to head off a cliff, or are we about to have the greatest society ever? We playwrights are supposed to know. I don't think we always do know, but I think we're at least trying to know, or we're attempting to be in tune with those larger forces. Here's an example from Shakespeare. He was writing about the issue of the unity of his country at a time when King James was trying to create Great Britain by unifying Scotland and England. Shakespeare's cleverly chosen metaphor in *King Lear* actually looks at unity's *opposite*. He asks us to consider: "What happens to a kingdom when it falls apart?" As playwrights, we're always looking for that riveting metaphor that deeply helps us understand our time.

Playwrights are stewards of the language. We seek to keep language alive—a fiery, theatrical language that transcends our time and place. In my opinion, language-centered theater is the most exciting theater.

CS *The idea of being stewards of language is interesting.*

JR We specialize in text; that's what playwrights do. We specialize in the written word for the stage. It's a wonderful thing. I'm really proud to be in a tradition that goes all the way back to Aristophanes.

That's not to say that text is not elastic or evolving, as technology evolves, as even the nature of our storytelling evolves, or the needs we have for story change as well. Text will change and be fluid and that's the beauty of it. But ultimately we make plays the way they've always been made: A word at a time, in isolation. Essentially we get in front of some actors, hand out these pieces of paper, then they stand up in front of a bunch of other people and they say the things that you've written, and it's always going to be that way. And there's something antique and kind of sweet and poignant about that. It feels to me that the act of storytelling was created and fixed for all time around the campfire, and we made the campfire cooler and more interesting. But ultimately that's still what we're doing. And the primitive, primal nature of that transaction between storyteller and receiver is encoded in us; its part of us, and it won't ever really change, no matter how much the trappings change. The trappings do change and it's great, but that contract is inviolable.

CS *Does the audience influence your writing?*

JR I would probably be more commercially successful if it did. No, never. I mean, I get mad at an audience sometimes—especially when doing a play with Latino themes and characters in front of a white audience where it can get frustrating because they don't get the jokes, they don't have cultural context, it's exotic to them. And that's a drag but, normally, I honestly don't think about the audience much. If I think about an audience at all, I think about writing for people like myself, not necessarily in terms of economic status or in age, or even in education, but people who are curious and willing to try something new. I believe that, across nations, there is a common artistic culture. You and I could go to Romania and meet some young artists, and we would all love the same books, we'd all dig the same movies and music and painting and TV shows. There is a common world culture, fed and shaped by common forces, and I guess I write to that culture.

CS *A lot of the writers in this book have been talking a great deal in various ways about mapping the self, as writers, when they face the page. Do you live in that world when you face the page? Do you feel "I'm mapping consciousness, I'm mapping myself"?*

JR What I do is endow all my characters with aspects of myself, especially the aspects that are contradictory—so that those contradictions could at least fight with each other. I don't write plays, and maybe I should, to understand myself. I write plays to understand an idea; it might be a passionate idea of mine, but ideas are central. And how those ideas are embodied through character and expressed through the basics: Conflict, spectacle, language, and story. I think all good writers can't help but talk about what's in their soul. I think we are merchants of obsession. We map our obsessions, we dissect them, we analyze them, we put them on the page. And I guess maybe our souls are just one string of obsessions that we're mapping, I don't know.

CS *Theater is civic engagement. The audience walks in, "Oh I'm going to see something." There's an opportunity there to offer transformation to an audience, not transformation through a story but more like, in your lives, there's something here you can then make change.*

JR I think that transformation is a great by-product of the storytelling activity. I don't set out to force that to happen, though. What I set out to do is write a compelling, complicated, original story that will hit an audience hard. If there is transformation, then I'm very happy, believe me. But I don't hold out a lot of hope that it happens very often. I think we can move an audience. I think we can get them to think about something they hadn't thought about before. But it may not happen the way you expect it to. For instance, we did *Marisol* at Hartford and I was walking out with the audience and I heard someone saying, "Oh, we better pay our credit card bills." So that's what they got out of it.

CS *For them!*

JR That was it! That was the transcendent moment for them. And sometimes you go, "Well, I guess that's the best I can hope for." On the other hand, some people will see your one-act play and their lives will change forever. By something you may have scribbled in twenty minutes. You never know. And to me, the beauty of doing any kind of theater anywhere is the potential and the unpredictability of fostering change. For instance, we did *Another Word for Beauty* for Chicago school groups. For two days, we performed for 800 inner-city public school kids. And I can bet you we changed lives. I know we did. They saw theater do things that they never imagined possible. True, the play featured a reggaeton contest and a lot of skimpy costumes.

CS *Which is fun.*

JR Yes, which is all fun, all cool, and all part of the experience. But I can't imagine they had ever known theater to be that way. I had the same experience when I was younger—I didn't know about theater's potential until I saw *Buried Child* by Sam Shepard in the 1970s. I would bet my house that we moved and changed some people in Chicago in those two days, forever.

CS *How do playwriting and the playwright fit into the digital age of storytelling?*

JR We tell and transmit stories digitally now—hardly anyone makes a film on film anymore. But as I was saying, the very primitive nature of storytelling is analogue, it's not digital. It'll never be digital, unless we find a way to shortcut the human brain. I think digital technology is another tool in the toolbox, and a valuable one, and I think it'd be great for a playwright to exploit those tools and at least seem relevant to other people . . . so let's at least pretend relevance. I'm not afraid of technology; I don't lament its ubiquity in our society at all. But I do feel that these are means to an end. The end hasn't changed. The end is: I, the storyteller, want to illicit awe in you the listener, to take you someplace you've never been to before. I want to expand your mind. I want to frighten you. I want you to fall in love. I want to elicit terror and compassion. That's what I want. Now, how I get there is a matter of the choices we have regarding the various technologies that exist. It's a matter of the evolution of the stage in America and elsewhere. But those primitive impulses are what's really important to me.

Steve Waters

Steve Waters' plays include *Limehouse* (Donmar Theatre, directed by Polly Findlay); *Temple* (Donmar Theatre, directed by Howard Davies, 2015); *Europa* (co-authored) (Birmingham Rep/Dresden Staatspielhaus/Teater Polski/Zagreb Youth Theatre); *Ignorance / Jahillyyah* (Hampstead Theatre Downstairs 2012); *Little Platoons,* "*Capernaum*" in *Sixty-six Books* (both Bush Theatre, 2011); *Amphibians* (Offstage Theatre Co; Bridewell Theatre, 2011); *The Contingency Plan* (On the Beach and Resilience; Bush Theatre, shortlisted for 2009 John Whiting Award); *Fast Labour* (Hampstead Theatre/West Yorkshire Playhouse, 2008); *World Music* (2003; Sheffield Crucible/Donmar, 2004); *English Journeys* (1998); and *After the Gods* (2002) (both Hampstead Theatre).

Future projects include an adaptation of Giles Foden's *The Last King of Scotland* (Paulden Hall Productions) and new commissions with Hampstead Theatre and the Michael Grandage Company.

Work for radio includes: *Deep Swimmer* (Boz Temple-Morris for BBC R4, 2016); *Scribblers* (BBC R3, 2015); *Bretton Woods* (BBC R3, 2014); *The Air Gap*, about Bradley Manning (Saturday Play BBC R4, 2012); *Little Platoons* (BBC R4 Saturday Play, 2011); *The Contingency Plan* (Radio 3, 2009); *Morning* and *The Parliament of Rooks* (both Fact to Fiction, BBC R4); and *The Moderniser* (BBC R4).

For the screen, Steve has written a version of *The Contingency Plan* (*Safe Plan,* BBC4) and is developing TV dramas with Forge Entertainment.

After running the Birmingham University's MA in Playwriting for five years, Steve is currently Head of Scriptwriting at the University of East Anglia. He is the author of *The Secret Life of Plays* (Nick Hern Books). Steve's plays are all published by Nick Hern Books also.

Caroline Jester *What is a playwright?*

Steve Waters Well, obviously it's somebody who writes plays—that's one side, that's self-evident—but also what's quite interesting about that is when you categorize yourself as one. I remember doing the MA in Playwriting at Birmingham University many years ago, and we had big debates about whether we were allowed to call ourselves playwrights until we earned money from writing plays. I think I came to the conclusion that actually if you want to call yourself a playwright, you can call yourself a playwright; nobody can stop you. Clearly you don't also just have to write plays: It's not an exclusive term because you can write screenplays, novels, short stories, all sorts of transactional documents—you don't have to be only a playwright.

My mind and my imagination, if you like, go toward constraint in storytelling rather than freedom. I suppose that's one way of thinking about being a playwright because you're writing for a medium that has inbuilt constraints, which I think create pressure, and which then dynamize stories in an interesting way. So if you feel like you tend to condense story into a very intense moment, then I suspect you're more of a playwright than a novelist.

I also think you tell stories through other people. There's a degree to which it's a form of writing [that is] by definition focused on others and voices and people that are not you. I think that's probably true of other fiction, but it's particularly true of playwriting.

CJ *That's fascinating, the first point you made about whether you can call yourself a playwright, about the professionalization of the word.*

SW Well, if you call yourself a doctor you could end up in court, but no one has been sued for being a playwright imposter as far as I'm aware.

CJ *Does the audience influence your writing?*

SW I think they must influence your writing; probably you would write differently if you weren't ultimately aware that your work would be in the presence of an audience. One example I've definitely learned as I've written plays is that it's absolutely of no point to say something in the play that the audience won't understand. So it doesn't matter if they don't initially understand, that's absolutely fine, but if they leave the theater still not understanding it, be it a word or a reference, then what the hell have you achieved? And in a sense that's a really difficult one because when I was doing *Temple*, one of the actors suggested that I should clarify who the Archbishop of Canterbury was, that no one would know who Rowan Williams was. I sort of refused to do that: I felt I had certain expectations of my audience that they are not coming in like newborn babies every night knowing nothing at all. On the other hand, why should I assume they would know something that has taken me quite a lot of time and labor to find out for myself? I certainly don't sit down and think, "how am I going to pleasure an audience? What will they find amusing?"

CJ *Do your ideas come from a sudden idea or conceit or are they more planned?*

SW Well, it depends how you categorize an idea. If I look back on the last twenty years' work, I do feel like I'm still interested in all the things I've written about. I wouldn't necessarily have written the plays again, but when I look back I think that there are things that are obviously part of who I am that keep popping in. You're carrying around instincts or your experience, which make you alert to particular stories or something you want to write about.

You catch me right now as I'm embarking on, I hope—I always start off in a pessimistic way—writing a play about trade unions. And I've been thinking about doing that for a very long time actually, and waiting for the contacts and the person to work with and the theater that's interested, the opportunity. Then I turn myself to it and think, "why on earth do I want to do it? And what on earth is interesting about it?" I go and spend some time reading lots of stuff and getting bored and annoyed about it, and now I'm waiting for the experiences and the encounters that are really going to enliven that. But yesterday I was doing some reading and suddenly I felt like I could sense the story coming into view, and that suddenly everything starts to fall away and you can see in it, you can see the scene, you can see the characters. You're looking for something where you can see the people and see the struggles, and I think I found that yesterday; probably today it'll go away again.

CJ *In your book on playwriting,* The Secret Life of Plays, *you write about plays staging behavior and revealing rooms, and what's inside those rooms and the relationship the characters have with those objects. And I started thinking about your play* Temple, *which is a play set in a room in St. Paul's Cathedral that is out of bounds to the general public. Yet through your play we get an entrance into that room. I'm thinking of location and narrative here; how important was this room in developing the narrative for that play and did the idea come from the Cathedral or the protests or somewhere else?*

SW You've hit the nail on the head, really, because once I can imagine place, I can write a play. So everything in *Temple* comes out of that room and its location with St. Paul's bearing down upon it. And St. Paul's Cross round the corner, and all the history of the city of London like a route underneath it, feeling that something reaches back into the past and forward into the future. As soon as you've got the room, you know the premise for the play.

If there is a theme in my work, then I am quite an environmentally influenced writer. I am interested in those questions that naturalism first raised that we are products of materially influenced detail, we are expressed by our situation and our environment. Obviously we shape those things, but we're also shaped by them. Theater says that quite clearly, way before naturalism. I think it goes way back to classical theater, Oedipus before the palace, or every one of those tragedies where place is chosen so brilliantly. I think much of the work is to find that resonant space and to work out how it functions. It could be outdoors but you've got to know how to get there, how to get out of it. It's where all the story comes from. I mean when the Dean leaves Chapter House at the end of the play, he's walking out at the end of his career in a way, at the end of that chapter. So the exit becomes relevant.

CJ *I was reading that you don't especially like your two plays that make up* The Contingency Plan *being described as a "double bill" about climate change because it is too complex to be spoken about as if it were an issue. We often hear the term "issue-based drama," but what is your definition of an issue and how should we talk about climate change then? What's the difference between a play and an issue-based play?*

SW Yes, good question. Well I think we've probably all seen perhaps what I'm alluding to, where something is only an issue, and the play arrives for the issue and remains intact throughout the play as an issue, remains in people's mouths as an issue, is passed around as an issue, and doesn't really affect anything at all. It just hovers in the play. I think that's what I guess one's getting at. But if we have themes I always feel slightly different about that, I don't know why. But the idea of a play not being about something is a play I'd not like to go and see, frankly, even if it was incest or passion or whatever. Everything is about something, but sometimes when it's politically about something, that's seen as reductive. And of course it can be, but it might not be, and I suppose that's what one's trying to avoid with the issue question. And perhaps with climate change, what I was getting at there is that it's like a "super issue." I mean the issues like trade union legislation, the minimum wage, or the right to have an abortion, those are things we can see as issues, they have existential meaning behind them, particularly so abortion, for obvious reasons. But they're quite isolable: You can pin them down; you can look at what they mean in society. With climate change, you can talk about it politically, philosophically, artistically, geographically—there are so many languages even to just describe it and what it means . . . it's global, there's no escape from it, it's everywhere and nowhere at the same time. You'd never capture that; it's like capturing a whale in a teaspoon. You can't grab hold of that thing; it's far too big for any one art work to be satisfactory about it. I think it's why *The Contingency Plan* was two plays. If you're clever you could subdivide the things it's about: It's about English political inadequacies relative to climate change, it's about a crisis of scientific knowledge; those sorts of things are perhaps more what the play is about. It came with the sense of "here's a play about climate change" when we were talking about it, but there wasn't actually any artistic representation of it. And it came in as if it was some sort of definitive statement about it, which it couldn't possibly be.

CJ *How do playwriting and the playwright fit into the digital age of storytelling?*

SW Well, I'm probably the least well-placed person to answer that question; I barely exist in the digital world of storytelling, but I think it's going to be more necessary. I get profoundly disturbed by what I see on public transport as I wander round this country, people not being where they are but somewhere else at all times. I think that looks very different from a bunch of people you see in a theater watching a play, which looks like people who are very human and alive watching other people who are really human and alive. So my feeling is that we need theater and playwriting more than ever, actually. And I do feel that people get that when they go and see a good play. We all have to acknowledge that going to see a bad play is the worst possible experience you can have and then we probably would prefer to be playing computer games. But in a way that's because when it is very good, it is an extraordinary experience.

Charlene James

Charlene James is an award-winning playwright and actor who trained at Birmingham School of Acting in the UK and The School at Steppenwolf, Chicago. She has been part of the Royal Court Young Writers' Programme, one of the 503Five at Theatre503, and Writer-in-Residence at the Birmingham Rep, where her play *Tweet Tweet* premiered. Her play *Cuttin' It* was awarded the Alfred Fagon Award, the George Devine Award, and Best New Play UK Theatre Award, as well as a BBC Audio Drama award for the radio adaptation. It was a Young Vic/Royal Court co-production with Birmingham Repertory Theatre, Sheffield Theatre, and The Yard Theatre. She is a Jerwood New Playwright 2016.

Caroline Jester   *What is a playwright?*

Charlene James   In its simplest form, it's someone who writes plays. A playwright is a good storyteller: Someone who takes a story they are compelled to tell and structures and shapes it from beginning to end. It's somebody who has an understanding of theater and writing for live performance as opposed to screen, as there is a difference between writing for the two mediums.

CJ   *Does the audience influence your writing?*

CJames   Yes, I think so, because when you're sitting down and writing it, you've always got the questions that you want an audience to ask. So it's about shaping it to think, "OK, how do I want an audience to feel at this point?" Or "what do I want them to take from it? What do I want them to be asking when they leave and get on the train and talk about in the bars?"

CJ   *Do your ideas come from a sudden idea or are they more planned?*

CJames Usually I will get an idea from maybe hearing a conversation, watching a documentary, or seeing a headline, so I guess in that way it's a sudden thing because you just get an impulse—"oh that's really interesting, I want to explore that more." I think it's harder to sit down and plan to find an idea of what to write about, to pick a theme about love or a play about homelessness, because I don't think that's as organic.

CJ *So it's a reactive process.*

CJames I think you've got to have a sudden reaction to something and go, "that's something I want to write about," but then it kind of marinades for a while as opposed to just going, "oh OK, what's relevant now, what should I be writing about, what themes are out there?"

CJ *Your play* Cuttin' It, *which is about female genital mutilation, it was an article you read about this that triggered a reaction in you that you had to write about it.*

CJames I watched a documentary by Leyla Hussein called *The Cruel Cut* on Channel 4 and I was just kind of blown away by it because I didn't realize there were different types of FGM, or that women could endure lifelong suffering from emotional and physical pain. I didn't know I wanted to write about it after watching the documentary, but I had a gut reaction to find out more. So I did a lot of research on it, I watched videos of girls being cut—those images will never leave my head. A lot of the research I did came from girls being cut in Somalia and other African countries, and then I read an article about girls in Scotland being cut and I just knew that if girls were being cut in Scotland, they were being cut in Birmingham, they were being cut in Bristol, they were being cut in London. And I think this was when I knew I had to write about it, because when it's closer to home, when it's happening down the road from you, it's harder to ignore.

I knew that I wanted the play to be from a young girl's perspective. We see that image of the older woman with the razor in her hand and I thought let's challenge that; what if it is a young girl who is assisting with the cutting, and what if it's happening here as well? How do you react when you know that it's happening in the tower block next door to you? So I had two characters and I knew that one was definitely going to be a British character who would talk like the girls on the bus and the girls I'd grown up with, and then the other one, we don't quite know her story and she might be a little bit further away from us, but she's trying hard to integrate into society. I wanted it to be almost like pages of a diary. These girls are sharing intimate moments with the audience and are intended to make you feel that after hearing them; you have to get up and do something about it because they can't, but you can.

When I was telling people I was writing about female genital mutilation, you kind of see them go, "oh God, it's going to be preachy, it's going to be a lecture," and I've seen work like that as well. It's great that you're trying to get this message across but I don't want to be talked at, I don't want to be preached to. I wanted to come to it from a different angle. So I think it's about having characters that are relatable, who you can at first laugh with and then cry with. It's about caring for them and then discovering that they have this secret, and you're so invested in these characters that you feel compelled to help them.

CJ *And another approach, which is really interesting looking at your work, is that you're working with RADA.*

CJames Yes, I wrote a play for graduating students at RADA with Tiata Fahodzi, who are an African theater company looking at the British African experience. We felt it was really important that actors of color are given the opportunity to play diverse roles on stage so that audiences of color feel represented when they go to the theater. It was great to be able to sit down with the actors and hear about the roles they'd like to play if given a chance. Then I went off and wrote it. I had a really short time frame, which is something that's quite new to me. With *Cuttin It*, I hadn't been commissioned to write it so I could really let it breathe and really tackle it.

CJ *How long did you have?*

CJames I think it was about three months to write, and usually it takes me about that time to do a bit of research and let an idea begin to germinate. So I wrote something and handed it in, and the feedback was that it was slightly stereotyped and something that had been seen before. I agreed that we could get something better, so I had about a month to either work at it or write something completely new.

CJ   *And did you write something new in a month?*

CJames   Yes, I wrote something completely new, and it was great because it might not be the most polished thing that I've ever done but I think it achieved what we set out to do. And it was helpful knowing the actors beforehand so you have the choice to be able to write with them in mind. I remember being in the first read-through and looking round the room at four actors of color taking on characters that were about more than just their color, and that challenged what they might be typecast as. Hopefully they'll be able to tell more of those stories when they graduate.

CJ   *And I read that this was also your experience at drama school.*

CJames   It was interesting that I'd left drama school ten years ago, and I was having some of the same conversations with the RADA students that I was having back then. It's been ten years, surely something should have changed? So it was a really nice opportunity for me to go, "well, actually, there are four actors of color who I can just write for and not think about any of that; let's just write for them."

CJ   *How do playwriting and the playwright fit into the digital age of storytelling?*

CJames   There is such a high quality of drama on TV nowadays, drama that we can download and watch instantly from the comfort of our own homes. We can turn it off and search for something else if we are bored. And we are bored easily. I think theater gives you that chance to immerse yourself in a live experience that's unlike any other medium. I think we need to make sure theater is accessible to all, though, as it can be quite elite. Theater can be expensive. I go to the theater a lot: I try and go at least once a week, and sometimes you have to go in the preview period because that's when it's cheaper. You can be looking at £60 a ticket. For me to pay £60, for me to come out of my house and invest in an evening, it has to be good, [so] you start to scrutinize things a lot more. Some theaters are great with offers and discounted tickets, and you can go to the cinema and see the stuff the National Theatre Live are doing, and other theaters are starting to stream their work too. I think that's a great alternative because I can't get to Scotland, but if they're streaming stuff, I think that's a good way to keep up with the digital age. I grew up on theater at the Birmingham Repertory Theatre and people sometimes forget that outside London, theater is just as engaging. Just take these stories out to people who don't know this is happening. I'd love more of that sharing work within theaters across the UK.

Quiara Alegría Hudes*

Quiara Alegría Hudes is a playwright, strong wife, and mother of two, Distinguished Professor at Wesleyan University, barrio feminist, and native of West Philly, USA. Hailed for her work's exuberance, intellectual rigor, and rich imagination, her plays and musicals have been performed around the world. They are: *Water By the Spoonful*, winner of the Pulitzer Prize for Drama; *In the Heights*, winner of the Tony Award for Best Musical and Pulitzer finalist; *Elliot, A Soldier's Fugue*, another Pulitzer finalist; *Daphne's Dive*; *The Good Peaches*; *Miss You Like Hell*; and *The Happiest Song Plays Last*. Hudes is a Playwright-in-Residence at Signature Theatre in New York; the Profile Theatre in Portland, Oregon, has dedicated its 2017 season to producing her work.

Caridad Svich   *What is a playwright?*

Quiara Alegría Hudes   Someone who dedicates her heart, days, and home to creating a long body of theatrical work. Someone who limits herself to conversation as the lone artistic tool of expression. A transcriptionist, a wind catcher, a composer with words, a lover, and indicter of messy humans. A lonely masochist kept company by the voices in her head. Not so much a manipulator of characters for her own dramatic purposes—but a cowgirl who can lasso her way onto the charging horse of a character mid-stride.

The role of a playwright is profound, sacred, and obscene. I did not choose this profession to feel comfortable or to be adored. I chose it to go deep, to expose my contradictions, to scream and thrash, to indict and sanctify, to make an ass of myself, and to find the music and humanity in that endeavor. I am interested in the contradictions we face within our own hearts. The inward battles. The multitudes. When I get

---

* Interview reproduced with the kind permission of the author and their legal representation.
© Quiara Alegría Hudes 2017.

confused, my agent centers me by saying, "What do you want to do? What does your heart tell you?" My mother centers me by reminding me about things like dignity, humility, and thunder.

CS *Does the audience influence your writing?*

QH Yes and no. I believe what Albee said—a playwright is not a servant. You must not alter your core vision based on an audience's reaction. Additionally, audiences differ—city to city, production to production, sometimes night to night. So if you write solely to suit the audience, you'll be chasing your tail. That being said, I study them very closely—where they laugh, where they lean in, where they "go fishing" in their minds. To me, the most telling kind of audience reaction is the electric silence—when you can feel them stop breathing for a moment. If I find myself in agreement with an audience's reaction, then I will rewrite.

CS *Where do playwrights find the ideas that become the stories and narratives within their plays?*

QH A combination of living life, recording its strange happenings and cadences in your mind, mindfulness, and daydreaming. Inspiration can come from anywhere—an overheard conversation, a news story, an accident, a coincidence, a social agenda, a grudge, or disappointment or sadness. All of these things are like seeds—planting themselves in our hearts, sometimes taking root and sprouting, other times yielding nothing. Every once in a while life catches you off guard and serves you up an unexpected thing that sparks your imagination—Joyce Carol Oates referred to this as a lit match dropped into a tank of gasoline. One day I was listening to Bach preludes and fugues, and suddenly it occurred to me that the music matched perfectly with the war play I had been thinking about for a few months. It was a confluence of disparate interests, in that case, that became *Elliot, A Soldier's Fugue.*

Place is important to me. I am asked sometimes if what I see onstage is comparable to what I had seen in my mind. I rarely *see* things. But I hear them, and I have a deep sense of place when I write. I know the air quality of a community, the temperature in the room of a house; I know how tense or loose a city block is. I know if that block has stoops or porches. I know how fast or slow people walk in a community. I know if the stairs creak in a house. I know how a kitchen smells.

I am continuously informed by the work of my predecessors and contemporaries. Baldly so. I have a character, and a revelation, that are direct responses to August Wilson. Here I'm referring to Lefty in *The Happiest Song Plays Last*. That's an August Wilson homage; it's me playing with his ideas that hit home the most. The end of *Happiest Song* is me grappling with *Joe Turner*'s ending. Especially the need for blood sacrifice and blood-letting.

I have structures that are arguments with *Angels in America*. Here I'm thinking of the plate-spinning I do in *Water by the Spoonful*, balancing multiple worlds. I studied how Tony Kushner approached it. Of course, *Angels* is his gloss on Shakespearean structure, and *Spoonful* is influenced by that bard as well.

Right now I'm working on a new one, *Daphne's Dive*. I exchanged early drafts with Amy Herzog and encountering the unflinching integrity of her naturalist dialogue reminded me to scrutinize my own work-in-progress by those standards. Every moment must be real. And in her case (and mine), when that reality is broken, it should feel shocking.

I use musical structures, too. Most notably in *Elliot, A Soldier's Fugue*, where I'm thinking: How can I dramatize three lives in relief against each other, much in the same way that a theme plays with and against itself in Bach's fugues?

CS *So, forgive me for asking, but those of us that identify as Latinx or hybrid Latinx playwrights deal with this all the time, and I just want to hear you weigh in on the "magic realism" box many of us are put in, in terms of the way we approach theatrical form and content as individual artists.*

QH I've been hearing the phrase "magic realism" less and less, and for me it's a good riddance. It was used a lot to describe my work when I entered the field, and it always struck me as colonial and condescending. "Magic" is not an accurate term for spiritual or sensual or colorful or ritual. "Magic" is a guy pulling a rabbit out of a hat. It's a limited concept in American English. Whereas grappling with ancestry, with palpable metaphor, with dramatized inward states, with possession—all of those things are *real* in a story.

In my early plays, I grappled with the legacy of Santería I inherited from my mother, who is a priestess/santera. I wrestled with ritual in particular—how it embarrasses us, exposes us, jolts our senses. I was drawn to the ritual language used—vibrant and jolting, and disturbing and strange. I witnessed animal sacrifice as a child, which was terrifying, but I couldn't look away, either. I also witnessed adults being possessed—also terrifying, marvelous, strange, and real. This was a big legacy I had to grapple with. I listened to Emilio Barretto's *Santissimo* and wrote plays directly addressing the fascinating contradictions I found in these practices.

I'm now entering a stage where I'm thinking about chaos and anarchy. I'm a child of the 1980s. I grew up in [a place where] silence = death. I grew up when crack was ravaging entire city blocks. There wasn't gentrification. Philly's streets were a mess. The murder rate was high. AIDS was a plague. Keith Haring was spray-painting walls. Cities were dangerous. There was chaos everywhere. This was the moment *right before* the NEA was defunded—a massive victory for the "cleanliness" of right-wing USA. That turning point led to what I see as a new era for us culturally. The moment we're in, to me it's defined by the magazine *Real Simple*, or *Martha Stewart Living*. Everything is *feng shui* now. Cities have been cleaned up and gentrified. Big box stores are *de rigeur*. Pottery Barn is the home decor of the American dream. Everything looks nice and slick. The Container Store has healed our broken spirits. It's a mask. It all looks so good and nice and orderly, we can pretend that the darkness is all gone.

Then along comes Black Lives Matter to remind us: This is criminal. It's a facade. It's a lie. We've gotten very good at sweeping shit under the rug—but it's there, stinking and rotting.

I keep returning to this order versus chaos dichotomy these days. I keep thinking about the aesthetics of it. The aesthetics of safety and danger. I think I will be writing about it soon.

CS *You hold a unique position as someone who works in music-theater as well as non-music theater, in addition to being someone who has worked on projects that have had commercial life like* In the Heights—*and the author of a children's book too—an entirely different platform for a playwright.*

aywrights must be hustlers. How will we keep the lights on other wise? There has to be some basic instinct for business. In my case, my stepfather, Mercedes "Sedo" Sanchez, is an entrepreneur in Philadelphia. I related to how he had multiple projects going at once. How he took pride in employing people in our community, offering jobs, erecting buildings where there had been an eyesore vacant lot. These are all things I do as well, just with words. I've created many roles for actors of color. Is this an accident? Of course not. Each role was a choice, a thrilling and delicious morsel of activism.

I put no limits on who those stories speak to. Though I'm baffled by urban theaters who don't show interest in the communities beyond their familiar comfort zone. It's 2015. I can't help but fume at (or at least regret) a New York or Philly theater with a homogenous audience.

But that's actually a skewed view of audience. Plays are documents as well, and this is where "audience" becomes wildly diverse. How did I get absorbed in theater? Reading *Death of a Salesman*—for free—at the Philadelphia Public Library. Producing a play costs a lot. Reading one costs a little, or nothing. My plays have been taught at Community Colleges around the country. They've been taught at military academies. These are my audiences, too. These are my people, too.

CS *We are in an age of rampant inequity. Many people around the world feel like "nobodies." Where do you see reflected in theater the strength of, and the necessity to, tell the story of those who feel they are such?*

QH There are many examples. The school children in *Sarafina!* The employees in *The Flick*. The idea of the powerful nobody is not unique to theater. Rosa Parks sat down on a bus. Malala wrote that girls should read books. These are simple acts. It is their smallness which makes them thunderous. I think women have had to use the strategy of smallness because it's what they're allowed. I think of a story about Dolores Huerta—at early United Farm Workers meetings, there was a lot of sexist language being used by the leadership. Did she quit? Did she curse them all to hell? She simply wrote down every sexist comment that was said, and at the end of the meeting, when it came time for new business, she read the list aloud. No accusations, just verbatim quotes.

At the next meeting she did the same thing and found that the list of sexist comments was about half as long. Again, in her kind voice, she read the list aloud to the men who had said the things. Pretty soon, there was nothing on the list. In her small way, she had helped people realize their own assumptions and ingrained behaviors. There is profound power in humility. As I was taught, humility does not mean letting oneself be insulted or slighted. It is a strong value and a useful tactic.

CS *How do playwriting and the playwright fit into the digital age of storytelling?*

QH It provides a rich new form of conversation—text messages, chat rooms, tweets. All of these are changing language in dynamic ways, giving us new palettes to work with.

Alecky Blythe

Alecky Blythe is a playwright and actress. In 2003 she set up Recorded Delivery, a verbatim theater company, creating and appearing in her own work. Her first show, *Come Out Eli*, at the Arcola transferred to Battersea Arts Centre and won the Time Out Award for Best Production on the Fringe 2004. Also for Recorded Delivery, she wrote and performed in *All the Right People Come Here* at the New Wimbledon Studio and *Cruising* at the Bush Theatre. As a writer her plays include: *Strawberry Fields* (Pentabus, National Tour); *A Man in a Box* (Channel 4); *I Only Came Here for Six Months* (British Council, Brussels); *The Girlfriend Experience* (Royal Court, The Drum and Young Vic); *Do We Look Like Refugees?!* (Rustaveli Theatre, Georgia and The Assembly Rooms, Fringe First Award 2010); *Where Have I Been All My Life?* (New Vic); *The Riots: In Their Own Words, The Rioters* (BBC 2); and *London Road* (National Theatre, Critics Circle Theatre Award 2011 for Best Musical). *London Road* has been adapted for film (BBC Films/ Cuba Productions) and was released in 2015.

Caroline Jester   *What is a playwright?*

Alecky Blythe   That's a very good question because I struggled for a while to call myself a playwright, as all my plays are from other people's words that I've collected and edited. Then the director I worked with, Matthew Dunster, pointed out to me that "playwright," being spelt the same way as "shipwright," actually means "play-maker" rather than writer in the traditional sense. So I thought that's absolutely what I am. So for me it crosses over into creator and a play-maker.

CJ   *Does the audience influence your writing?*

AB   I've become more aware of an audience with success and I try to fight that because I don't necessarily think it's helpful. Probably, when I was starting out I was working in a much more instinctive, freer way.

There might have been less craft there in terms of storytelling, but it was very instinctive. I have to encourage myself to trust my instincts because they've always served me well in the past.

CJ *Do your ideas come from a sudden idea or conceit, or are they more planned?*

AB It's not really one or the other; they come from all different areas. It might be something that I read about in the paper, see on the news, or even an idea or subject that a producer suggests to me. But once I act on them, they tend to come together in quite unbound fashion. When I start to develop that idea, I don't have too much of an agenda and cast my net quite wide so that I'm led by the people I talk to rather than know I want to write a play about the terrible effects of fracking or something. I will go into it more open-minded and the story will develop as the interviews go along.

CJ *Every play is unique but is there something you look for, whether it's an event you can pin the interviews to?*

AB It helps enormously if you have an event that you can structure your interviews around as it provides a point of focus. However, I've tried to keep exploring different settings and scenarios. I discovered that if you have strong enough characters who have clear objectives, as I found with both *Cruising* and *The Girlfriend Experience* for example, then you need not be limited to creating purely event-based narratives.

One element that I try to incorporate in all my work is to capture scenes on tape that are active; verbatim can often be very static. One way of getting round that is to gather your interviews in situations that have action within them. Rather than you going to interview somebody about a party, for example, you want to go to the party. By going to the party itself, you will get a much truer representation of what the party was actually like rather than someone telling you about it a week later in the comfort of their living room. Inevitably there will always be retrospective material, which is fine if it's brought to life with enough other more active material recorded in the present. Of course, it's not possible to be present at every single key moment in a story, so there will always be moments talked about in the past, but I try to keep those to a minimum. Fundamentally, it's about sniffing out situations you know will lend themselves to some kind of buoyant chat rather than trying to set up a formal interview.

CJ *I'm thinking of* Cruising, *where the framework of the action is of the friend getting married, so it's a reaction to something.*

AB Yes it is, although that wasn't actually the starting point. The starting point of that was the central character, Maureen, who had been a small part in *Strawberry Fields* in a rough-cut presentation. When we did the play for real she was cut from the final play; she was a little bit off message even though she was a gorgeous character and wasn't part of the central narrative. So I went back to tell her, "I have to cut you from the final show," and she said, "Oh, let me tell you about my cruises." So two hours later I thought, "OK, I think this is the beginning of another play." The idea was that I would interview her and she'd put me in touch with various people she'd been on dates with. And then wanting that present tense action again, she was a real sport and agreed to record one of the many blind dates she went on. We made sure her date was happy about the recording beforehand. It was a great moment in the show to suddenly be at the date with her. I thought the ending was going to be when she finally found the new love of her life and of course, in reality, her best friend gets married and she ends up getting a cat. In a way it's a bit clichéd isn't it, old lady gets a cat. If you wrote that as a writer I think the theater would go, "oh, it's a bit of a cliché," but when it's true, it's true, and with verbatim there's so much detail in there [that] it stops it from ever being a cliché.

CJ *There must be a trust that you set up and develop in the interview process that certain people feel open to you going back to them.*

AB Yes, so much is about trust. The more I want to stretch things and push the narrative, the more of a challenge that is. I can see that in the work that I'm doing now. I'm hungry for making things have a stronger narrative, so it is very important that people trust me. I had to choose the right moment to explain the musical dimension to the London Road residents. I think if I'd said that from the beginning they probably would have said, "sorry, love," as I can see the idea does sound a little odd, initially. However, after building good relations with them, I had earned their trust enough for them to be surprisingly open to the idea.

CJ *I saw the interview after the screening of the film* London Road, *and you talked about it being the National Theatre who came to you and said they'd put you with composer Adam Cork, so working with a composer wasn't your starting point for this, if I understand correctly. How did this push your craft?*

AB The way I structure a piece is to go this is the bit where everybody talks about being scared. With *London Road* those sections became potential songs, and then it was a matter of working out what should be verse and what should be chorus. I actually found it quite easy to choose as certain lines jump out at you. "Everyone is very, very nervous" summed up the mood brilliantly and was clearly what everyone was feeling. What I discovered was that repeating a line enabled me to build the mood to a more dramatic effect and that was an exciting breakthrough. The songs allowed me to push my structuring techniques further and therefore deliver a more potent mood and strengthen the narrative. But it was already a way in which I was working, without realizing how that correlated to songwriting. Adam explained to me about big numbers being created from shared sentiment and I thought, "OK, that naturally fits with what I do anyway." And then I think there's another thing in not knowing too much about song structures. The structures I was giving him were maybe interesting to him because they didn't follow proper musical patterns. Maybe lines were really quite long and messy and he was saying, "this is great" because this is what makes it interesting.

CJ *In terms of storytelling, playwriting is for me a living artform; it constantly changes. We're living in a society where there are multiple perspectives: There have always been multiple perspectives but even more today, with things coming from so many different angles. It feels like your approach resonates with the times we're living in.*

AB I walked into this field of verbatim at a time when *Big Brother* was starting on the telly. Documentary, that whole reality side of things was taking off. It just seems to be, not planned on my part, a thirst for the authentic. Yes it's important to get those other opinions so it's not all work made by—well, I am white middle class—but to reach out and capture those other voices that aren't so often heard on stage. That was what was interesting, what first drew me to this type of work. My Dictaphone gives me license to really go into the lives of people that I wouldn't otherwise get to meet, let alone really get to know. I thoroughly love that, that it's outside my own social sphere. I'm less interested in making something about my world. When Brexit happened, it made me realize how much of a bubble we live in. Everyone I knew was going round saying, "I can't believe it happened, I don't know anyone who voted OUT," including myself: That's because we are all living in the same bubble and that's clearly not a good thing. I think now more than ever it's important to reach out to hear the voices outside our own bubbles, in an attempt to understand what happened on June 23rd and to work through it with empathy.

CJ *And you've led the way in verbatim.*

AB I just want to think about trying to keep reimagining how you can use verbatim rather than lead the way.

CJ *How do playwriting and the playwright fit into the digital age of storytelling, do you think?*

AB What do you mean, the digital age?

CJ *We gather stories, whether that's digitally through media or whether it's digital forms of storytelling through gaming, how do live performance and the playwright . . .*

AB . . . Fit into that?

CJ *Yes.*

AB I think we have to adapt. I wouldn't be surprised if some playwrights were working with gaming companies. I think you have to embrace it, but I think a good play is active. When they really work, the audience is engaged, so I don't think we'll disappear. I think there is a real thirst for the more interactive sort of theater. And you know, I think that's all fine, that's all great, it's just when it becomes a trend for the sake of it. You can sit in your seat and watch a really good Chekhov or something and go on a much better journey. I think good writers probably don't have too much to worry about; they keep the audiences' minds engaged through their storytelling.

Steven Sapp

Steven Sapp is a playwright, poet, actor, and director. He co-founded THE POINT Community Development Corporation (Hunts Point) in 1993 and UNIVERSES (poetic theater ensemble) in 1996, both in collaboration with Mildred Ruiz-Sapp. With UNIVERSES Sapp has co-created and written *Party People*, *Slanguage*, *Ameriville*, *The Ride*, and more. Their work has been seen on HBO's DEF Poetry Jam, and at venues across the US and abroad. The ensemble is currently under commission from the Oregon Shakespeare Festival.

Caridad Svich   *What is a playwright?*

Steven Sapp   A playwright should be a storyteller. The griot. The bringer of their truth. Unapologetic, fearless, gentle, angry. The voice of the people. Social commentator.

CS   *Does the audience influence your writing?*

SS   I think in the early days of UNIVERSES we were really speaking to our community, and our artistic circle of artists and activists. As our artistic voice matured, Jo Bonney (our first major director) suggested that we use her as "Joe Public," [that] she would be our sounding board. If she could understand what we were saying, our growing fan base would be able to follow us. She wasn't trying to change us, but wanted us to be aware of the different audiences that were beginning to listen to us. We are very much aware that in some cases, we are bringing the voices and opinions of people to an audience that may not have ever heard this before, or we may be bringing these same voices to an audience that has never heard their voices on stage. And we speak to both groups, and make sure that we try to write from a place of sincere love for our communities, with all of the complexity that comes with it.

CS   *Do your ideas come from a sudden idea or conceit, or are they more planned?*

SS   Our ideas come from where we are in our lives at the time. We are an ensemble that got started in the poetry and open mic scenes in New York City. So we were always out performing in different venues around the city as a poetic musical group. Our early material was being generated and refined in poetry houses, and it really reflected where each of us were at creatively at the time. It was very exciting for us because there were no rules and we would create these ten-minute poetic, musical, theatrical pieces that reflected what was going on in our communities or what was going on in the world. And since we were an ensemble, the ways of creating these pieces started in different ways. Sometimes it started with a song someone was riffing on, or someone had a poem. And as an ensemble we found different ways to support each idea. With movement, a capella arrangements, stomping, and hand claps, spliced with original poetry and original monologues. As we have grown as an ensemble we still allow our process to be organic; even when we get commissioned by theaters, we still approach each process listening to what the universe brings to us.

CS   *How do you intersect with different, varied communities when you present or tour your works?*

SS   Not only are we a theater ensemble, but we have traveled extensively performing in performance art spaces, colleges, prisons, and community centers, as well as theaters. So we like to be where the people of that particular city and town are. We don't look at our art as a place where only the elite or wealthy can see it. We make sure that we get out and see the places where we travel to by doing workshops in the local schools or showing up at any open mics and signing the list and going up to work on new material, so people can see us who might not come to the theater or who can't afford it. We try to do talk-backs after our shows so people can interact with us and we can unpack some of the themes that come up in our work. It is through these interactions, from the classrooms to communities, which has helped us in our conversations with venues on how we want our work to be promoted and who we want to see our work outside of who the theater already has coming in.

CS   *How has the field changed since you started?*

SS As an ensemble that has been in existence for twenty years, as you can imagine we have seen the field shift in a variety of ways. I feel that the word "ensemble" has been embraced in the field in more ways. This is largely due to having funding regulated specifically for ensembles. For us, it allowed us to work using our own money to start developing material. We didn't have to wait for a theater to express interest in us, and "commission" us to create. We had resources to be able to subsidize the ensemble in ways that were liberating.

I also think that artistic directors started to look at work created by ensembles a little bit closer. With our first major show, *Slanguage*, we were invited to a summer retreat by New York Theatre Workshop to help develop our work. During this time, we had an opportunity to interact with Jim Nicola, the artistic director of New York Theatre Workshop. For us it was about having an institution get to know us, as people and what we stand for as artists. Then, we feel that the theater will truly be able to engage with our work in a more intimate way. Giving them an understanding of what they would be producing and what type of artist they are bringing into their "house."

UNIVERSES has built and sustained a career mostly from touring. The National Performance Network (NPN), which has a network of theaters and performance spaces across the country, was a place where we learned how to tour. The Network of Ensemble Theater (NET) connected us to the bigger ensemble community. It allowed us to see that there was a community of ensembles out there, and also embraced us as one of their own. We were able to engage with other practitioners from a variety of experiences. The young companies who were hungry and excited about connecting with everyone, and the older companies who have a real history, a legacy of work, who were continuing on their mission but were also looking to engage with the new voices and aesthetics that were entering the field.

CS *How crucial is the idea of company to you? Being in a company and making with each other?*

SS The idea of company and collaboration is very important to me. I feel the artist starts alone, learning to find their voice and then finding like-minded folks to share it with—fellow ass kickers in the struggle. So for us, it started very simply with the poetry/hip hop scene, where there were many different souls who were trying to find their voice. It was this scene that first gave us a sense of artistic self, where we felt we were part of something that embraced what we were trying to do. The conversations about art, life, politics, music, and the hustle to just stay current and reflective was life-altering for us. This scene gave us a foundation and sense of self before we even truly "arrived" in the theater scene. So for UNIVERSES, we knew who we were and what our voice was; it really was about finding theater allies who would help us move forward. It is this extended "family" of people who provided us with guidance, and friendship. We were challenged and encouraged to push further than we were even thinking this UNIVERSES thing could go. But it also allowed us to dream and to challenge and encourage their idea of what theater could be.

CS *How do you sustain an artist's life?*

SS It might seem strange but we don't allow the field to completely define us in terms of what happens to artists. We know of the pitfalls of the artist's life trying to balance art and life. Trying to stay alive, pay bills, and be productive. But we have tried to leave ourselves open to many different ways to function as a company. So for us we are now ensemble-in-residence at the Oregon Shakespeare Festival, but we also continue to tour as a traveling music theater ensemble outside of the regional theater model. We don't sit and wait for a theater to commission us. We have many different ways of expressing ourselves, both artistic and as activists. That does not mean that we are not challenged trying to make our way as a company, but we refuse to be pigeonholed into any one mode of working and performing.

CS *You have worked with a wide range of directors. I am fascinated by the notion that you are an ensemble, but over the years have not worked with one director exclusively, which tends to be somewhat the model in terms of how other ensembles establish themselves.*

SS The directors that we have collaborated with have become a part of UNIVERSES' development as a company. They each have become an essential link in our artistic journey. Jo Bonney was not only our director but also acted as a dramaturg. So our relationship became very close. She was able to sit with us and learn what our process was, and then merge that with where she wanted to see the company go. Our time developing and writing our first major show, *Slanguage*, with Jo for New York Theatre Workshop was very important for us because she was a very respected director, so even though we were a new company there was a huge interest in what this collaboration would bring.

Mildred and I worked with Talvin Wilks on our production *Eyewitness Blues* for New York Theatre Workshop in 2004. Talvin was the artistic director of New World Theater in Massachusetts and had become a friend. It was an enriching experience to be able to work with someone who we considered a friend but who was also talented as a director in his own right. So the process for that show felt more like having conversations with a friend than working for us. Also, we were very excited about helping Talvin become the first black director on the main stage at New York Theatre Workshop.

Chay Yew came into our artistic picture right after that. He brought us to Center Theatre Group, where he was in charge of the Asian Initiative, and introduced us to the artistic director Gordon Davidson, as well as Luis Alfaro, Brian Freeland, and Diane Rodriguez. It was this introduction that helped set up CTG producing *Slanguage*, with Luis Alfaro acting as the lead producer. So as we began to think about our next show after *Slanguage*, we thought Chay would be an interesting choice for our show *Ameriville*. Chay is a writer as well as a director, who we felt was looking at text and writing as fast and complex as us. So the synergy was amazing. We felt he actually was able to keep up with what we were doing text-wise, and stretch us even further. Chay was bringing ideas to us and getting the company to riff and collaborate on these ideas.

Liesl Tommy worked with us on our next show, *Party People*. We interviewed her for director after we saw her production of *Ruined* at the Oregon Shakespeare Festival. She was able to collaborate and help develop the piece as we began to stretch as a company, writing for other actors outside of UNIVERSES. So after we did the research and interviews we were able to bring that material and craft collaboratively with Liesl on the script. I think that Liesl's strength was being able to stage *Party People* with the actors at the Oregon Shakespeare Festival. And we were able to introduce her to the activist/artist strength of UNIVERSES.

CS *How do playwriting and the playwright fit into the digital age of storytelling?*

SS It really gives writers an opportunity to write anywhere, and at any time. From computers to cell phones, there is the opportunity to send and pull up information instantly. To have access to articles, music, art that can be used for research is priceless. This new generation is listening to things and receiving information at a rapid pace, and we as playwrights need to be able to speak in that same language.

Chris Goode*

Chris Goode is a writer, director, performer, and musician, and
lead artist of Chris Goode & Company. His diverse body of work has
been seen in venues ranging from Sydney Opera House and Tate
Modern to the most marginal spaces on the London fringe. His
credits include four Fringe First award-winning shows: *Men in the
Cities*, *Monkey Bars*, *Kiss of Life*, and (with Unlimited Theatre)
Neutrino; he also won the Headlong/Gate New Directions Award for
his radical version of Chekhov, . . . *SISTERS*, at the Gate Theatre.
Chris is a former artistic director of Camden People's Theatre in
London and he now directs the all-male ensemble Ponyboy Curtis.
He is the author of *The Forest and the Field*, a book on theater and
performance published by Oberon.

Caridad Svich   *What is a playwright?*

Chris Goode   I'm sure I won't be the only respondent to this question
to lament the cruelly deceptive homophony of "write" and "wright,"
which has done so much to cement the activity of playwrights (in the UK
and US at least) unhelpfully within a literary tradition. As my friend, the
actor Gemma Brockis, passionately insists: Plays are not *written*, but
wrought—that is, *worked*; and the work of playwrighting may or may
not involve writing—or, for that matter, the "play" object, as we tend to
understand it.

I'd like to consider the playwright to be the author/maker of play (or
of the space for or container of play) rather than of *a* play. I like Peter
Handke's thing, in *The Long Way Round*, where he contrasts the world
of nature with the world of games. When you get to the end of a game,
you say: "What next?" But nature continues, limitlessly. It may be true

---

that play cannot extend itself without territorial boundaries, but one can, as a playwright, shape or inflect play without ever having to accept or concede to "the play" in its commodity form.

Another way of articulating the same idea: These days I tell people that I don't really make things: I make the space for things to happen in. That said, I don't often call myself a playwright. Maybe I will now.

CS *Does the audience influence your writing?*

CG This is wonderfully hard to track, but I'm inclined to say no. I'm quite sure, in a way, that it can't. Audiences are specific groupings of people under particular conditions, in anticipation of and response to certain events. We struggle to meet them, especially as writers. Actors glimpse them, at best. The audience that attends a specific occasion is unique to it, and the next audience is its own separate entity. It makes no sense to talk of "the audience" in a generalized way. What we are talking about when we talk about "the audience" at the point when we are writing is, necessarily, our fear of the audience, our projection into the void where the audience will eventually convene.

There are, of course, moments of practical judgment that have to inform writing. Do I have to explain this reference? Do I need to signal this dynamic shift more clearly? (The one I try to expunge from my thinking: Will an audience get this?) My rule of thumb is that there's no reason to suppose an audience is, generally, any less intelligent or informed than I am or my colleagues are: But I guess I will, sometimes, spell something out a bit more, just to be sure, if the fluency of communication in a passage feels crucial and I don't want anyone to get hung up on something they think they may have misunderstood. Or, alternatively—and perhaps more successfully—I'll make it fuzzier and more hospitable, so that an audience that completely understands what I'm getting at isn't necessarily at an advantage over one that doesn't.

CS *Do your ideas come from a sudden idea or conceit, or are they more planned?*

CG Occasionally, it's a sudden high-concept idea that comes like a lightning bolt, more or less fully formed. *Monkey Bars*, for example, came that way—an unforeseen inspiration which took five minutes or less to unfold into its final shape, as I walked down a road in Oxford on my way to a gig. More usually, I'm suspicious of ideas that seem to be complete: I'll often hang on to a proposition until something wholly or largely unconnected with it comes additionally into my head and some kind of exciting dissonance is produced.

For example, I really wanted to write a play for the fiftieth anniversary of the Windscale nuclear accident, but it didn't have enough energy to it until I allowed it to rub up against an unconnected urge—to write about the death of the film actor River Phoenix. You're then frantically positing connections and torsions that might allow these two topics to coexist. The resulting play, *Speed Death of the Radiant Child*, contains— or can't quite wholly contain—both those strands, for better or worse, and the strangeness of their entangling becomes, in a sense, the traction in the play, where the "drama" would otherwise have been. I'm excited by complexity (because it seems to me to be blessedly true), and not least by moments where complexity is a product or function of the irrational being taken seriously.

CS *How do you negotiate areas of trouble in your work, in terms of your engagement with content and form, and your relationship to the audience?*

CG There's been quite a strong shift for me in recent years around these questions. In pieces like *The Forest and the Field* and *Keep Breathing*, my aim was to create for the audience a "safe" space to dwell in while questions hopefully arose from the work, concerning the whole category of the social, and the ways in which radical change might become possible without that potential immediately becoming occluded by defensiveness and fear. It is both a strength and a weakness of those pieces that they attempt to foster a fairly gently tremulating serenity, a sense of movement arguably less like revolution and more like head massage. This partly has to do with my role as "storyteller" in those spaces: I present myself as a trustworthy guide to a reimagined future of which, I tacitly imply, we don't need to be afraid.

From *GOD/HEAD* onwards, I suppose I am starting to strain at that leash. The "safe haven" of the work feels like it can't be an end in itself; on the contrary, what I'm putting in place is a set of frames and crash mats that support the idea of risk-taking and jeopardy and the attempting of difficult moves. Only a more turbulent scene, in which my role is not just to embrace but to agitate, can permit the ethical questions embedded in the form of the work to come through dynamically and unsettlingly.

Sometimes, it's true, I've used the gentler "host" voice in the service of misdirection: For example, in *The Adventures of Wound Man and Shirley*, I tell a story about (essentially) a romantic relationship between a young gay teenager and an eccentric middle-aged man who's clearly into boys; but the magic realist tenor of the work and the trustworthiness of the storytelling voice I employ always tend to neutralize what in other circumstances might be, for some audiences, a pretty disquieting narrative. In part, five years down the line, *Men in the Cities*, my next fictional storytelling piece, is energized by a determination to refuse that voice that soothes as it provokes: And it's no accident that, among many strands, that piece presents a much more confusing and volatile picture of a sexually fixated boy and any number of confounded older men in his orbit.

With the exception, I guess, of my 2008 play *Infinite Lives*, about an agoraphobic porn addict, *Men in the Cities* is perhaps the first time since *Past the Line, Between the Land* in 2003 (a devised piece responding to the UK's baleful involvement in Iraq and Afghanistan) where I start to want to dig down past the (to me) appealingly liquid, paradigmatically queer ethical speculations of the work, and really engage with the most fundamental root-position moral questions around patriarchy and capitalism, and around individual freedoms versus state oversight. I'm currently writing a play called *Freedom*, which pressurizes these questions still further, particularly in the half-light of recent strains of accelerationist thought. This turn from ethical thinking-aloud to moral excavation feels in a certain sense untheatrical, but in a way that I like. Paul Goodman says: "What you needn't watch— for instance, what you can read—is not part of a play, and too much of it kills a play." In that sense, subjecting a scripted play to a raft of possible moral orientations is a kind of self-harm or masochism, which, again, can have the function of drama in an otherwise largely postdramatic terrain. As Ron Sexsmith sings: "How can this song survive?"

CS *I am deeply interested in the idea that the "small" or what may be perceived as a "weak" voice in society actually can radiate out with the power of its own truth and integrity.*

CG I think theater is, first and foremost perhaps, a technology of weakness. Weakness is the index of its appeal to intimacy; and when, as it will, for various reasons, it sets its heart on spectacle, it doesn't so much scale up as balloon out, so that its vulnerability remains permanently embedded in its condition. Those who seek to eliminate the fault line in theater fundamentally misunderstand its nature. It is *all* fault lines: It is *itself* the fault line that we can introduce into other social configurations to make them ecstatically collapse.

I have been very influenced in recent years by John Holloway's work on the idea of the "crack": That captialism will not be overwhelmed, but undermined. Theater is extraordinarily well placed to author cracks in the ideological edifices that dominate our lives under capitalism.

And yes, I'm a fan, too, of smallness, and the ways in which the small can signify. For several years I collaborated with a performing artist, Jonny Liron, under the duo name Action one19: And much of what we did, we did behind the closed doors of an extremely marginal live/work warehouse space, just the two of us, each other's audience—or perhaps, more accurately, each other's witness. Because the collaborative partnership was so small, and so intense, it could contain anything and everything we brought to it. It was intrepid and queer and, on the whole, exceedingly accurate. I would sometimes watch Jonny improvising an angry fractured text, or cutting his arm with a scalpel, or wilfully and romantically making his exposed asshole the centre of attention within the performance frame, and no one else would be present, and yet I'd feel quite justified in saying to him that what we were doing was the most important work being done anywhere at that time. Which in one sense will seem a new standard by which to measure vanity and delusion: But *also* it still rings true to me. If we truly believe—as Jonny and I did—that theater is uniquely able to change a world that desperately needs changing; and that we are developing a theatrical vocabulary and syntax that is designed wholly and explicitly to help us create that change; and that we don't know of any other project that so insistently and urgently and unstintingly addresses that objective: Then provided we find, at the right times, a way of starting to share the work with others, we are justified in thinking of our work as being exactly *as important as all that*. If nothing else, this gives the work a kind of altitude that most theater and live art understandably refuses and even disdains. We save each other's lives by saving the life of the work.

CS *How do playwriting and the playwright fit into the digital age of storytelling?*

CG There is, to my mind, a profound, and not unproductive, tension here. The fundamentally intrinsic medium of theater, it seems to me, is real time, while the dynamic permissiveness of digital is predicated on nonlinearity. Perhaps the contemporary play-maker occupies a pivotal position at the crux of that tension. I remember being told as an undergraduate, by the director Ceri Sherlock, that the task of theater-makers of my generation would be to free ourselves from the tyranny of linear narrative; to some extent that's still on the to-do list, twenty years on.

It is true that some of my works for theater—I'm thinking above all of *Men in the Cities* and *Weaklings*—operate through a syntax that borrows heavily from the hypertextual, jump-cutting across layers of material and different orders of speculation and reality. There's lots that storytellers can do now to harness the energy and sheer velocity of digital, even in the most rudimentary oral or literary formats. I also think we're in desperate need of a much more fully developed ethics of the digital, and storytellers have an important role in sounding out those new relational maps. But maybe the burgeoning of digital forms will ultimately promote the divergence of play-making and storytelling as distinct disciplines? At any rate, theater-makers will still have to account, always, for the movement of time through their work.

Sylvan Oswald*

Sylvan Oswald is an interdisciplinary artist originally from
Philadelphia who creates plays, texts, publications, and video. Plays
include: A Kind of Weather (Playwrights Horizons/Clubbed Thumb
Superlab); Sun Ra (Joe's Pub, Jerome Travel and Study Grant);
Nightlands (New Georges); Pony (About Face Theatre, Chicago); and
Vendetta Chrome (Clubbed Thumb). Sylvan created the web series
Outtakes starring Becca Blackwell and Zuzanna Szadkowski—full
seasons are posted at outtakestv.com. His current project is High
Winds, an artist's book created in collaboration with graphic designer
Jessica Fleischmann. He is an assistant professor of playwriting at
UCLA's School of Theater, Film and Television, an affiliated artist at
Clubbed Thumb, and an alum of New Dramatists. sylvanoswald.xyz

Caridad Svich   *What is a playwright?*

Sylvan Oswald   For me, the role shifts with the project. Sometimes
I'm a playwright—responsible for the whole shebang of narrative and
character and action. Sometimes my role is more like a musician
contributing text as a rhythmic backbone or unexpected riff. Someone
else, or the group, is responsible for the clarity of the whole in those
cases. Either way, I consider it my mission to break form to explore how
we and the world are changing.

CS   *Does the audience influence your writing?*

SO   The struggle of the process can overtake me at times, so I often do
not have the energy to think of the audience while I am writing. I think of
them in separate stages, sort of a part of editing, but also a part of

---

* Interview reproduced with the kind permission of the author and their legal representation.

refining the text in rehearsal with cast and director. This is perhaps because I am driven by language and concept. Also, I live more in my head than in my body. My collaborators become representatives of the audience, and by watching them embody the writing with their full humanity, I'm able, finally, to see the work how the audience might see it.

CS *Do your ideas come from a sudden idea or conceit, or are they more planned?*

SO While it's not my tradition, I love reading about the old-school way to make kimchee, the Korean staple. It's buried underground. Chop and combine ingredients, add spices and liquids, seal in a pot or jar, dig a hole, bury it, wait. My ideas emerge from a similar process of combining disparate elements and stewing in my own juices for a long time. I wish I could work more outside-in or just faster — but that feels forced. Inside-out seems to be how I develop my richest and most satisfying projects. The networks of meaning grow within the piece like a nervous system with hubs and spokes and tendrils connecting distant limbs. When I must conceptualize in writing before I've had time to live with the images and sounds and thoughts, I end up having to recreate that lost time of wandering somehow.

CS *What is your stance on representation and gender parity in the theater and on stage?*

SO The way we produce our identities fascinates me. In *Nightlands* and *Pony* I look at how our identities are contorted by shame, and the work we do to dismantle that shame and remake ourselves. Often this story appears in the queer lives I depict. So my moral compass points toward representing the nuanced subjectivity of people who are not normally given ample space and time to be heard. I hope that, by dramatizing the vibrant self-hood of under-represented people, other audience members might discover inspiration for their own lives and greater empathy for those they don't yet understand.

Gender is a charged reality of my everyday life. As I move through the world, people read me based on their own gender literacy. Sometimes they see me as male, sometimes trans or queer, sometimes butch — and these variations depend on whom I'm with. We're living in a moment with more transgender awareness than ever before. When I was just starting out as a playwright, I was writing roles for women to play men and calling them "pants roles" because I had little vocabulary around the possibilities for gender non-conformity. As I've come out as trans, I have intentionally created trans roles and made a point of casting trans actors whenever possible. While it's true that in representational theater the character is a fiction, we are always, underneath that, seeing the reality of the performer's body.

When a straight actress is cast as a butch lesbian, the chemistry is usually off. Either that person is put in an unbelievable wig, they are performing masculinity stiffly, or they are cast in a supposedly romantic pairing no one spent enough time considering. Butch/queer people in the audience attend a show hoping, finally, to see themselves reflected, only to feel more misunderstood and invisible than ever.

When playwrights resist lazy and offensive casting, I find it thrilling. It's our job as writers to insist upon appropriate representation. If we do not make those obligations clear to producers, casting directors, and our collaborators, this troubling inertia will continue. They, in turn, must take up the charge.

Identity is not theoretical to most people. It can be hard-won. It can be a source of danger. I've been inspired by performance work outside the traditional American theater that uses non-actors or performers-as-themselves. In work by ensembles as disparate as 600 Highwaymen, Gob Squad, or Rimini Protokoll, we can find the potent suggestion that there is a tremendous amount of resonance to be found in turning our attention to the virtuosity required by people in living their everyday lives.

CS *We often make families in the theater—i.e., a particular company gravitates toward our work, or a band of actors, or directors. Who do you identify as family theatrically and how does this affect the way you think about stories and narratives?*

SO The writers with whom I shared my graduate school experience feel most like my family, as do colleagues from writers' groups I've been a part of at Soho Rep and Clubbed Thumb. With many of those individuals I share a curiosity about the limits of the play form and a history of rebellion against it. Maybe because I always gravitated toward the historical avant-garde, I feel most aesthetically visible in the downtown New York scene. My work sits precariously between the dramatic and the postdramatic. This year, in teaching Hans Thies-Lehmann's seminal *Postdramatic Theatre*, I realized that the writing I love most is driven by the knowledge that it doesn't need to exist, generating its urgency through a rigorous self-awareness. So I find myself seeking community among those artists who are willing to let go of the idea of a play. *Play A Journal of Plays*, the publication I created with Jordan Harrison, is alive with this conflict.

CS *What do you see as some of the turning points in your evolution as an artist?*

SO An inspiring theater history teacher I had when I studied abroad in London introduced us to the etymology of tragedy—"goat songs." I was about twenty and heartbroken/obsessed with a girl back home and felt alienated from my peers on the trip. So I lived in the library and read all the time. When I got back, I had to come up with a substantial project at school and, through a combination of other minor obsessions, became consumed by the idea of choruses in theater. I had seen the Bulgarian Women's Choir, images of Robert Wilson's productions, and had a desire to fill Wilson's cold visual landscapes with some kind of passion. I started playing with language and found text even though I didn't even know what it was at that time. The writing that emerged was like nothing I'd ever written before. It became a short play called *Goat Songs* (2000), with a somewhat convoluted narrative and a fearsome/charming chorus of psychic grandmothers and a gender non-conforming main character. This was a moment when I felt supercharged as an artist and I consider it to be the arrival of my "adult writing."

I wrote a couple more plays in this vein (2001–2003) with heightened language exploring the agency of characters that, with hindsight, I can read as transgender. Unusually for someone attending a women's college at the turn of the millennium and identifying as sort of gay (I guess), I didn't know anyone trans. So it was uncharted territory on a couple of levels.

Outside of a daring cohort from college, no one would touch those plays! Thank goodness for the ensemble Polybe + Seats, led by director Jessica Brater, who played a grandmother in *Goat Songs* and then produced my next two plays on shoestrings in New York.

The more recent significant turn in my work has been toward video with my web series *Outtakes* (2013–2015). Making that show gave me a chance to write through directing and editing, which really reshaped my brainwaves. After a decade or so of writing in isolation I was making something in the room with people—the show was largely improvised and very loosely planned (for better or worse!). That immediacy and the relief from isolation gave me another much-needed boost of creative energy and confidence.

Earlier I mentioned *Play A Journal of Plays*. Along with *Outtakes*, those projects do not fit easily into their respective disciplines (literature/drama and performance/video). There's something naïve in the approach. The boundary blurring is only a problem when it comes to institutional funding. Creatively, that's what excites me. I get the most traction artistically when I'm ignoring categories.

CS *How do playwriting and the playwright fit into the digital age of storytelling?*

SO Some people think that virtual reality will require theatrical brainpower in significant ways—that there's something about our expertise in liveness that's going to be required. Maybe the virtual will finally collapse the distinctions between "theater" and "performance." Film directors and TV creators are fascinated with shoots that run like rehearsed plays. Playwrights are the backbone of the Golden Age of Television, which is also a renaissance of digital distribution. This is all significant to playwrights because our options for making money on playwriting itself are sorely limited. So while we largely lose ownership of our work in the digital space, we may make discoveries that transform our approach to theater. Isn't that what we want? To be transformed?

Naylah Ahmed

Naylah Ahmed has been writing since the late 1990s for stage, radio, and television. She won the Bruntwood Prize for Playwriting with *Butcher Boys* in 2008, and was one of the writers of *These Four Streets*, which premiered at Birmingham Repertory Theatre 2009. *Mustafa* was awarded a Special Prize by the National Theatre Foundation 2013 and produced by Birmingham Repertory Theatre and Kali Theatre. *Ready or Not* toured the UK in 2017, produced by Kali Theatre. Naylah also writes for radio and television and has been a Script Editor and Producer for *Silver Street* (BBC Radio Drama Birmingham).

Caroline Jester   *What is a playwright?*

Naylah Ahmed   Simply put: Somebody who tells stories on the stage. I'm always very aware of how unaware I am of the academic world of theater! Theater folk go on about different forms and theories and choices that I don't have an in-depth knowledge of, so for me, it really is simply telling a story in a space that's seen as or called a stage. Not having that in-depth knowledge doesn't put me off. Like most areas in my writing life, if I like it, or like the idea of it, I give it a go and see what happens—there's always plenty of people willing to let you know if the work isn't good! It's been the same with playwriting; I really liked the idea of it and so had a go.

CJ   *Does the audience influence your writing?*

NA   I would like to say no because I think that's the best way to deliver to an audience. But with the play that I'm working on now, *Ready or Not*, I was slightly overwhelmed for a time thinking about all the different possible perspectives people in the audience might have, how to navigate them. It wasn't in order to say something to please one of those groups—or try and please all of them. It was in order to try and avoid misinterpretations, because it is a political play but not in the traditional sense, and at its heart it's about people, individuals. Thankfully, when the characters came into their own, I realized that I don't have to navigate any opinions or political leanings. I simply have to be true to the characters and situation and write the best play I can—one that I'd want to engage with.

CJ   *Could you say something about the story?*

NA   *Ready or Not* is a play I've had in my mind for about six years in some form. Even before that it's been in my head—a desire to address something slightly unpindownable, because it's still unfolding. Everything that's happened since September 11, 2001, really, a response to that. Obviously one play or story will never address it all, but given the lack of Muslim voices addressing our perspectives in the arts, considering what's happening globally and within our communities (I hate that word!) . . . it's important to me. That happened to be the year that Dad died, 2001, and it was a big change in many ways. The changes in our home were reflected by changes in the world outside—especially being Muslim. I just wanted to cope with it all, to stay on top of it, but increasingly I really wanted to address it, to tie it down and examine it, to try and see what it was. That doesn't really answer the question as to story—but if I start on the story, I'll be going on for ages!

The play is essentially about collateral damage; the outer concentric circles of collateral damage. The seed of the play when it first started as an idea was, what it would take for the kind of person you would least expect to be capable of doing the things that we all think we're incapable of.

CJ   *Do your other ideas come from a sudden idea or conceit, or are they more planned?*

NA   The idea itself, the nugget, is very often something that just comes to you, or comes to me, because I can only talk about myself! It's rare I get an idea without a character or characters attached. I love character—it's what leads story for me. I can sit through things where the story might not quite cut it if the character works for me.

Strangely, *Ready or Not* wasn't so much like that because it was the result of years of churning lots of stuff, news reports, the day-to-day experiences of people you know, the language around Muslims and Islam. You can't deal with all of it and *Ready or Nor* doesn't: It couldn't, it's one play. I guess the situation preceded the characters in this case—aside from Pat, she was with me from the start. With all the continuous references all around us about Muslims and Islam and foreigners, I kept thinking, "when is there going to come the day that a 'normal' British white person grabs the nearest person who looks Muslim and says, 'You guys fuck with us, well I'm gonna fuck with you'?" There are people that do. They fall off the edge and they do that, of course they do that, and with all this fear-mongering, that used to be my biggest fear. But it's never because of melanin; we are all in our own situations, coping with different eases and difficulties . . . That was the start of the situation, "what would it take . . .?"

I have a love of character so it's never enough for me to say "so there's political unrest in the world and an older white woman takes a young Muslim man captive and does terrible things to him." It had to be about why, who they are as individuals; it had to be about those tiny circumstances that build.

CJ *In your other plays, the majority of your characters are male.*

NA Yes.

CJ *Is that a conscious decision you make?*

NA It's never a conscious decision. It's only ever what I want to explore.

My play *Butcher Boys,* for instance, came from the most memorable summer I spent with my Dad. He wasn't well so he did half-day shifts in his Halal butchers in Small Heath. I would drive him to work and pick him up again at 12 pm or 1 pm and there came a point when I thought I may as well just stay with him. Actually, I thought I may as well sit at the desk he has on the shop floor and write. After a little bit of "is she OK? Does she need anything?" from the men who were working for my Dad, they realized "oh she just sits at his desk and fannies about with a bit of paper," and they just went on with their business. After a while I was invisible.

I was really intrigued, truly intrigued, by these characters I thought I knew. It's so easy as a British Asian Pakistani person to dismiss "Pakis" that come over because there's that whole thing of wanting to play down people that you fear you may be seen as. I grew up around it and it was really the first close up observation I had of non-British-born Asian Muslim Pakistani men in a male setting out of sight. You usually don't even notice them because they're either not visible in your life, or not an active part of your life. They're the ones that are carrying your Mum's heavy shopping to the car from the Asian supermarket. You don't even remember what they look like. And here they were laughing, joking—getting and giving life advice. You could just see the texture of their lives, how they lived their vibrant, brightest lives in that safe place where their language was understood. My characters were based on the ethos of my Dad's employees—the vibe. I didn't take from their lives: It was more their spirit, my dad wasn't just the boss, he was their "Uncle," a father figure, someone to be respected. They were understood. They were valid. And I loved that; to be able to explore that in a play was a treat.

CJ *How do playwriting and the playwright fit into the digital age of storytelling?*

NA I don't even know that I'm aware of that: The digital age of storytelling. The magic of stage is the stage for me; the magic of stage is the event. Filmed theatrical performances don't quite work—not that I think they shouldn't happen.

However many people have Kindles, it should be quite a while before people think of ditching [print] books completely. In the same way, however people take their stories now, I think the magic of theater is a space where something happens. You're there to witness it and that, for me, will never go away. What interests me about the future is how this engaging form of storytelling can become affordable—both for theater-makers and audiences—how it can reach wider audiences, and how we can respond theatrically to things unfolding around us more swiftly. Of course, great creative minds and talents are doing this already, but it's not reaching out to me. I don't want it to be for people "in the know"—I want theater to reach out to us in our daily lives. It may well be wishful thinking, but I would love a time when it's a real choice to take my son to the cinema or an affordable theatrical performance (whatever the performance space).

Paula Vogel

Paula Vogel's plays include *How I Learned to Drive*, which received the 1998 Pulitzer Prize in Drama, *The Baltimore Waltz*, *And Baby Makes Seven*, *The Mineola Twins*, *Hot 'n' Throbbing*, and *Don Juan Comes Home from Iraq*. *Indecent*, which was developed with director Rebecca Taichman, marked her Broadway debut in 2017 after productions at Yale Rep, La Jolla Playhouse, and the Vineyard Theatre. In 1985 she took on the directorship of the MFA program in playwriting at Brown University. She became an adjunct professor at the Yale School of Drama and Playwright-in-Residence at Yale Repertory Theatre in 2008. She chaired the playwriting department at Yale until 2012.

Caridad Svich   *What is a playwright?*

Paula Vogel   A playwright is someone who writes for a living audience; crafting a script to be performed by collaborators in a space shared by the audience. A playwright is a writer who embraces the ephemeral quality of performance and knows that the script is one element only of performance. In a way, playwriting is playing a three-dimensional game of chess . . . trying to calculate how different responses by directors, actors, designers, and production artists will still get through (that is, communicate) the playwright's intention.

CS   *Chess is a fascinating analogy! This takes us back to the notion of crafting text architecturally for different areas of a playing field, with the knowledge that text is merely one component!*
   Does the audience influence your writing?

PV   Not really. I believe that I am the first audience, and I want to have a broad aesthetic so that every play engages a different emotional and intellectual muscle than the play I wrote before.

CS *Where do playwrights find the ideas that become the stories that become their plays?*

PV I think by constantly writing plays I now think in dramatic structure. Often plays begin with a moment of plasticity. Or a moment of conversation. A character that won't go away. Like most playwrights, I have a long, long list of plays I won't get the time to write, but that I play with in my head. Only the ideas that stalk me relentlessly get written.

CS *Being obsessed with something. Yes. The ideas that rise to the surface and will not go away. This notion is key. As well as the ability to chase that idea to its fullest extent.*
   Will there be playwrights in another fifty years?

PV Of course. We may be writing for media at that point. The real question is whether or not societies will underwrite theater. America has abnegated its support of all of the arts, not just theater. By relegating it as entertainment in a marketplace economy, America has seriously weakened our arts . . . and this is a form of political and economic censorship.

CS *Invisible censors, in a way, if you look at this abnegation from the impact of neo-liberal capitalist systems set in place about thirty-odd years ago in US culture (and increasingly, globally). Unlike, say, countries where censorship is evident and there may even be a state censor, in the US, censorship of a kind occurs through the ties between power-broking in politics tied to economic structures that keep said political operatives in place. It's a tough nut to crack. But I think that we have a responsibility to actually, through our writing, crack through such systems, if only through how we present what we present and the choices that we make as artists. Call it a moral compass.*

PV About the moral compass of playwriting, Caridad: I have been seeking to arm younger writers with whom I've worked with tools to underwrite playwriting: Through teaching skills and skills for television. Like you, I am a believer in theater as an important literary form that questions and disturbs our status quo. I only write to share my concerns about the world we inhabit; my sense of loneliness and outsiderness is too great for me to bear without some purposeful sharing.

I am not often mentored by theaters and theater-makers, perhaps because of my perceived success—but I must answer with gratitude toward the Vineyard Theatre and Yale, as well as Sundance, which have provided me with homes, process, and an openness to my voice. I am so very grateful to that. And I work with directors who also mentor me, who have an aesthetic and political view beyond mine.

All of my plays are written with a sense of me trying to understand what disturbs me. For *Don Juan Comes Home from Iraq,* I am greatly disturbed with the cultural invisibility of veterans and the rupture between the military and civilian society, the lack of discussion about our wars and our sending off women and men to fight wars that have been left out of political discourse in Congress. A dangerous state for a so-called democracy. *Indecent*, for me, is a way to examine how anti-Semitism and a nativist movement in America has led to our culpability in censorship, and how censorship can lead to genocide. *How I Learned to Drive* was written as a way for me to express concern over how we participate in abuse against children and adolescents, and how our culture perpetually sexualizes the young.

But the key importance of theater is that it is dialectical; I want to explore being a perpetrator as well as a survivor. I want to see the argument for those who espouse censorship, war, and see relationships with the young as a natural state of being, a necessary state of being. So I need to write as well from the position of being the predator, the censor, the adult who strays over the boundaries. This is, for me, the greatest thrill, challenge, and responsibility of playwriting . . . to explore the gray areas, and eschew the black and white. Theater calls upon us to examine the position of Iagos as well as Othellos. As a queer woman, my call is to examine the Desdemonas of the world as well.

CS *How do playwriting and the playwright fit into the digital age?*

PV First of all, I think of playwriting and screenwriting and television and media under one title: Dramatic writing. We are, when we write for the stage, writing for a very different audience than, say, Tennessee Williams or Eugene O'Neill wrote for. They wrote for an audience of readers. Our audiences consume work visually, with a much different notion of dramatic time. Plasticity, the physical reality of the stage, plays a much larger role. So, too, does the way we design time. It is difficult to insist, as many critics do, that dramatic form be syllogistic with a beginning, middle, and end that fit the nineteenth-century well-made play.

2
HOW DO YOU PUT IT ALL TOGETHER?

Paula Vogel leads us into this chapter from the previous one by connecting the audience's experience of consuming theater to the times they are living in. She states that audiences consume work visually now and that the "physical reality of the stage, plays a much larger role" than audiences in the past. She links this with the craft of the writer and how their role in designing time may not follow the nineteenth-century model of the well-made play, as this chapter explores. We asked each writer two core questions:

1 Does the narrative you're writing dictate the dramatic structure you select to tell the story?
2 How much do you consider where the play will be staged when you begin the writing process?

Chris Thorpe rejects the first question and positions narrative as an option, one of the many tools a playwright has when creating a piece of work that asks a central question. But it does not dictate the way he chooses to create his work.

Mia Chung is positioned next to him and has a different perspective. For her, once narrative and structure are in place they work together to push the creative process forward: "A tight relationship—conceptually, something like the double helix of DNA comes to mind."

Kaite O'Reilly comes singing onto the page, "TA DA DA DAA," and rejects narrative as not being of interest to her at all. She writes dynamic and is interested in an experience between the spectacle and the spectator.

Alexander Zeldin reminds us of the origins of theater. He feels it was to do good to people and a space where every type of person could be brought together. His interest in theater's architecture seeps into his clear connection with the stage and the environment he creates for his audiences.

Our connection with ancestors continues as **Naomi Iizuka** describes how she experiments with existing dramatic structures to see if they will "hold" her story. It feels almost battle-like at times and the structure begins to bend to the new stories as they take on a different shape.

"The potato doesn't give a shit about the laws of symmetry," says **Sibyl Kempson** from the next seat at our playwrights' table. And for her the time of current Western dramatic structure has passed. There's a need to discover the way the plays want to be told by listening to "our authentic imagination" and becoming more in line with our intuition.

But what happens when you're working on one of the country's largest stages? **Carl Miller** describes how being attentive to an audience and their reactions to watching a play that you have written can not only indicate how the play can be improved, but also how to understand the stage you are writing for.

George Brant challenges Carl's notion of the play being instructions for others to create the playwright's vision, as there were almost no stage directions in his play *Grounded*. This resulted in different productions varying radically from the other.

Lisa D'Amour talks about the birth of her play *Anna Bella Eema* and how she struggled with writing this using conventional, proscenium-style naturalism. When she let the process lead her, she started hearing a heart beating inside the play and listened to what was calling out to her.

David Greig needs old forms to create new forms. Each new play should have something new to say.

This chapter does not wholly reject the past but it is fully alert to its present. As stages can be anywhere, the way writers tell their "stories" or "dynamic" is constantly adapting and reinventing itself.

Chris Thorpe

Chris Thorpe was a founder member of Unlimited Theatre and still works and tours with the company. He is Artistic Associate of live art/theater company Third Angel and has worked with Forest Fringe, Slung Low, Chris Goode, RashDash, Belarus Free Theatre, and mala voadora, where *Your Best Guess* opened at Lisbon's Almada Festival in 2015. He plays guitar in Lucy Ellison's political noise project *#TORYCORE* and works with the National Student Drama Festival. Other plays include *There Has Possibly Been an Incident* (Manchester Royal Exchange), *Confirmation* (a collaboration with director Rachel Chavkin from New York's TEAM), *The Oh Fuck Moment, I Wish I Was Lonely* (collaborations with Hannah Jane Walker), *Victory Condition* (Royal Court), and *Chorus* for *The Iphegenia Quartet* (Gate Theatre). Chris is one of the Jerwood New Playwrights 2017.

Caroline Jester   *What is a playwright?*

Chris Thorpe   To me it's someone whose chief responsibility within the team of people who make a performance happen is to form the language, not necessarily narrative, or the literary construction of something, and also articulate the question at the heart of the work, the unsolvable question that is always at the heart of the work.

CJ   *When you use language is it necessarily words?*

CT   Certainly the most important meaning of that for me is text, before character, before setting, before any choice about whether to use narrative or not. [That means] The actual words being used, the form of those words, and then the form in which those words are going to be communicated.

CJ   *Does the audience influence your writing?*

CT   The idea of the audience and people being there used to influence [for me] it in a really negative way. When I started out I was scared of the audience; I didn't have an idea of them as a scary bunch of people, but there was an over awareness, a second guessing of what people might think. And that's something that I really had to dispense with, actually. The flip side of that isn't that you cease caring about them, the flip side is you recognize that none of this is useful or alive without those people, in terms of their relationship to it, and how a piece of work needs to be crafted in order for that relationship to be as good as it can be, as useful as it can be.

The only hurdle you truly need to get over is worrying that people think you're an idiot. Once that ceases to be a worry, it doesn't mean that you're not an idiot, it means you stop worrying about it and I think there's a similar thing in life and with writing because then you can really interrogate what you're producing and have a useful perspective on whether it's doing what you want it to.

CJ   *Does the narrative you're writing dictate the dramatic structure you select to tell the story?*

CT   It's a fascinating question and the answer is no, because that's not where narrative occurs in the writing process for me. Narrative is an option. You find the question at the heart of the work, then you find the language that might best serve that question, then you find the form, and for me that's quite often not about setting or narrative but about a specific relationship with the other people in the room. So narrative for me is one of the things I would consider as an option, but whether I use it or not would be entirely dictated by the question at the heart of the work and what kind of form that question suggests.

CJ   *That's interesting that you say "whether" you use it or not.*

CT   Or how you use it. It's an option, and I've created a piece of work that has an overarching narrative, absolutely, and that can be an intellectual narrative or an emotional narrative, or it can be a series of events, or a combination of those. I don't think I've ever created anything that has a plot because narrative to me isn't about driving a plot. It's only useful in so much as it serves the piece that you're making, and that will change from piece to piece. For example the work I've done with Portugal, with mala voadora, the largest scale piece I've done with them was conceived as an explosion of the elements of the well-made play. That's the thing they wanted me to do. So all the narrative, all the plot you would normally find in a well-made play is there, but it's collapsed into a single scene, which is a fifteen-page monologue of a guy explaining in forensic detail the plot of the play you would be seeing if you weren't seeing this piece. And that's narrative. That's a use of narrative that has to be constructed and chosen and shaped in the same way that any narrative is, but it's isolated and used for a different purpose. In a piece like *There Has Possibly Been An Incident*, there's a series of narratives in there but they're broken up in a way that makes a reading of a single overarching narrative difficult, but they exist, the narratives exist to serve a purpose in that world, which is to make people think about choice and heroism in that room. So yeah, narrative is an option. As is character, as are any of the conventional elements of playwriting, they're all up for grabs, any of the conventional and unconventional elements of performance.

CJ *In* Confirmation *we follow your journey in trying to process the central question of the piece, trying to explore* how *a white supremacist thinks and not* what *they think, and how your process informed structural choices for the play. I remember watching it and witnessing you going to America to an academic and then . . .*

CT . . . And then having a series of very intimate conversations with someone whose point of view is absolutely reprehensible to the vast majority of people, yeah.

CJ *How did that process inform the choices you made in the play?*

CT Because again, *Confirmation*, the purpose of *Confirmation,* is to ask if it is even possible for someone to become aware of the mechanics of how we believe what we believe and to engage in a series of dialogues and to see collaboratively if me and that other person can come to some understanding—that we perhaps operate in the same way even though the material of the world looks very, very different to us. For example, he believes that the Holocaust is entirely fake and I don't, and aside from any repugnance in me for his viewpoints or in him for mine, there's another conversation we can have about taking a perspective, taking a step back and asking how we believe that. In *Confirmation*, the form of it, you have to feel the repugnance, you have to have an honest and accurate account of those beliefs, but you also simultaneously have to be in an environment where the person is in front of you, and is also me, and that environment itself is asking you to engage on a personal level with your own beliefs and how you're constructing and holding them. So the choice is for it not to be a "play," as in a dramatization of those conversations, but to cut out the acting and write language that can simply be said, as a person, to the other person in the room.

CJ *How much do you consider where the play will be staged when you begin the writing process?*

CT   That entirely depends on who has asked me to write it. My initial premise, my initial feeling, is that it should always be stageable in as wide a variety of places as possible, obviously within the limitations of whatever technical requirements you will need. And you would be stupid to ignore that because technical requirements are one of the tools, like narrative, because when you use them you use them for a reason—but I think the initial position should always be as many places as possible with as few resources as possible. But then for specific projects, such as *Victory Condition*, which I've written for the Royal Court, I think it would be possible to perform that piece in a huge variety of places, but they asked me to write it and it's written with that theater downstairs in mind because there are elements of what it's asking the audience participating to think about as they watch it, elements of the history of that place that work really well to support that place, that thinking, because it's written for that theater. They are not just in a theater but in the Royal Court theater. So because of the look of that room, because of the feel of that room, and because of the things that go on in there, you can open that up, encourage people to think about everything else that is going on while we're sitting watching this piece in that room, rather than narrowing it down to just a functional stage.

CJ *You've mentioned your work in Portugal, and you and your work have travelled outside the United Kingdom and have been produced a lot in Europe. Has the decision to leave the European Union influenced the ideas that you're exploring now?*

CT Well I've scrapped a show that I was writing and I'm rewriting it because of the Brexit vote. I think it's absolutely incumbent on certain pieces of work that you take into account the things that happen in the world.

I'm writing a piece for the Royal Exchange in Manchester about as a community expands in size, how people's needs stay the same in some ways but how they express themselves differently. It's based on research—a lot—from six different places around Britain of communities of different sizes. Now, I had to scrap most of it: It wasn't about Brexit, although Brexit was a large part of the conversations I had in those places even though the show wasn't about that. But the fact that that decision had been made influences the tone of the context in which the show takes place, not only when it's finally produced but as it's being written. So yeah, for that particular show I threw away most of what I had written and I started again. Because I was writing in a fundamentally different world to the one I thought I was writing in—well, maybe not a *fundamentally* different world, but the world had factually changed in a really big way. So of course you take it into account. But I could have been writing a different play about a totally different subject and it would have made no difference whatsoever.

CJ *How do playwriting and the playwright fit into the digital age of storytelling?*

CT I'm really glad that the Internet wasn't a thing, a usable thing, until I was essentially a young adult because I think you're presented with a multiplicity of ways to tell a story now at a very early stage of your development as a writer, and that would have replaced the essential thing of learning how to use language for me. Obviously the writers that are coming up now are born into that world so they are much better at that than I am, but I'm personally glad that I got to do a little bit of my development before the digital age. That said, I find it incredibly fucking exciting. I was down at the National Theatre Studio trying out some VR [virtual reality] stuff and thinking about the theatrical possibilities of those all-consuming experiences that are only going to get more convincing, and I was very, very excited by that. But what excites me more than the technology itself is the ability as a writer to watch those things happening and to imagine, it's kind of your job to imagine, how they might affect us in the future. So I'm very excited by the technology, in terms of its potential effect on society. Of course I'm excited by the fact that I can communicate with someone instantaneously across large distances, how is that not going to be a good thing in a lot of ways? But I also think there's a huge opportunity for us to engage, grapple with the possible effects of this on us in a way that academia does, in a way that industry does, in a way that politics does. And there's a way to draw it all together as a writer which gives a really useful perspective. I'm very excited by technology.

Mia Chung[*]

Mia Chung is author of *You for Me for You, Catch as Catch Can,
This Exquisite Corpse*, and an adaptation of *The Orphan of Zhao*. Her
works have been produced at the Royal Court Theatre, Woolly
Mammoth, Ma-Yi Theatre, InterAct, and the Guthrie Theater. Her work
has been supported by Berkeley Rep, Hedgebrook, Magic Theatre,
South Coast Rep, and TCG. She is an alumni member of the
Huntington Theatre playwright fellows. She has degrees from Yale,
Trinity College Dublin, and Brown University.

Caridad Svich   *What is a playwright?*

Mia Chung   Impossible to define with any finality.
   But for me, right now, the key thing is live performance. Theatricality.
There needs to be a reason that I have to witness a performance in
person. So: A playwright conceives and constructs a live performance—
often with language, often with the purpose of telling a story, often with
characters and dialogue and environments. But keep in mind, what is
best expressed through live performance keeps shifting as what we
experience in life and how we experience life evolves.

CS   *Does the audience influence your writing?*

MC   I write for performance, so I am inherently invested in the notion
of an audience. But I do my best to protect the writing process from
being shaped by perceptions of "what the audience will think" and
especially "what the audience wants." I believe the best, most original,
most authentic writing comes out of listening as carefully as possible to
your own voice. So in that way, if we define "audience" as the recipient
or spectator or witness, then I am my primary audience. At least in the
initial act of expression.

* Interview reproduced with the kind permission of the author and their legal representation.
© Mia Chung 2017.

This is not to say that I only "write for myself." Without question, I write to communicate to others, to contribute to the world. When workshopping a play, my ears are wide open for responses from anyone in the room. Because at that point I need to know if what I want to say is clear or not. At that point, I am listening carefully to others' reactions to the play in order to reduce unproductive static due to imprecise language or ambiguous theatrical devices. And I am listening carefully to the play . . . so again, I guess I am a primary audience.

CS *Does the narrative you're writing dictate the dramatic structure you select to tell the story?*

MC Completely. Or rather, they dictate each other. In other words, they are absolutely complementary. Sometimes the story comes first, other times the theatrical device or a structural image. But once a few key pieces of both components (narrative and structure) are in place, they dictate and propel and complement and reflect back at each other. A tight relationship—conceptually, something like the double helix of DNA comes to mind.

Moreover, this tight relationship between structure and narrative can sometimes be useful for the writing process itself. For instance, how a structure is built might then evoke a piece of story and then that original structure might be renovated or even abandoned to serve the evolving story and plot and characters. Especially during the initial draft, this back-and-forth conversation between structure and narrative can be so productive and even exhilarating.

CS *How much do you consider where the play will be staged when you begin the writing process?*

MC I love site-specific plays, but I have not yet written any. But I think site-specific work can be beautiful, extraordinary responses to an environment (or a theater or city). I simply haven't found the right project or opportunity. Yet. But with regard to my work thus far: To be frank, I generally try to put all practical, stage considerations aside to better consider the ideas, stories, characters, and theatrical moments. Those are my guides for the writing of a play. My feeling is if/when a play is produced, there is ample room for flexibility of How the play lives in the world; and for me, the How includes Where. Each Where—whether stage, alternative space, theater, city, country, etc—has its own questions and solutions.

CS   *Your play* You for Me for You. *It's had quite a journey from Icicle Creek Fest to Woolly Mammoth, Company One, the Royal Court, Portland Playhouse, Mu Performing Arts at the Guthrie Theater, Crowded Fire Theater, and InterAct Theatre. Years! No reason to think the first draft is the same as the draft audiences saw in London, of course. But I do wonder: a) how did the play first begin its journey?; b) how did it change along the way?; and c) what was it like to work on it in the US and then in the UK?*

MC   Even after *You for Me for You* had been professionally produced multiple times, published, and honored with awards, I kept revising. Along the way, I heard lots of wise counsel on perfectionism as "the enemy of the good," the importance of letting go, how being "finished" is a choice, a state of mind, etc—and frankly, I agreed. But the reason I kept going back to the play was not dumb perfectionism. The reason was Minhee. This character—one of the two sisters fleeing North Korea over the course of *You for Me for You*—was not satisfied with how I'd depicted her perspective. With the endurance befitting a woman who had suffered mind-warping loss and survived via cognitive dissonance and patience, Minhee had gamely persisted through sundry script workshops and rehearsals and productions, multiple name changes, and dramatic re-workings of her back story. In effect, she had waited for me to grow as a writer.

I wrote the first draft as my grad school thesis. In this draft, Minhee was a minor character, too sick to leave North Korea; her younger sister Junhee was the singular heroine: She took Minhee to the US, first in spirit, then in physical form—a complex transfiguration that *might* have been legible as a novel but was indecipherable on stage. Several drafts later, Minhee came into her own as an essential co-heroine. In 2012, the play premiered at Woolly Mammoth—an exceptional production—but though Minhee now had equal time on stage, she was not equal as far as dramatic interest. Junhee had various diverting adventures in the US, while Minhee was literally stuck at the border. Not very dramatic. Lots of telling, not showing. (By having Minhee stuck at the border,

I was attempting to dramatize how North Korea has been frozen in time, stuck in the political moment of the mid-1950s Cold War—just after the Korean War ended and the land was divided into North and South.) On the heels of the Woolly production, that same draft had a second production at Company One. A very different production that I also loved dearly. But the play wasn't done.

The play's *raison d'être* was to give as much access to, and engender as much empathy as possible for, a figure that is mystifying (especially for a Western audience): The North Korean who is sincerely loyal to the brutal NK regime. But in that draft, Minhee's scenes were inactive, dormant, and frankly, rather boring. I just couldn't stop working on the play until Minhee's complex, delicate psychological journey—from loyal NK citizen to determined defector—was as dramatic as Junhee's adventure in the US. I took the play apart to the nuts-and-bolts level more than once, finding better narrative strategies and deeper sensitivity for Minhee's perspective each time.

All this took a few years. I never thought the play would ever be produced again.

Luckily, I am often wrong: In early 2015, Portland Playhouse made a production offer; it felt like a good omen. A few months later, the Royal Court Theatre in London announced the UK premiere of *You for Me for You* in their Fall 2015 season.

In London, they were particularly attentive to the play's investigation of thought control and social programming; in rehearsal, they often drew parallels to Orwell's *1984*. They also assumed that Minhee's fall into a well was an intentional reference to Alice's fall down the rabbit hole. (I actually was inspired by a Korean aphorism about frogs in a well looking up at the sky and believing they are seeing the entire world.) The links to these Western literary classics were really useful reference points for the creative team as they built performance and design vocabularies for interpreting North Korea and its shifting levels of reality. The same was true for critics and audiences seeking a foothold in the play's investigation of a country that so many in the West find utterly bewildering.

The Royal Court production was followed by productions at the Portland Playhouse (Oregon), at Mu Performing Arts/Guthrie Theater (Minneapolis), and in 2017, at Crowded Fire Theater (San Francisco) and InterAct Theatre (Philadelphia).

Without question, *You for Me for You* has been the most thorough and superlative writing teacher I've ever had.

CS *Matters of language and translation affect how dramatists consider structure of their work, too. The shape of words, the shape of language. I notice that one of your new plays, workshopped at Berkeley Rep, is called* Bloken Engrish, *and focuses on translation. Could you talk about it? And also about language and shapes in your plays?*

MC When I realized that I wanted to write plays from the perspective of characters that were non-native English speakers, I remember having a sinking feeling inside . . . because I have an allergic reaction to broken English on stage. The accent is so often inaccurately generalized and inaccurately syncopated—just poorly rendered. It makes me break out in hives. And I believe it can keep audiences from truly seeing, hearing, and, most importantly, identifying with these characters. So, out of this internal conflict, I was intent on finding theatrical devices that eliminated the risk of hive-inducing broken English. In *You for Me for You,* I wanted the North Korean characters to be our primary points of access into the play; they are our baseline, the norm. And so, when Junhee's journey takes her to New York City, I abstracted the language of the American characters. In other words, we hear America from Junhee's perspective: When Junhee first arrives, not knowing any English, she hears fast-paced sounds.

In *This Exquisite Corpse,* I have the main character—a Korean immigrant to the US—wear a plastic mouth piece when she converses with native English speakers in order "to convey that speaking in a non-native language can feel like fighting with your tongue." Instead of being distanced by (poorly rendered) "broken English," I hope audiences will lean closer and listen more carefully to this abstracted rendition of non-fluent English, this English that has, in fact, been broken by a physical impediment.

Now I'm developing a play called *Bloken Engrish,* which drives straight into my discomfort; it will consider how English morphs and adapts when spoken by tongues accustomed to other languages. It may also look at what translation is, and how it works and doesn't work. I'm in the early stages of research and exploration so right now anything related to transformed language feels relevant. But what I can tell you is that I hope to render "broken English" with forensic accuracy and as a sort of music.

CS *How do playwriting and the playwright fit into the digital age of storytelling?*

MC To be honest, I flinch a bit whenever I'm asked this question. I think this is because human beings have a fundamental appetite for live performance. Watching a play has the indescribable potency of being simultaneously inside and outside of human action. On fulfilling that need, TV and film categorically cannot compete (other than with live broadcast events, such as, say, a presidential debate). This sounds like I have blinders on (and sure, I probably do) because the general public rarely goes to the theater, there is so much dramatic content at our fingertips online, theater is so expensive, and productions are so momentary.

But maybe another way to think about how plays fit in the digital age of storytelling is that theater can more easily be a site for innovation. In recklessly simplistic terms: There are endless ways to write a play, but there are formulas for writing TV and film. Obviously, there have been exciting innovations in TV and film, particularly when you step away from the mainstream, but my understanding is that innovation and risk are not really a priority.

Anyways, I get uncomfortable about grand pronouncements on art-making. Simply: I believe that three-dimensional, living performance is special and valuable. And something that humans need. I don't subscribe to the contest mentality that pits digital storymaking against plays. For me, they are categorically different. I think this live vs. digital question is really about access and quality . . . and access to quality. And that is a critical issue: Theater's current economic models of success don't make a lot of sense to me for a medium that has historical roots in and inherent potential to serve democracy.

Kaite O'Reilly

Kaite O'Reilly's awards include the Peggy Ramsay Award for *Yard* (Bush Theatre) and *Manchester Evening News* Best Play of 2004 for *Perfect* (Contact Theatre). She was also one of the winners of the Susan Smith Blackburn Award 2009 for *The Almond and the Seahorse* (Sherman Cymru). Her version of Aeschylus's *Persians* won the 2011 Ted Hughes Award for New Works in Poetry. She works extensively within disability arts and culture and wrote the groundbreaking *peeling* for Graeae Theatre in 2002. *In Water I'm Weightless* was produced in 2012 by National Theatre Wales before transferring to London as part of the official celebrations for the Olympic Games. Other plays include *The Echo Chamber*, and *Leaner, Faster, Stronger*. She is a Fellow of International Research Centre "Interweaving Performance Cultures" at Freie Universität, Berlin. Kaite has written radio plays for BBC Radio 3 and 4 in addition to writing and directing a Screen Gem for Channel 4/Sgrin/British Screen. Her collection of plays, *atypical plays for atypical actors,* is published by Oberon Books. www.kaiteoreilly.com

Caroline Jester *What is a playwright?*

Kaite O'Reilly It's funny, I started to go, "Ummmm . . . what is a playwright?" and I thought "I don't know if I would like to say *what is* a playwright, but I would like to say *what kind* of playwright I am, or what I do." I get nervous sometimes if we end up with these general "this is what a playwright does" [statements] because I think that's bollocks, frankly.

I think when I describe the work that I do I say, "I write dynamic," and it's something that's come up in all the years I've been teaching. I'll always say a playwright, in my definition, from my experience, is someone who writes the invisible: We write the invisible, we write structure, we write dramaturgy, we write atmosphere, we write dynamic, we write tempo rhythm, we write pace, we write subtext, we write everything that you can't tangibly see on the page necessarily, but you can see when it goes into live medium, performed by other people. So a playwright writes the invisible and does all those things that are, I think, structural. I think they are to do with energy and dynamic, the ephemeral and being in the moment, but it's when it's translated with the imaginations and skills of the rest of the company, the directors, the scenographers, the designers, the actors . . . that's what I think a playwright creates—the invisible thing that we then see when we work with our collaborators.

CJ *You were quite specific with the word "dynamic" at the beginning.*

KOR   Yes, that's what I think I do. I think I write dynamic.

CJ *I've never heard that phrase before.*

KOR   I've never heard it said before, it's just what I say and have been saying for about fifteen years, now. I might "do" characters but I'm not so interested in stories, I'm not so interested in characters; I'm interested in an experience between the spectacle and the spectator and what I do is I write dynamic. It's energy, it's atmosphere, it's relationship, it's tempo rhythm, it's the mind in thought hopefully expressed through your collaborators, the actors, and director, and scenographer. I always think of myself as a composer. I talk about music and terrified a group of poor writers I was giving a workshop to once, because I burst into Beethoven's Fifth (*sings*)—"TA DA DA DAA"—and they all jumped. "What's this strange woman doing?!"

(*sings*) "TA DA DA DAA, ta da da da da da da daa de de de de de de de dee, de da da DAH da, da da da DAH da, da da DAH, DAH, DAH, Da da da." When you think about it, the variety, the tone, the pace, the unexpected . . . everything is there in the equivalent of what we want to do in text. So I'm thinking all the time as a playwright, I'm thinking of the textual, variety, the unexpected, I'm thinking of the movement of the language and the action, the dramatic action, the way I imagine . . . I don't play an instrument, but I think it's similar to the way a composer thinks about writing music: It's moving, it's dynamic. So I think about that. I don't think about "Oh what's the story, what's the character?" because that bores me, actually.

CJ *Does the audience influence your writing?*

KOR It's the first thing in my mind, the audience. Of course it is, of course it is!

If I'm writing dynamic and I'm writing something that will be live and interpreted through my collaborators, it is about the relationship between the spectacle and the spectator, so I am constantly thinking about an audience. But I'm not thinking about an audience in the very patronizing attitude I've come across sometimes where people go, "Oh let's make sure the audience knows what we're thinking about," or "Let's not make it too complicated," or dumbing down. I'm not thinking of the audience as a consumer, as the person who has paid for the ticket, I'm thinking about the important second part of the equation that makes theater happen.

It's not that I'm thinking of the audience as a way of inflicting ideas or perspectives or political aspects on them. When I'm writing, I know what my intentions are. That's the other thing, teaching, I always say to people straight away, "What are your intentions?" Because that is our relationship and our contract with the audience.

CJ *Does the narrative you're writing dictate the dramatic structure you select to tell the story?*

KOR I'm not interested in narrative. I'm really not interested in narrative, I don't think about narrative at all.

CJ *Could I ask you to expand on your definition of narrative?*

KOR I often came unstuck when in the past I was working with literary managers and sometimes now, when I'm working with dramaturgs and they start using that language that feels very alien to me and not how I work. So they'll often say: "Well, what is the story? What is it really about? What's the journey you want to take the audience on?" And I understand all that intellectually, but that's not necessarily what I'm doing when I'm in the process of making work.

So for *peeling* for example, I knew very specifically and politically what I wanted to do with that piece. I wanted to challenge preconceptions of disabled and Deaf* women. I wanted to make all sorts of comments about the profession in which I work and their attitudes to "the tick on the equal opportunities form," as I think one of the characters says. I knew I wanted to tell stories that maybe hadn't been told before and I wanted to represent these female characters and voices and energies that were not necessarily the usual representation of impairment that I'd seen previously.

In the 1990s I volunteered with playwright Christina Katic for Suncokret, a grassroots humanitarian relief aid agency working in frontline towns and cities of former Yugoslavia during the war and post-war reconstruction, and we kept hearing about rape being used as a war tactic. We heard about genocide, we knew about young men and the boys being taken to the stadium in Srebrenica, and then the women raped by the Serb soldiers to basically ensure that the next generation was not necessarily Bosnian Muslim. We keep hearing about it all the time again—we keep hearing about how in Africa rape is being used consistently as a war tactic—and for me there was something about genocide that connected deeply with all these ancient Greek plays, going all the way back to *The Trojan Women*. It's like nothing's changed. We have always been shackled by war, we always have been given to the victors, the children have been killed and yet the war continues. And so for *peeling*, because I had all those things I wanted to work with—I wanted to talk about disabled women having control over their reproduction, and I also wanted to talk about women in the context of war having control over their reproduction—and it was by identifying what I wanted to address, and what I wanted to say in a mash-up of apparently opposing and opposite scenes—how on earth will they ever meet?!—that that was when the narrative came in. Because I then sit down and consider: "How could I do this? What could this story be? Ah, the characters could be a chorus, they could be a chorus in a war play, and all parts can come together."

CJ *How much do you consider where the play will be staged when you begin writing?*

---

* I use capital D for Deaf for those who identify as culturally Deaf, and who do not consider themselves disabled, but rather part of a linguistic and cultural minority group.

KOR   It depends, because my work is so broad. I have worked site specifically (most notably with Mike Pearson's production of my reworking of Aeschylus's *Persians* on a firing range on Ministry of Defence land for National Theatre Wales in their inaugural year). I've worked in different contexts; I collaborate a lot with Phillip Zarrilli and the Llanarth Group, his company, playing with the different projects. Each project is distinct and unique and then I formulate it and we approach it fresh. I don't ever want to reproduce anything.

CJ   John McGrath, in the preface to your collection of plays atypical plays for atypical actors, *wrote that: "Kaite O'Reilly is not a playwright. She is an artist of possibilities. A great one." I wonder how you respond to this?*

KOR   I was very humbled and surprised and grateful. And now that I've got over that incredible compliment, I like to think that theater is the exploration of what it is to be human and I try in my work to embrace all the possibilities of human variety. So if that makes me an artist of possibilities because I'm trying to provoke or present the variety of what it is to be human, or the breadth of human variety, I'm very proud to be called so.

CJ   Could you say where the idea for the title of this collection came from?

KOR   I was doing *In Water I'm Weightless* with John McGrath in 2012, an Unlimited commission with National Theatre Wales/Wales Millennium Centre and Southbank Centre as part of the official Cultural Olympiad festival. We think we're right in that it set an important political and cultural precedent—the first production of an all Deaf and disabled cast on a national platform with disability content written by somebody who identifies as a disability artist. I think the Paralympics did a lot of good for us because we would often be there trying to explain how disability is the norm, challenging notions of normalcy etc., etc. I kept coming back to this notion: Let's be really broad in our interpretation of what it means to be human and let's embrace all the potential of human variety. And when I was writing essays as Fellow of the International Research Centre "Interweaving Performance Cultures," attached to Freie

Universität in Berlin, I began thinking about something that is "atypical." "Disabled" is such a loaded term now. I don't want to project what I think somebody should think or believe: Just because someone has impairments, that doesn't necessarily mean that they're working from a disability perspective or that they even want to identify as disabled. I choose to, that's my own identity politics and I choose and I celebrate the fact that I identify as a disabled woman. I see it as something very positive because it has broadened my perspective, completely opened up all the possibilities of what it is to be human for me. And I just found using the word "disabled" is often seen as negative, and people will come with preconceptions of that word. Academically I was writing about the atypical body and I was talking about people who were neuro-atypical and then I just suddenly realized: That *atypical* was the word I wanted instead of talking about *disabled* actors—*atypical actors*. And atypical plays? Because it reflects the breadth of the form and the dramaturgies that I use in that collection. We have everything from what seems to be almost-realism—it's not quite, you know—to character-driven plays (*The Almond and the Seahorse*), as well as montage (*the 9 Fridas*), and open texts for people to take and remake in the shape they want (*In Water I'm Weightless*). There is a family saga (*Cosy*) and others like *peeling* that are in a very different aesthetic and form again, and so it seemed the plays themselves are atypical. And usually when you say you write plays, people have a set idea in their heads, that it's maybe realism and character driven and that's not how I perceive my work. So that's why I decided to say they were atypical plays and for atypical actors, to hopefully throw a fresher perspective on what is an actor, what is a play, and what theater can do.

CJ *How do playwriting and the playwright fit into the digital age of storytelling?*

KOR I don't know. I think that's something that other artists with other specialisms can address. I'm not quite sure what digital storytelling is, or the digital age. I do work a lot with video, with different theater languages, with projected texts, with soundscapes . . . I suppose that could be included in "digital storytelling." I don't really know what the phrase means.

Alexander Zeldin

Alexander Zeldin is a writer and director for theater. He trained on the Jerwood Young Directors course at the Old Vic and has taken part in residencies at the Egyptian Centre for Culture and Art at Studio Emmad Eddin in Cairo. His critically acclaimed play, *Beyond Caring*, had its world premiere at the Yard Theatre in Hackney before transferring to the Temporary Theatre at the National Theatre in 2015. It had a UK tour in 2016 and a US production in Chicago. In 2015 Alex was the recipient of the Quercus Trust Award and appointed as Associate Director at the Birmingham Repertory Theatre. *Love* opened at the National Theatre in December 2016.

Caroline Jester *What is a playwright?*

Alexander Zeldin I think it's a mistake to think of it [theater] as literature because it goes away from what it could be, which is a guttural, physical, messy, unpredictable, and totally fluid thing. The very fact that theater is different every night is part of its quality.

CJ *Does the audience influence your writing?*

AZ Yes and no. I write poetry and other forms of writing for myself, but I think theater is a way of helping me and the people I'm with have a better understanding about ourselves and our place in the world. One of the great qualities of theater is that you can concentrate time, you can look at life in a way that is increasingly difficult to do so. I read lots about the origins of the theater and in those days I think theater was there originally to do good to people; to help crops grow, or rain fall, and to have a space in which every type of person can be brought together. One need only to look at the architecture of certain theaters, be they Greek or Elizabethan, to notice that one of the particularities of the theater is that a whole different range of people can come together. Theater is for me a very effective tool for thinking and crucially feeling a little bit of what it's like to be in the world now. So the audience is absolutely crucial to the point of theater in the first instance but theater is an invitation to think of oneself as part of a group of more than one.

CJ   *How much is there a distinction between yourself and an audience?*

AZ   One of the strongest experiences I had was when I went to Egypt when I was twenty and I saw an exorcism ritual performed as music. In this exorcism these extraordinary women were singing a song and they got everyone to stand and dance until they were exhausted. They got their audience to get up. That felt very alive and was powerful and that's in a way what I want to do with an audience, even if they're just sitting still. I think it's good to disturb people. I don't think that's a separation; I think quite the opposite, it's a penetration. It's the opposite of a separation, in that it's a togetherness but in a very intense way.

CJ   *Does the narrative you're writing dictate the dramatic structure you select to tell the story?*

AZ   Yes and no. Somebody who I admire very much, Joël Pommerat, says he tries to create structures of moments. My work is quite different to his but in that way I'm quite inspired by him.

CJ   *How much do you consider where the play will be staged when you begin the writing process?*

AZ   It's everything. Before *Beyond Caring*, I did plays in drama schools where I wrote by devising with the students and that's how I learned my way of doing things. I knew where it [the play] was going to be performed. So there were no technical possibilities and in one instance it had to just be a community center room. Now at the Dorfman, for the first time I've had to really think together with the designer, Natasha Jenkins. What could this architecture be? I need to know the place. I remember when I did *Romeo and Juliet* in Naples, I wanted to actually stage it on a street corner and I chickened out of it because I didn't have the confidence that I have perhaps now—I hope I have now. I'm quite fascinated by traffic going past a small space and that's of course what the theater is. It comes back to that point about concentration; it's just one space. I'm quite simple in that sense and I don't like changing location too much. I know where it's set, I make the actual space so the lights are on, I transform a space into an environment where something can happen.

CJ Beyond Caring *is inspired by* The Night Cleaner *by French journalist Florence Aubenas, but you also went and applied for zero-hour contract jobs in the development of this piece. Can you describe how this experiential process informed the structural development of the play?*

AZ For me, making a play is an experience from the beginning to the end. From writing notes in my book to going for a walk and fantasizing from the notebook. But with *Beyond Caring*, it wasn't just about doing the jobs but meeting the people and having them be involved in the process with the actors. The question for me is really the meeting point between an actor and their personality and the person, a real person. That often is a moment of theater that is one of the strongest ones, stronger than what we end up making. So that meeting of individuals is often at the heart of what I try and do, and it's very experiential not just for me but for the actors as well. Who the actor is is also a big part of who the character becomes. There's no point lying and saying I'm going to invent some character and then the actor will just have to transform into them; I think that's not possible. For me it's very important I use the actors who have a certain quality in them that will meet with elements I have in my mind, and of course they are big collaborators in creating those characters.

CJ Love *is a piece about homelessness.*

AZ It's families living in temporary accommodation. One has got small children, one of them is an older woman living with her son who is fifty who has never really left her and they're living together in over-intimate conditions, and then there are two asylum seekers whose English is quite basic and they speak in other languages without surtitles. So it's just these people sharing this shitty common room and we're turning the Dorfmann into a shitty common room. These people live in cramped and salubrious conditions which is all over the country and it's a forced intimacy. Really it's a play about boundaries and borders as much between individuals as between groups and families. It's about love in the most extreme circumstances, which of course then has a way of talking about a whole load of other stuff which is very important. I knew what I wanted the characters to be and the way I work, it's almost musical, there's almost a score eventually in the room. It's a mixture between total freedom and total control.

CJ *Multilingual work without surtitles: How is that informing, or does that inform the score that you've just described?*

AZ I think I have to proceed in my work through my nerves; I have to sense my way. I can't write a whole structure; that won't work. I have several possibilities for structure but loads of material that's written. Very little will go in because the actors will need to reappropriate the scenes by improvisations, and sometimes I just have bullet points, which I ask the actors to improvise, and then I go away and write from that. But the writing process for me can be quite seamless. It should feel like they just say this but it is all intuitively constructed with quite clear decisions. In terms of the foreign language, it comes back to this really obvious point that in this country, and I'm trying to just be aware and acknowledge the reality in which we live, there are loads of languages other than English being spoken.

CJ *I've read in interviews that you don't see your work as political theater and I'm interested in why you don't see it that way, or why you don't see that in your work.*

AZ I think that the danger is it should speak for itself and I'm just interested in telling really concrete stories. The theater is fantastical enough with its make-believe and I just want to tell simple, concrete stories. I just want to tell clear stories about people's lives and I'm going to keep doing that.

The problem is that you sometimes invite people to think of a situation as an issue and it dies dramatically. To make it live dramatically, it needs to remain a true situation and the person in that situation isn't thinking, "I am in a political situation about zero-hour contracts." They're thinking, "shit, I'm too tired to get up, my legs are frozen or I haven't got enough money for the bus"—just show that and the whole "political" thing becomes real.

CJ *Because it's about not having the luxury of being outside of that present, it's survival: Where is she going to go to sleep? She's going to try and sleep in her workspace.*

AZ You just said about not having the luxury of being outside that present, but wouldn't you describe the theater in exactly the same way?

CJ *Yes.*

AZ You see, so in a way one of the reasons I do this is to find the situation that tells us more than the sum of its parts. That's precisely what we look for as dramatists; we look for the richest situations

CJ *How do playwriting and the playwright fit into the digital age of storytelling?*

AZ It's a chance to forget your phone for a couple of hours.

Naomi Iizuka

Naomi Iizuka's plays include *36 Views*, *Polaroid Stories*, *Anon(ymous)*, *Language of Angels*, *Aloha, Say the Pretty Girls*, *Tattoo Girl*, *Skin*, *At the Vanishing Point*, *Concerning Strange Devices From the Distant West*, *17 Reasons Why*, *Ghostwritten*, *Hamlet: Blood in the Brain* (a collaboration with CalShakes and Campo Santo + Intersection for the Arts), *War of the Worlds* (a collaboration with Anne Bogart and SITI Company), and *Good Kids* (the first play commissioned by the Big Ten Consortium's New Play Initiative). Iizuka is an alumna of New Dramatists and the recipient of a PEN/ Laura Pels Award, an Alpert Award, a Joyce Foundation Award, a Whiting Writers' Award, a Stavis Award from the National Theatre Conference, a Rockefeller Foundation MAP grant, an NEA/TCG Artist-in-Residence grant, a McKnight Fellowship, a PEN Center USA West Award for Drama, Princeton University's Hodder Fellowship, and a Jerome Fellowship. She teaches playwriting at the University of California, San Diego.

Caridad Svich   *What is a playwright?*

Naomi Iizuka   For me, being a playwright encompasses an eclectic range of roles. When I began writing, I had what might perhaps be viewed as a more traditional understanding of that role. I wrote scripts that became blueprints for the performance. I still do that, but I do many other things as well. I facilitate story circles, conduct interviews, lead workshops, help to organize community-based events around specific projects, adapt, and edit. So much depends on the project. I would say my understanding of what it means to be a playwright has grown over the years.

Being a playwright, by definition, means that you are writing for a live theater event. That entails working within certain constraints imposed by time and space. You're also working with a lot of variables, including the dynamic between your text and a particular constellation of actors, the many decisions made by directors and designers, and the particularities of the performance space, whether that be a traditional theater or a site-specific location. You have to create a piece of writing that can adapt to all these variables as well as the continually shifting circumstances of a given performance, embodied most of all by a live audience who bring with them a very specific, yet unpredictable, energy and mode of engagement that varies from performance to performance. As a playwright, you are creating a living, fluid storytelling structure in which an audience is seeing, hearing, and taking in a multivalent array of information in real time. I bring that awareness to my writing.

CS *Does the audience influence your writing?*

NI Absolutely. I'm about to start rehearsals for a play at Children's Theatre Company. Much of the audience will be elementary-school-aged children. I think a lot about how to make the story as vivid and surprising as possible for a theater full of bright nine- and ten-year-old children. I worked on a play not too long ago that was set in Louisville, Kentucky. Some of the characters were based on people from the area. And I knew a large portion of the audience would have a firsthand knowledge of the world of the play. I thought about that a lot as I wrote and rewrote. I wanted the piece to resonate for that local audience, and that awareness of who would be seeing the play absolutely informed the writing.

CS *Does the narrative you're writing dictate the dramatic structure you select to tell the story?*

NI I look at existing dramatic structures as a starting point. There are so many potent storytelling conventions that have been passed down over centuries. As a playwright, you want to know them fully. You want to understand how they work in a deep-tissue way. I think the challenge is to find how those familiar narrative structures can hold the story you want to tell. Sometimes that requires a pushing back. Sometimes you push back hard enough, and the structure begins to buckle, bend, and take on a different shape. It may look very different from what you had when you began, but that original architecture is still very much present.

CS *How much do you consider where the play will be staged when you begin the writing process?*

NI I don't.

CS *How do you begin the writing process?*

NI It sometimes feels as if I arrive at the inceptive idea for a play suddenly, but I think that's an illusion. Though an idea may feel as if it appears out of the blue, it almost always has a root system already in place that's been growing over time. It may come from a question or a story fragment that I've been turning over in my mind for months, sometimes years. More and more, I write with specific audiences in mind. One of the earliest pieces I wrote where the audience was clearly defined was a project that I worked on with CalShakes and Campo Santo. The piece was inspired by *Hamlet* and created with and for various Oakland communities who had some kind of relationship with violence. I spoke with people who had lost children or siblings to violence. I spoke with young men and women who were, or had been, incarcerated for violent crimes. I did interviews in people's homes, community discussions in churches, and writing workshops in youth detention facilities. Over the course of the almost four years it took to write the piece, I had many conversations about family and violence and ambition and revenge. What emerged at the end of that process was a play that was as much a version of *Hamlet* as it was an embodiment of the stories of the men and women who had participated in the process. There were community members who were constants from the beginning, including some who became actors in the production, and others who dropped in at different points of the process, going away and then coming back again. In working on this piece, what became very clear to me was that the making of the piece was as important as the piece itself.

CS *Your plays are often structured as ghost stories—spirits enter the material world and leave again, and characters are affected by the traces left behind or what they carry from the stories and legacies of these ghosts. The invisible is made visible in many of your plays. What draws you to this?*

NI I'm drawn to the question of how we see the world and what we miss. There's a character in *Concerning Strange Devices* who speaks very directly about our literal and figurative blind spots, all that we don't see or choose not to see, and the ethical implications of our inability to see the world around us. A play like *Polaroid Stories* is about a segment of the population that was in many ways unseen. I remember vividly the kids that inspired the play panhandling in a neighborhood filled with pedestrian traffic, and people walked by them for hours in a day without making eye contact, without engaging in any way. Writing that play was in part fueled by a desire to make visible people who had been rendered invisible in their daily lives, to honor their lives and their stories. I'm also interested in the struggle to make sense of what we see, of how we live through the same event, and yet see that same event very differently. Though they are very different plays, both *36 Views* and *Good Kids* are centered on competitive and irreconcilable narratives about the given world. And at the heart of these plays is an awareness that who gets to tell the story, who gets to say what the truth is matters in a deep way.

CS I was chatting with a colleague recently about how much the field has changed in only twenty years! In terms of the kind of works that get produced and don't, there exists, oddly enough, more "risk-averse" mentality amongst producers at venues that program new writing. What changes do you see in the field and how do you think things can be improved in ways of working?

NI I would like to see theaters be more adaptive to the different ways that theater-makers actually work. Not all work lends itself to a few weeks of rehearsal followed by a few days of tech. I would wish for more time to make the work with everyone in the room from the beginning. I would like to see critics enter the process in a way that felt more like a far-ranging conversation with a community of artists rather than a thumbs up/thumbs down appraisal process. For an audience, I would wish for a different kind of experience. I think about seeing bands in small clubs in LA or San Diego or Louisville, and the excitement of hearing something electrifying and new that I haven't heard before. I think about going to hear music in parks and outdoor venues where it's all ages and generations, and kids are running around, and the audience ranges from toddlers to their grandparents, and seeing how the act of coming together to hear live music is this event that stands out from the everyday, and is celebratory and a little bit unpredictable, and very much alive. I want the experience of seeing theater to be like that.

CS   *How do playwriting and the playwright fit into the digital age of storytelling?*

NI   I think the answer to that question is a work in progress. I have seen some intriguing and ambitious pieces that have explored the marriage of live performance and cutting-edge technology. That being said, more and more I am drawn to the kind of simplicity that playwriting can offer. We do indeed live in the digital age of storytelling, and yet I find that the simplicity of live actors speaking to an audience in real time, the intimacy and immediacy of that encounter, remains the most powerful kind of storytelling a playwright can engage in.

Sibyl Kempson[*]

Sibyl Kempson's plays have been presented in the United States, Germany, and Norway. As a performer Kempson toured internationally with Nature Theater of Oklahoma, New York City Players, and Elevator Repair Service between 2000 and 2011. Her own work has received support from the Jerome Foundation, the Greenwall Foundation, and the National Endowment for the Arts, among others. Her works include *Crime or Emergency, Potatoes of August, The Secret Death of Puppets, and Fondly, Collette Richland*. She is a MacDowell Colony Fellow, a member of New Dramatists, a USA Artists Rockefeller Fellow, and an Artist-in-Residence at the Abrons Arts Center. Her plays are published by 53rd State Press, *PLAY: Journal of Plays*, and *Performance & Art Journal (PAJ)*. She gained her MFA at Brooklyn College under the instigation of Mac Wellman and Erin Courtney. She teaches and has taught experimental playwriting at Sarah Lawrence College, Brooklyn College, and the Eugene Lang College at the New School in New York City.

Caridad Svich *What is a playwright?*

Sibyl Kempson To me, a playwright is someone who puts images, events, emotions, and words together in different combinations. These have the potential to be sacred combinations. Usually unbeknownst.

CS *Does the audience influence your writing?*

SK They help determine what the meaning of what the writing is. They are there before I write it—there is a thing that hangs in the ether and it's trying to get to them. My job is to step out of the way so it can do so.

CS   *Does the narrative you're writing dictate the dramatic structure you select to tell the story?*

SK   I believe I don't so much have a thought as a thought has me. I have found that there is another pattern at work that is mostly out of the conscious reach of my rational mind. It takes time and many hours in the writing and research saddle for the larger pattern to reveal itself. It's scary. Because it means I have no control, and also because it rarely fits neatly into a production timeline. I'm learning how to plan a production timeline in a way that allows for the discovery process.

I really try to keep Apollo and his orders and structures out of my thinking until the thing is up on its feet, and even then I work in a more visceral, almost biological, way that contends with how the writing feels in the room where it is being spoken. The time for the current Western dramatic structure has passed. It is no longer serving us. It's time to find new structures, and new ways of uncovering those new structures, that are more in line with our intuition, our authentic imagination, and our direct experience. It's time to own up to the tremendous power our human minds exert on everything in and around us, to stop thinking that we are helpless, and to change the images and stories we tell for the better, wider, longer future purpose.

CS   *How much do you consider where the play will be staged when you begin the writing process?*

SK   Consciously, not as much as I probably should. It's hard to write to a particular space unless you are resident there from the very beginning. But I do try to bear it in mind if I know the place where eventually it will be performed.

CS   *How do you see your work within a feminist framework of writing, especially in regard to structure? Are there certain formal structures to which you are drawn, and if so, in what way?*

SK   My work is feminist because I focus on details just for themselves, not as subservient to an overall structure. I do not impose structure on my work. Rather I allow it to emerge on its own. If I'm working in the best way, the play will tell me what it wants to be. I try not to boss it because it takes the fun out of it. I don't work from a recipe, I see what's in the fridge and I make something out of it. When I start having to think about structure in any way, my creative self completely shuts down. I immediately begin to find ways of subverting it, and usually that takes the form of some kind of excess that floods the system. Excesses of words, images, events, behaviors, scale, scope, budgetary expense, mannerisms, architectures, landscapes—whatever—will bust open the seams and bring the whole thing crashing down until it's something that is unrecognizable. It maybe has traceable patterns but even those are unpredictable and don't obey the laws of logic. I am drawn to patterns. I think the best patterns are those found in the chaotic workings of nature. So I look for those in the wreckage of what I have written.

CS *What makes theater theatrical? How do you think about structures and stages, even in your process?*

SK When I wrote *Potatoes of August* I was obsessed with potatoes and alchemy at the same time. I grew potatoes, filmed the plants, read everything I could find about the potato, looking at the same time at so much imagery of alchemy and famous alchemists, architectural blueprints for alchemical research labs, filmed myself digging up the potatoes, did research into music with divine components, making contemplative videos that combined all these elements, and at the same time I was writing the play. It's a very active but not always fully cognizant process.

The play ended up being about religion and science, and the kind of writing that humans were doing at the time when the two were intersected instead of opposed. And the potato figured in as a sort of trickster figure—defiant of the laws and the ideals. And a comic relief from such heady topics. The potato doesn't give a shit about the laws of symmetry. And the potato was showing up in herds and legions and swarms, ready to take over our outworn belief systems. And all the while I'm also playing around with ideas about what it means to have herds and swarms and legions of potatoes on a stage. How do we stage a storm of potatoes? What would it mean to have to actually have a sack of potatoes dressed up as a doctor performing in a scene with a woman about to have a colonoscopy? These kinds of questions— ridiculous!—the kind of questions I would pose as a restless kid feeling constricted by too many rules. Not long after *Potatoes of August*—that was in 2009, I think—I strayed from staging my own work and entered a period of writing on commission for other groups. I had been performing in all my work too, and in the work of others, and got burnt out. The period of writing for others taught me a great deal, and now this year (2015), I have founded my own company for the express purpose of staging my own writing again, and taking the performing out of the equation in order to survive it. I should say, however, that even though I'm not performing these days, I think my writing and staging is taken directly from my own performance experience. The energy put into the writing is my own physical performance energy. That's why I started writing—to give myself a performance vehicle. And the writing still contains that energy.

CS *How do playwriting and the playwright fit into the digital age of storytelling?*

SK Plays are texts that are meant to be performed within a shared time and space. Television and telephone came along and made it so we could hear stories from wherever we were, so it took the shared space out of the equation. Then the Internet came along and you can watch your stories any time you want, as well as any place. So that takes the shared time out of the equation too. When we were all turning on the Simpsons at 7pm on Sunday night, Fox, we were still all together in a way because everyone was watching at the same time. Now everything is scattered. For a little while there it seemed like plays were going to slide off the face of human experience. But now it feels like they are re-emerging as something we need to do and share in that same old way that we used to.

Carl Miller

Carl Miller trained as a director at the Royal Court in London on the Regional Young Director Scheme. He has been Artistic Director of the Royal Court Young People's Theatre, and an Associate Director of Birmingham Repertory Theatre and Unicorn. As Writer-in-Residence at the Theatre Royal Bury St. Edmunds, Carl adapted a number of late eighteenth- and early nineteenth-century plays for the "Restoring the Repertoire" project. He wrote the book *Stages of Desire: Gay Theatre's Hidden History*, and is a member of the BML and MMD Lab workshops for musical-theater writers. He has devised many playwriting projects with young people and adults. With the Royal Court International Department, he has worked with playwrights in Brazil, India, and Uganda. Plays and adaptations include: *Ostrich Boys* (Belgrade Theatre, Coventry, and National Theater Company of Korea); *Emil and the Detectives* (National Theatre); and *Red Fortress*, *The Three Musketeers*, *The Tempest*, and *The London Eye Mystery* (all for Unicorn Theatre).

Caroline Jester   *What is a playwright?*

Carl Miller   For me, playwrights don't just write the words that are spoken: They create the structures within which those words are spoken and the world from which all the partners—the actors, the director, the design team, whoever happens to work on the production—can create that world. I think one of the frustrating things sometimes is when some of that information is seen as irrelevant or dispensable with. I had an incident recently where I was working with a writer whose director's process was to cross out all the stage directions in a writer's text. Maybe if you were looking at a classic play, those stage directions may be instructions appropriate to the theater production forms of that time, and crossing them out might liberate the spoken words of the play from its original context and refresh it. But I also think there's a danger sometimes in seeing playwrights as dialogue writers, and I think that's something to do with the complex relationships between writers and directors in film and television, particularly in film where there's a sense that dialogue, what people say, is just one layer and maybe not even the most important layer of what's happening. So I suppose for me a playwright is the person with the responsibility for creating that whole world and that you do that by the words you put down on the page as a set of instructions or guidance for the team, and I feel that includes all of the information you give about what people are physically doing, what the setting is, and all the rest.

CJ *I wonder in terms of your understanding of a playwright, you've worked at theaters, you've worked at the Royal Court Theatre, you were in charge of the young writers' programme . . .*

CM At the time I worked there it was the Young People's Theatre, and in fact what shifted during that time was that it moved to a much closer focus on writing as the one thing that the Royal Court had as a sort of speciality in, so it moved from working with primarily young *performers* to working primarily with young *writers*.

CJ *And you were Associate at Unicorn Theatre and Associate at the Birmingham Repertory Theatre . . . that's a lot of work with writers, encouraging writers; do you think that has informed your understanding of you as a playwright?*

CM A lot, partly because I think I trained as a director and so I have that sense of what a rehearsal room is like and simple courtesies or facts. I remember quite early on we were producing a play by a young writer in a young writers' festival and had to explain to her that yawning a lot during rehearsals was quite off-putting to the actors and she hadn't realized; it was quite a long day, but she would just be at the side of the room while the actors were rehearsing her play yawning loudly. You suddenly go from something that you very much do on your own to something where you're with loads of people, all of whom have slightly different temperaments, some of whom may be good with people themselves, and some of whom aren't. So I certainly think it's helped me in those moments when it's been stressful or difficult.

CJ *Does the audience influence your work?*

CM I think the point at which I learn a lot about the rhythm of a scene and a play is being in a room with other people watching it. Sometimes I can guess that earlier, but it's definitely true that in a room with an audience it's much more obvious to me that, for example, a scene's just going on too long, people are fidgeting, people are not focused . . . [I notice] the points where, for some reason, there's something wrong. And it may be actually the timing of that information is wrong, and they're more confused than they should be. I think sometimes it's a broader thing and it just feels like everyone's been in the room for too long, and that actually we could do with losing five minutes off this half, or whatever. So you can learn from the audience by being in with them watching your own work.

In terms of targeting and who you're writing for, people have different views about that. I think I'm always writing for people who are excited or interested by the stories, ideas, or characters I'm interested in. And again I think that may be a dilemma because sometimes I might be astonished that nobody is interested in a thing that I find particularly fascinating. I don't think I could write well about something that I *don't* feel fascinated by, so I just have to hope there are enough people out there who do find it fascinating, and maybe for some pieces that's quite a narrow group or a small group and for some that's wider. I'm reluctant to assume that something is only of interest to a particular group, although things are slightly different when I've been specifically asked or I've wanted to write work for young audiences. I think one of the ways that I've thought about it is it should be a piece which in some way gives greater weight to the perspective of that young person in the audience, so I'll often be thinking about what that perspective is.

In terms of the gender, social–political background, and ethnicity of characters, I ask myself: Are those characters peripheral? Are they active? Are they driving the story? Do they matter most? Those aren't necessarily questions that I'm choosing because I'm thinking, "oh, those will apply to an audience or a particular sector of audience," but because they are questions about what kind of stories do I want to tell. And many, many of the stories that are told in our culture are about white male adults doing things. They're great stories, but they aren't the *only* characters who can do things and make things happen, and so if you're writing now I think it's useful to consider whether you're writing something because it's a habit you've got into and those are the stories you've always seen.

CJ *Does the narrative you're writing dictate the dramatic structure you select to tell the story?*

CM Ideally, content and form work together beautifully, so you need to find the way to tell the story that's right for the form. Taking *Ostrich Boys* as an example, though, I've now written two completely different versions of one story. That's the same story but I've now written two versions which are completely different. The specifics of that choice were, the first commission was for a large youth theater cast, so one of the dilemmas there was I knew it would involve a large mixed-gender group of performers and the central story of *Ostrich Boys* is about a friendship between four boys. So working out how best to tell that story with a mixed group had quite a big influence on the structural choices. For example, leaping into the story midpoint to a crucial narrative moment when the three boys who are on the journey meet three girls felt like a good way of making those characters vivid from the very beginning simply in terms of when to start telling the story.

When I then rewrote a new adaptation essentially for a small cast, I made the choice to just have the four male actors, which meant that we could have a more chronological telling of the story. It then posed a different technical problem because you've then got to have a scene where the three boys meet the three girls and we only had four boys to act them, so that and other technical challenges meant that that form of role-playing in the story had to be different. So from the particular choices of cast size in both those cases came some quite big choices about form and how to tell the story. And I think they both work, even though you get a very different feel from the adaptations; one maybe gives you a much "bigger" world, while the other is much more focused in on the psychology of the four boys.

CJ *How much do you consider where the play is going to be staged when you begin the writing process?*

CM I think about it more and more, and it was a huge learning experience to do *Emil and the Detectives*, which was on a huge open stage, the Olivier, where I'd never imagined I would have a play on, so I'd never thought about what the implications would be and a lot of them hit home only when I was sat in the auditorium looking at it and realizing what did and didn't work in the writing, or where the writing did or didn't help in the space.

The things that I think I've learned from watching *Emil and the Detectives* in the Olivier are that in that space, focusing the audience's attention becomes really important because it's quite hard to choose where to look, whereas I suppose a "picture frame" stage has a vanishing perspective, and it's much easier for the staging to focus your eye. The nature of the Olivier, particularly when you've got more than one performer on it, is that it's very easy to be looking anywhere and so what the writing I think would benefit from doing—and didn't always in the adaptation that I'd written for it—is going "look over here." So as a character comes on, you kind of know that's someone to focus on; they want something, they're after something, and this scene is going to be about this struggle. If I was doing a show in The Door or the Theatre Upstairs, on the other hand, I could allow the audience to find that out for itself as the scene goes on. If you look at plays that are written for big open spaces—Greek, Elizabethan, Jacobean—and often the most successful ones have a very vivid way of making it clear to you what matters at the top of the scene. The challenge then is to also be subtle.

CJ *How do playwriting and the playwright fit into the digital age of storytelling?*

CM Playwriting has been going on for a long time: The idea that you imagine something, you write it down, and other people act it out has existed in different cultures in different ways for thousands of years. I'm optimistic that there's something it [still] offers us and that other forms of storytelling—the novel, radio, or anything else—don't threaten it, so I'm not sure that all these things necessarily have to kill each other off. I think that the way that we tell stories changes. So one of the things that does offer opportunities for a playwright today is that audiences are very literate with different types of narrative structure, so in the musical piece I've just been working on, a lot of the time we've been talking about the way scenes dissolve into or cut to each other. Or the language of film feels like something that is quite possible to do on stage and that an audience will be able to follow because actually that language is in their head; references in an Elizabethan or a Jacobean play to classical culture might be part of their education. So what's in the collective knowledge enriches the possibilities of what you can write. I think the attention span question, which is not just about playwriting but maybe about how we live now, is a dilemma.

George Brant

George Brant's plays include *Grounded, Elephant's Graveyard, Marie and Rosetta*, and *The Mourners' Bench*. Brant's work has been produced internationally by such companies as the Public Theater, Trinity Repertory Company, The Atlantic Theater Company, Cleveland Play House, Gate Theatre of London, and Traverse Theatre. His scripts have been awarded a Lucille Lortel Award, an Edgerton Foundation New Play Award, the David Mark Cohen National Playwriting Award from the Kennedy Center, the Smith Prize, the Keene Prize for Literature, and an NNPN Rolling World Premiere. He is published by Samuel French, Oberon Books, Fischer Verlage, and Smith & Kraus.

Caridad Svich   *What is a playwright?*

George Brant   Most often, my role as playwright to an audience is to say, "Hey! Look over here!" When I researched drones for *Grounded,* my mind was blown—I had no idea our pilots were flying the UAVs (unmanned aerial vehicles) from here in the United States, and no idea that the pilots were going home every night after a day of work/war. The play is an attempt to share that information, as well as ask an audience to consider the psychological damage such a set-up might provoke, and to consider the costs of strikes on the drone's targets.

CS   *Does the audience influence your writing?*

GB   On a micro level, the rewriting process is all about the audience. One specific example: The life of a drone pilot is for the most part a boring one, so I knew that boredom had to be part of *Grounded*— calibrating how much intentional boredom an audience can handle was certainly a new and fascinating challenge.

CS   *Does the narrative you're writing dictate the dramatic structure you select to tell the story?*

GB I'm often inspired by the dramatic structures and strategies that other playwrights hit upon, and frequently try my hand at what has come before, influenced by both the triumphs and missteps of others. Ultimately, I try to follow Sondheim's advice and match story and form, whether that means trying something existing or new.

Sometimes it's an image that won't let me go, sometimes an odd historical detail that stays with me. That then leads to research, where hopefully there's some detail that strikes me as worth exploring, that helps define the angle with which I want to approach the subject. As far as planning, I usually have some sort of outline before I begin writing, sometimes as detailed as the scene-by-scene events, sometimes merely a few scribbles of ideas, all of which is subject to change once I turn the characters loose.

When I began my writing career in Chicago, I wrote mainly comedies, generally satires of the theater, poking fun at its conventions. I remember reaching a point where I felt I had hit a dead end with this style, that I should stop writing plays that made fun of theater and be brave enough to express why I thought it was a valid form, and to share and define myself without hiding behind another's structure. It wasn't easy: I felt quite naked without a convention to poke fun at; even now, I feel that I'm still discovering what my own comic style is.

In fact, I shifted away from comedy altogether at that point, but even so, I feel strongly that even the most serious tragedy is in need of a joke every now and then. I find that there is no substitute to opening up an audience member than making her laugh.

CS *But at some point, when you're building a playtext, the writer's moral compass comes into play, no? What we sometimes call "responsibility." That is, going beyond mere structural work and thinking more globally about what we have in hand before us and how we wish to engage the audience in civic dialogue.*

GB The moral compass most definitely comes into play at some point in the art-making process, whether in the initial draft, where one chooses whether or not to censor or steer what's spilling out, or in the rewriting process, when the cold light of day strikes a play, and you question the morality of what your subconscious has created.

I suppose there are two moral compasses at work when writing a play. The first lies with the characters in your script, allowing each of them their own moral compass, and not censoring it. The second lies with the circumstances in your play, which in a sense are where you share your personal moral compass.

The Mourner's Bench has a moral universe at work; the characters all know the tragedy they've endured was horrifically morally wrong, but how they deal with it is where their own morals are tested—each is desperate to create their own moral universe in response to the violence that has come before. Circumstance-wise, the play could end with Bobby and Melissa's story, but it doesn't; it ends with a story of hard-fought love and sacrifice.

Elephant's Graveyard's many characters each face their own moral quandary; one choice I faced with the play was how horrific its conclusion should be—in this case, my moral compass steered me to take it further than I was comfortable with, the discomfort being the ultimate point.

The Pilot in *Grounded* doesn't feel she's in much of a moral quandary, at least consciously. She every once in a while questions if what she's doing is fair, if it doesn't fit the definition of combat, but other than that she doesn't give much thought to the morality of her actions. Her subconscious is at work, however, and ultimately saves her—or is her downfall, or both. As for the circumstances she goes through, I spent a few sleepless nights over whether I could stand by the conclusion of the play, but ultimately was morally comfortable siding with the Pilot, the individual, over the military structure she exists within.

CS *How much do you consider where the play will be staged when you begin the writing process?*

GB I'm increasingly interested in inviting designers, directors, and actors into my plays, inviting true collaboration. *Grounded* is perhaps the most extreme example of this: There are almost no stage directions in the play, and I offer only a few notes on the presentation. As a result, the productions have each been radically different from the other, which has been equal parts fascinating and gratifying.

Chris Haydon of the Gate was guided by a strong sense of presentation: He knew he wanted to place the Pilot in a cube, creating a physical fourth wall that would not lessen the sense of intimacy the play requires, but rather increase it. On the other hand, Ken Russ Schmoll in the Page 73 production was guided by the physical expression of the play, eventually coming to the conclusion, no less radical than the cube, that the Pilot should never move at all. Julie Taymor, perhaps unsurprisingly, was guided by a series of images that came to form and define the world of the play.

With each director I've personally been in the rehearsal room with, I've attempted as best I can to allow them the space to create, offering my opinion, but not smothering their creativity. I will admit that part of what made this easier was that, unlike some of my plays, I wasn't entirely sure myself how *Grounded* should look or sound, and was genuinely interested in how others interpreted it. This doesn't mean that I didn't sometimes disagree with these interpretations, but I tried to hold my tongue and allow exploration before shutting down others' creativity that might pay unexpected dividends.

When the Gate's production of *Grounded* opened in Edinburgh, I had a moment of panic, wondering if the international audience was going to connect with what struck me as a very American character and concern. I even flirted with changing a few references (J. C. Penney was one) to make them more international, but the director, Chris Haydon, rightly talked me down from that ledge, insisting that the references gave the play a ring of American authenticity, whether the audiences fully understood them or not.

If I could, I'd wish for a theatrical world in which courage was rewarded, instincts were trusted, chances were taken, and audiences craved work that challenged them.

CS *How do playwriting and the playwright fit into the digital age of storytelling?*

GB I think we are going to increasingly need an escape from these devices around us, and I hope that theater can be a part of that. It has been fascinating to see how *Grounded*, a play about the digital age, has connected with audiences using the oldest story telling method we have; one woman telling a story. And at any play I go to now really, the moment when everyone turns off their phones feels increasingly like an act of resistance, of acknowledgment: More than ever before, those of us in this room are choosing to distance ourselves from the world around us and commit to spending the next hour or two together, in one room, sharing one story, at the exact same time. It makes me hopeful that what we playwrights provide may become even more necessary than ever before.

Lisa D'Amour*

> **Lisa D'Amour** is a playwright and co-artistic director of PearlDamour, an OBIE-award winning interdisciplinary performance company. Most recently, Lisa's plays have been produced on Broadway at Manhattan Theatre Club's Samuel J. Friedman Theatre, Steppenwolf Theatre (Chicago), The National Theatre (London), Playwrights Horizons (New York City), and Southern Rep (New Orleans). Her play *Detroit* was a finalist for both the 2011 Pulitzer Prize for Drama and Susan Smith Blackburn Prize.

Caridad Svich *What is a playwright?*

Lisa D'Amour A playwright is a trickster who frames human experience through performance texts in the hopes of getting what she wants: The truth. Since truth is relative, the playwright, like the trickster, will always become ensnared in her own trap (i.e. frame, i.e. play). The play will always be imperfect, and the playwright will always be driven to try again, using new strategies, reaching just far enough outside of her own grasp that she will become ensnared again.

This process can be delicious—like what I imagine a healthy S & M relationship to be. A cycle of submitting to and then dominating your play, trusting that you know each other, staying as present as possible, in order to break through to the *new*. Look too far into the future— toward critical success, financial success, trying to make every imagined audience member happy—and the energy dies.

CS *Does the audience influence your writing?*

LD The play takes place in the audience. I learned this most radically when I performed Yoko Ono's *Cut Piece* for the first time. *Cut Piece* is

---

* Interview reproduced with the kind permission of the author and their legal representation.

one of Ono's instruction pieces—the instruction can hang on the wall of a museum, or it can be performed live. There are two sets of instructions running around for *Cut Piece*. I've seen one that says simply "Cut" and another that says "Performer sits on stage with a pair of scissors in front of him. It is announced that members of the audience may come on stage—one at a time—to cut a small piece of the performer's clothing to take with them. Performer remains motionless throughout the piece. Piece ends at the performer's option." The first time I performed the piece I prepped in a state of nervous self-absorption. Worrying about how many layers to wear, feeling star-struck that I would be performing at The Walker Art Center, obsessing about what was going to happen when people started cutting—would it be boring? Would it be violent?

I came onto the small stage and read the instruction, sat on the floor (because that is what I'd seen Yoko do in the film of her performing it at Carnegie Hall), and put the scissors in front of me. Immediately a line formed to cut pieces of my clothing—the audience began "writing" the script. Each cut revealed something about the person cutting, and the cutting became a conversation: The punk rock boy with the wild hair cuts a large piece out of my shirt; the older woman approaches, cuts a piece out of her own sweatshirt and covers me up. For forty-five minutes, I stayed as neutral as possible, and let the story unfold. At times it was a healing ritual, at times it was a public shaming—the story morphed and shaped itself, instigated by Ono's one instruction.

CS   *Does the narrative you're writing dictate the dramatic structure you select to tell the story?*

LD   Yes, it does. I don't always realize it when I begin writing, and the structure often hits me early on, and becomes a kind of carrot dangling in front of me to keep me writing.

I'm thinking of my very early play, *16 Spells to Charm the Beast*. I'd become fascinated with wills through a day job I had at a law firm, and I wanted to write a play about the will of an angry woman who disinherits her daughter completely in one sentence. At this time, I was also interested in extreme language experiments in my plays. I began the play with the woman reading the will out loud to a beast, like a fairy tale beast, who was kneeling in front of her. She reads seven items/instructions, one of which informs the beast that he gets nothing.

Immediately after writing that scene I thought: "Oh, right, there will be a scene that deals with each item, and the scenes will leap back and forth through time, giving us an abstract snapshot of this character's life. And I will also write scenes with the beast alone, spying on her and making gifts he will use to woo her." And I kept writing, alternating a will scene with a beast scene, which eventually became sixteen "spells" plus a coda.

I tell the story of the birth of my play *Anna Bella Eema* to students all the time. I was blocked—completely out of ideas. And so of course I went to whine to a friend. When he was thoroughly sick of me, he reminded me that I had told him months before that I wanted to write a version of the golem myth in which a woman created a woman out of mud. I kind of shrugged: "Sure, why not try, it'll either work or it will be the end of my writing career." I started writing the play using conventional, proscenium-style naturalism: *"Lights up on the exterior of a trailer in a run-down trailer park. Annabella runs in, kicking up dirt behind her . . ."* and so on. It went nowhere. I kept writing scenes and tossing them. I was about to abandon the whole project when I said to myself "is there one thing you have written that rings really true to you?" And I said to myself "yes, the monologue where Annabella's mother, Irene, tells her life story to a werewolf who visits her trailer home." And I let Irene start talking, without thinking about the set, or where the play was going. And as I wrote, I realized that this was a three-person, spoken and sung ghost story, told directly to the audience by Annabella, her mother Irene, and Anna Bella Eema, the girl made out of mud. This play about a supernatural mother–daughter bond/rite of passage needed to shapeshift between epic fable and intimate exchange; I found that structure through the voice of the character.

CS *How much do you consider where the play will be staged when you begin the writing process?*

LD This varies for me, depending on whether I am writing for a theater, or making a collaborative piece with PearlDamour. With PearlDamour's recent piece, *Lost in the Meadow* (created with designer Mimi Lien), the space came first. We were invited by People's Light Theatre to explore the vast Longwood Gardens and pick a performance site. Much of Longwood is beautifully manicured—bonsai gardens, award-winning chrysanthemums filling a majestic glass conservatory. PearlDamour was immediately drawn to the Meadow Garden: Eighty-six acres of tall natural grasses and sunflowers that can be viewed from a nearby lawn, or explored on paths cut through the garden. We loved sitting on the lawn, watching people walk, run, and discover things many yards away from us. We decided to create a piece for audiences sitting on the lawn, wearing headphones, and watching a group of pilgrims travel the paths of the meadow. These characters would "pop up" in different parts of the meadow, all the while getting closer to the audience. Audience members could listen in on the characters conversations, and track interlocking stories. It was a bit like watching a Chinese landscape painting come to life. The writing was tricky: We realized early on that the meadow was so vast, we needed to begin almost every scene with a sound or large action in order to draw the audience's eye. And so the script reads like a radio play.

CS *What advice would you have for sustaining a life in the arts, especially during these times of economic austerity?*

LD You are dangerous. I spent a lot of time working within the glorious bubble of downtown New York theater. I thrived on radical theater experiments—plays that tried to re-invent language, site-specific train wrecks. I still love and am a part of that world. But I learned much more about how theater can shake us out of stasis when I began PearlDamour's *Milton* project. The project began with a naïve desire of two "big city" women to learn more about small towns and see how a small-town audience might differ from the audiences we'd been making work for in New York, Austin, Minneapolis, and New Orleans. We began visiting five towns named Milton and interviewing residents about their lives, town and worldviews, then created an experimental performance that reflected our experience of the towns. When we started visiting the five Miltons, many residents really didn't know what we meant when we said we were theater artists. They would introduce us as "the girls writing the book" or "the girls making the movie." Some people were reluctant to meet us, questioning our intentions, worried that we were just there to swindle them out of something. After multiple visits, we built trust with a core group of community members in each Milton, and people could understand what we wanted: To bring our play to their town, and collaborate on arts activities that might bring their community together to work on issues that were important to them. Once there was trust—once we could all truly hear each other—well, things really started cooking. We started to see people imagining their own town—taking matters into their own hands instead of sitting around being scared by what the TV or Internet was telling them about the world. It's been beautiful to watch, and really makes me mourn the days of the Works Progress Administration, and the lack of community arts funding in general; and then I start thinking about how gathering for theater in small towns is an easy, efficient way to gather lots of different kinds of people in the room to find common ground and take action. And then I think: "Oh, right. There are many people running this country who might not be so happy about that. A country is harder to control when the people living in it feel they can act in their own best interests and imagine their own world . . ."

You are dangerous. You will question your own motives. You will feel like the art you want to make has no value. You will feel like there is no place for your skills, for your voice, for the new paradigms you will propose.

Find your people. Ignore the noise. Make the work.

CS *How do playwriting and the playwright fit into the digital age of storytelling?*

LD Playwrights can sit around all day and compare the number of people that have seen an entire run of one of their plays to the number of people who have seen one episode of *Game of Thrones*. Or we can spend our time writing a moment that requires the breath and presence of both the actor and the audience.

Now, we're in a golden age of TV. Free from the prison of three networks, dozens of platforms are creating adventurous shows in new formats, bringing all kinds of characters center stage. It's beautiful. And is that the work? Do we need theater too?

Yes, we do. Because theater is harder to turn off, and it will always be a different kind of communal experience. I adore some of the new TV shows that are shaking up the field. I eat them up, but they don't *rattle* me. They don't make me laugh till I cry and hit the hand of the person sitting next to me. Or gasp collectively in a room of 200 people. They don't make me argue with the people I came with as I walk out of the theater. It's a completely different chemistry.

And even as TV grows more diverse in content and representation, it still can't create a moment of true, shared spontanaeity. A moment that each audience member and performer experiences slightly differently. Sparking a diversity of perspective and opinion, altering the rhythm with which an audience member walks through the world. And because of the *Milton* project, I'm especially hopeful about these small rooms—more and more in the United States, it's nothing short of a miracle to gather people with opposing viewpoints in the same room, to experience live performance and discuss it. It's frightening to most people. It's easy these days to huddle inside one's tribe.

We can use theater to bring people *out*. To promote spontaneity, idiosyncracy, flexibility, and a spectrum of points of view, rather than just two or three to which people cling for dear life.

David Greig*

> **David Greig** is a playwright and theater director. His works
> include: *The Events*; *Pyrenees*; *The American Pilot*; *Yellow Moon*; *The
> Strange Undoing of Prudencia Har*; *the Yes/No Plays*; *The Architect*;
> and the book for the West End and Broadway musical of *Charlie and
> the Chocolate Factory*. He has adapted works by Camus, Strindberg,
> and Euripides, among others. In 2015, he was appointed artistic
> director of the Royal Lyceum Theatre in Edinburgh.

Caridad Svich   *What is a playwright?*

David Greig   A person who has written a play which has been
performed in front of a paying audience.
   A structurer of shamanic rituals.
   A crafter of vehicles in which actors travel.
   A manipulator of emotion through time.
   A poet.
   A Turkish carpet salesman.
   A psychic stripper.
   A naughty girl, showing all the boys her pants.
   I could go on . . .

CS   *Does the audience influence your writing?*

DG   Well . . . of course . . . but not in the sense that I anticipate their
reactions, in the sense that I *am* the audience, as I type I play, the work,
to myself.

CS   *Structure informs narrative and narrative informs structure, but
how can the stage, whatever form that might take, inform the playwright's
creative process?*

* Interview reproduced with the kind permission of the author and their legal representation.
© David Greig 2017.

DG I don't know, because I don't quite understand this question. I could answer it this way: When I write a play, I am always aware of the stage upon which it will be first performed. That shapes, the type, of story I will tell, the length of it, the size of cast, the tone of it etc. But that is not the stage as a physical object as much as it is the stage as a space with a particular audience, a particular history, and a particular geographical location.

I have a number of tests, which I like to apply to any play I'm working on. One test is "How would I explain this play to my friend Ugg?" Ugg is a man who lived 10,000 years ago with his tribe of hunter-gatherers. With every play I imagine I'm talking to Ugg and proposing that this evening, round the campfire, my tribe of the future wants to give his tribe a story. Ugg, who understands this time-traveling nonsense, has agreed to vet the idea to see if it will be appropriate, or if it might cause offence or be a disaster. So Ugg sits with me by the river and I explain the show.

— So, Ugg, this is a play about the death of the Labour Party . . . a new young MP decides to . . .

— David, I have to stop you there, what is the Labour Party, what's an MP?

— OK . . . right, sorry, this is a play about . . . a man who . . . a man whose tribe is dying and he decides to try and fix it . . .

— Ah, now I get it. Sounds interesting . . .

And so on.

The point being that I feel every story should be very particular on the surface. Very precise. But deep down, it should be easily explicable to Ugg. It should be the sort of play Ugg and his tribe would be able to connect to as well.

On the other hand, recently I have tried to create another filter whereby every idea I have for a play has to be set in present day Fife. This is not completely possible—of course—but somehow this filter acts as another anchor. It forces me to be precise and particular.

CS *Sometimes I like working with an existing structure, even if only in my mind, as a way to anchor the work. Say, Brecht's* Baal *or Euripides'* The Bacchae. *The pre-existing structure—its bones—will become the foundation for a new play on top of which an entirely new piece gets written!*

DG I take a very simple approach to this. Every new play should say something new about the world and something new about theater. I always cleave a play to an older form or writer but then I look at the way I will twist it into something formally new.

So—*Monster In The Hall* is a farce. *Yellow Moon* a road movie. *Europe* a Brecht play. *The Architect* is Ibsen and so on. In the new work I am doing, I am writing a Western, and I'm also writing a drawing-room discussion play.

With all of them, the key is to learn how that form works. To understand what its mechanisms are. Then to find a way to twist it and break it to make it feel new.

I need old forms in order to create new forms.

CS *Writers dig trouble. We shake the trees. We rattle the cages. We look at stuff that troubles us but which also troubles the times in which we live. We write to that, and from that we go from the hyper-local to the national and trans-global. So, there are strategies for doing so. There is a quest. Perhaps, dare I say, a shamanic one.*

DG a) Always ask a question to which you genuinely do not know the answer. This is vital. This is the fuel. Otherwise why write at all? So therefore, with *The Events*, don't ask, "Is this bad?" Of course it's bad! You write, "Does evil exist or is all bad action explicable by politics, sociology, medicine, etc.?" I genuinely don't know the answer to that question. I wrestled hard with it in the play. Not pretend wrestling, either; I challenged every thought I had which gave me any kind of comfort. So in the end, *The Events* says, I think, "We can't know, and we must let the question go, but in order to earn the right to let the question go, we must wrestle with it until we are broken." That process is as close as I can get to in thinking of playwriting as a moral act.

b) The truth. You must always, always be pushing for the truth. In every line. In every thought. "Is that true, or is that just a comforting thing I would like to be true?"

c) Jo Clifford said: "Empathy is a muscle, theater is the gym." With every character and every moment, ask yourself if you have truly put yourself in their shoes. Never assume, never pity, never patronize . . . listen.

d) Representing "the Other" is never easy, but it is your responsibility. You cannot speak "for" people, but that doesn't mean you should ignore them or not let them into your imaginary world. If you have a platform and the power to speak, then you have a responsibility to include. In *Damascus,* I write Arab characters and so I run into the danger of orientalism and cliché. But it's no good to say, "I won't write it, then." You have to redouble your efforts to truly imagine another person's perspective. You have to challenge yourself. You have to invite challenge from others, listen, and respond. Also, a play like *Damascus* comes out of a long, long process—ten years—of working with young writers from Syria, Palestine, and the wider Middle East. So, for me, engagement with "the Other," whether it be racial, gender, sexuality, class—all of these things—is a central challenge that any writer has to engage with. You can't shirk it.

Then, you must use what power and voice you do have to create space for voices coming from the "Other" place. So, write *Damascus*, but make sure to do festivals where you stage plays by young Arab writers. Write female characters, but make sure the theatrical space you control is feminist space.

CS *Breakthroughs, sometimes we know where our own breakthroughs are before anyone else does. And I can totally point to exact moments, too: Exact plays where a kind of turning occurred: A different way of thinking about form or space or language or time. Can you?*

DG For me there are two moments.

San Diego was the end of a long journey of exploration into the fragmentation of narrative. The next play I wrote was *Outlying Islands*, which was a direct response to Gregory Burke's *Gagarin Way*, which I had recently seen. I felt I had battered at the story like a child banging its furious fist on the tummy of a benign parent until finally you collapse in tears and into a hug. *Outlying Islands* is me falling into the arms of story and looking for a hug; believing in story as a motor for ambiguity and power; letting story take me on an adventure.

But *Outlying Islands* came out first, *San Diego* second. As a result, critics misunderstood the journey of the work.

The other moment is around *Yellow Moon*. This was the moment when I realized that I could be particular. I could set my stories in the real world around me—Fife, Scotland, the present day. And yet within that, I could tell every story that ever needed to be told.

I feel that I am coming toward the end of a cycle of works just now. This mine is just about exhausted and a new type of work is coming. There will be another break soon.

I did some work for Ramin Gray in a workshop recently. He was very taken with it but he observed: "You're working in a new font." I used to write everything in Arial, [but] this piece I was writing in Times New Roman. It may seem small, but that for me is the equivalent to going out dressed as a woman. It feels like something fundamental is different. Not sure what, though, and I have no idea how people will react to it.

I guess I have to wait until the work I'm doing in the new font starts to hit the stage.

CS *How do playwriting and the playwright fit into the digital age of storytelling?*

DG Perfectly. The playwright crafts drama unmediated by screens. The theater is the last unmediated public space. It's the place we gather together, next to each other, no phones or screens, and we watch the unfolding of life through time. The playwright is the person who organizes this. So, as long as we yearn for common experience—and we do, witness the increasing need for live events—we will have a place for playwrights, because they structure these events for us in such a way as provokes emotion, thought, catharsis. The digital age is no more of a threat to theater than every age since 2500 BC . . . from Rome to Ford to the Internet . . . theater is a basic human need as primal as joke-telling, singing, or sex.

3
DON'T PUT ME IN A BOX

As playwrights in this chapter were asked the question "Can a playwright cross into other artforms?" a glazed look in their eyes would appear. Their interest had been lost as yet again they were being asked such an unimaginative question. Why is it such a surprise that storytellers can do their job and tell stories in multiple ways? And why start with the playwright as if you come out of the womb telling a story for the stage and are immediately being defined as a playwright?

Philip Ridley just doesn't find the discussion around categorization interesting at all. He tells stories and has always done so. Storytelling is the medium. But it's the question he's been asked ever since his writing was first published after exhibiting his artwork. He's like "the dog that spoke."

Jordan Tannahill isn't convinced that art-makers discover their ideas in the disciplinary silo they have been directed toward. It is people who feel beholden to disciplines rather than ideas. The label of "playwright" can be stretched to encompass and contextualize all of his work.

Sabrina Mahfouz feels all artforms seem to be cross-artforms in some way. The term "spoken word," often used to describe some of her work, has become the mainstream definition of non-traditional poetry and not one she uses often about her own storytelling. Playwrights should just keep making plays that are important to them.

Daniel Alexander Jones isn't following a formula but making an equation. Who is making the boxes and who are they serving anyway? "It also has a lot to do with reinscribing the centrality of the unquestioned norm, an unnamed but implicit privileged white heteronormativity that picks and chooses its houseguests."

Caridad Svich not only switches artform to suit story but steps inside the minds of other writers and adapts their prose and translates their text. Does the ability to work inside the brain of another writer enable a different way of thinking about storytelling in theater?

Tim Etchells wonders if people who have a strict sense of their role in terms of a job title like "playwright" might not be able to cross from one mode of storytelling to another with ease. He thinks of himself as being interested in language, performance, and making things with other people. But we're in an era that enables multiple approaches.

Willy Russell's *Blood Brothers*, which is still playing to packed theaters thirty years after it first hit the stage, didn't appear to him in script format. He heard it and knew instantly that the idea was to be sung through. Was it his ability to cross artforms and write music, lyrics, and text that sprinkled magic onto it?

J. T. Rogers believes that new work that resonates have good stories at their core, well told and using new tools. When he returned to playwriting after screenwriting, this didn't distance him from writing for the stage but brought with it a new economy of language and swiftness to his storytelling.

Lin Coghlan thinks one of the reasons she has been able to stay working for so long is because she can diversify and do different things. She didn't listen to producers who told her she couldn't cross artforms and has even found herself using her storytelling skills in the gaming industry. You should be able to have fun with your storytelling skills and let them lead you into new arenas and opportunities.

Robert Schenkkan believes this is a healthy pursuit for an artist. They expose the artist to different ways of approaching story and text and performance. Some of these are radically different in approach.

So if the playwrights or storytellers in this chapter aren't afraid of being exposed to new ways of storytelling and reinvention, why can't we release the need to categorize them and let the stories lead the way?

Philip Ridley

Philip Ridley was born in the East End of London. He studied painting at St. Martin's School of Art and his work has been exhibited widely throughout Europe and Japan. As well as three books for adults (*Crocodilia*, *In the Eyes of Mr Fury*, and *Flamingos in Orbit*) —and the highly acclaimed screenplay for *The Krays* feature film (winner of the Evening Standard Best Film of the Year Award)—he has written many highly regarded and hugely influential stage plays: The seminal *The Pitchfork Disney*; the multi-award-winning *The Fastest Clock in the Universe*; *Ghost from a Perfect Place*; *Vincent River*; *Mercury Fur*; *Leaves of Glass*; *Piranha Heights*; *Tender Napalm* (nominated for the London Fringe Best Play Award); *Shivered* (nominated for the Off West End Best New Play Award); *Dark Vanilla Jungle* (winner of an Edinburgh Festival Fringe First Award); *Radiant Vermin*; *Tonight with Donny Stixx;* and *Karagula*. He has also written several plays for young people: *Karamazoo; Moonfleece* (named one of the 50 Best Works about Cultural Diversity by the National Centre for Children's Books); *Sparkleshark;* and *Brokenville* (collectively known as The Storyteller Sequence), and a play for the whole family, *Feathers in the Snow* (shortlisted for the Brian Way Best Play Award). His books for children include: *Scribbleboy* (shortlisted for the Carnegie Medal); *Kasper in the Glitter* (nominated for the Whitbread Prize); *Mighty Fizz Chilla* (shortlisted for the Blue Peter Book of the Year Award); *ZinderZunder*; *Vinegar Street*; *Zip's Apollo;* and the bestseller *Krindlekraz* (winner of both the Smarties Prize and WH Smith's Mind-Boggling Books Award), the stage play of which— adapted by Philip himself—was premiered at the Birmingham Repertory Theatre in 2002.

He has also directed three feature films from his own screenplays: *The Reflecting Skin* (winner of eleven international awards, including the prestigious George Sadoul Prize); *The Passion of Darkly Noon* (winner of the Best Director Prize at the Porto Film

Festival); and *Heartless* (winner of the Silver Meliers Award for Best Fantasy Film). For the latter two films, Philip co-wrote a number of original songs, one of which, "Who Will Love Me Now?" (performed by P. J. Harvey), was voted BBC Radio 1's Top Film Song of 1998 and has since been covered by the techno-house band Suncreem (as "Please Save Me"), becoming both a club and viral hit. In 2010, Philip, along with songwriting collaborator Nick Bic_t, formed the music group Dreamskin Cradle and their first album, *Songs from Grimm*, is available on iTunes, Amazon and all major download sites.

Philip is also a performance artist in his own right, and his highly charged readings of his ongoing poetry sequence *Lovesongs for Extinct Creatures* (first embarked on when he was a student) have proved increasingly popular in recent years.

In 2012 What's On Stage named him a Jubilee Playwright (one of the most influential British writers to have emerged in the past six decades).

Philip has won both the *Evening Standard*'s Most Promising Newcomer to British Film and Most Promising Playwright Awards, the only person ever to receive both prizes.

Caroline Jester *What is a playwright?*

Philip Ridley Mmm . . . Well, if you want to know what a shark is, don't ask a shark. So I'm not sure I can answer that, you know? "Oh, I just swim about happily and snack now and again," says the Great White Shark.

CJ *That's fine. I read that you—*

PR Sorry, sorry. Of course, having *said* I couldn't answer it, I've *now* thought of something: A playwright is someone who has a need to create a live storytelling experience that requires an equally live audience to make it complete. The aspect of audience is what it's all about. The audience's reaction *changes* the piece being performed. I should add that when I say "storytelling experience," I don't necessarily mean "narrative." My definition of a story is something that changes the way you feel. The *journey* of that change is the story. A rock on a beach can tell you a magnificent tale or two.

CJ *I read that you don't like your work being categorized in the medium in which it's told. So does it go back to story?*

PR Well, it's not that I don't like it being "categorized"—that's inevitable, to an extent—it's just that I don't think "categorization" is a very interesting discussion. It's like eating a roast dinner and endlessly discussing why this combination of meat and vegetables and gravy has been put together on the same plate, as opposed to just eating it and enjoying it, or not enjoying it. Either way, the *meaning* of the experience is what it makes you *feel*, not in an endless discussion as to why it's not a soup or an omelette. The meaning is the feeling. Also, I guess, I'm a bit touchy about the subject as I sometimes feel that's all I'm *ever* asked about, the idea that I tell stories in different mediums. But, honestly, for me it's just one medium. The medium of storytelling. I just tell the story in the way I think is most suited to that story.

CJ *I've got a sense of stories bursting out of you. How do you navigate? Do you follow rather than navigate?*

PR I deliberately get as lost as possible. I don't plan anything. I don't pre-judge anything. I never know what the next thing is going to be. In fact, I deliberately try not to *think* about anything at all. Thinking can be very unhelpful when you're trying to create something. It puts you into a room that's too well lit. And you need to be in a dark room where you fall over things. It's the things you fall over that are worth writing about. Especially if the fall scares you. So, yes, I want to be surprised and—hopefully—scared by what comes along. It's why I find it very hard to take on a commission. If I could tell an artistic director so *clearly* what I intended to write (which is, usually, the way it's done), I wouldn't feel the need to write it in the first place. I discover *what* the piece is *while* I'm writing it. Now, that's not to say that—once I have a first draft—I don't re-work and shape and all of the usual things. As anyone who's worked with me will tell you, I'm constantly re-writing and trying to make things better. But the initial "discovering" has to be a journey into a very dark and unsafe place. As soon as I feel I'm on safe ground, I run for the nearest minefield.

CJ *You talk a lot about your work in terms of images. That's your background as a painter?*

PR It might be. But I've always seen things primarily in terms of "images" first, which is why I had some resistance to the word "idea." I don't think I've ever had an "idea" for anything in my life, but I have had an "image." Or a "character." Or an opening line. It's hard to explain really. I'm not even totally convinced that what I'm saying now is correct. It's probably not. I maintain my right to contradict myself in the future. Or, possibly, in the next few minutes. It's like asking someone, "How do you fall in love?" An easy question to ask, impossible to answer.

CJ *And you know what you're working on is going to be a stage play and not, say, a novel or film?*

PR Oh, yes. What the story is and *how* it should be told usually happens at exactly the same time.

CJ *Given your experience of being a visual artist as well and training at St. Martin's School of Art, do you think the experience of creating art that way has enabled you to hold onto that authenticity?*

PR I've no idea, to be honest. I loved my time at St. Martin's and I was lucky to be in a very exciting year of fellow students. We all inspired each other and dared each other and I was taught by some truly exceptional tutors. But the way I work—the way I'm working now— well, it seems to me I've *always* been doing that. I was very sick as a child. I suffered from chronic asthma. I was a regular at the Chest Hospital in the East End of London for most of my early life. At home, I had an oxygen tent round my bed and I was in it for weeks—sometimes months—at a time. All I wanted to do was draw and write. My parents bought me reams of typing paper, because it was the cheapest paper they could find and I was getting through *a lot* of it. And, of course, I was reading. Marvel comics mainly. *Spider-Man*. I knew Spider-Man far better than I knew anyone in real life. He was my first real friend.

CJ *When you first left St. Martin's, you were primarily known as a painter, though. Is that fair to say?*

PR Yes, that's true. While I was still a student I'd shown a drawing at the Institute of Contemporary Arts called *Corvus Cum* and that got a fair bit of attention. And then I had my first one-man show, at the Tom Allen Centre in East London, a few years later. But I was always doing all the other things as well. Photography, for example, is something I've been doing since I was a child. My parents bought me a camera when I was seven. I exhibited some of them at the Bernard Baron Gallery in London in 1986. But I was also constantly writing. I used to perform my own durational monologues. When I say "durational," I mean some of them could last eight or more hours. They were delivered at breakneck speed. I performed them in art galleries and night clubs. Anywhere that would have me, basically. Soon after I left St. Martin's, some of my writing started to get published. The first was a short story called *Embracing Verdi*. Then there was an adult novel, *Crocodilia*, then a children's novel, *Mercedes Ice*. It was when I published these things that I realized people found it hard to compute that I did paintings *and* took photographs *and* did performance art *and* poetry as well. Right from the first interviews I ever did, this is the main topic anyone has *ever* wanted to talk about. Not the work itself, just the fact that it's expressed in different forms. I remember discussing this with one of my tutors from St. Martin's a few years after I'd left and she said, "This will always be the main question you'll be asked. You're like the dog that spoke. It's not what you're saying that people want to talk about. It's the fact you say it like you do at all!" And she was right.

CJ *But it's the boundaries that we try to put around artforms. It's like we're trying to contain them.*

PR And many people have *very* strong ideas of what they consider each of these "artforms" to be. I remember when *The Pitchfork Disney* premiered, there were a lot of people coming up to me and saying, "It's not a stage play!" Because what I had done was a visceral journey of skin and sex, and it was primarily about images and claustrophobia and there was no obvious political agenda or conclusion reached, and it was heavily influenced by both horror films and science fiction, with more than a dash of performance art. Not your "normal" stage play at all. And it annoyed people. *Really* annoyed them. One man threw his programme in my face in the bar afterwards. The same thing happened when I wrote *The Fastest Clock in the Universe*. It was becoming quite a ritual.

CJ *Does the audience influence your writing?*

PR If you mean am I writing to *please* an audience, then the answer's "no." I'm not doing that. I don't think that's what I'm *meant* to be doing. In fact, I think it's a very *dangerous* thing to do creatively. But, of course, there are occasions when the audience's reaction can help me *finesse* something. Like in a stage play when you're in previews: Then I'm watching the audience's reaction so I can gage if I need to explain something a bit more, or if I need to cut something. But that's long after the play itself has been created. I don't think the audience that comes along to see my work *expects* me to "pander" to them anyway. I think they like to be surprised by where I'm going, just as—like I said earlier—*I* like to surprise *myself*. And, you know, some of my plays were not liked at all on their first outing. *The Pitchfork Disney* wasn't. Neither were *Vincent River* or *Mercury Fur*.

CJ *A great many of your plays have been very controversial and shocked people.*

PR Oh, that's a thing people throw at me a lot. "You're setting out to shock." And that is *not* the case. All I've ever done is try to be true to the play I'm writing. To not censor myself. To be totally honest. In *Mercury Fur*, for example, I had a gang setting up a party where a rich client could enact his darkest fantasy. So . . . I had to pick a dark fantasy. What's the worst thing I can imagine anyone ever wanted to do? To wilfully hurt a child. So that's what I wrote. To have chosen anything else would have been dishonest. It would have been artistic cowardice. I got a lot of flak for it when the play was put on. I was personally attacked in the press. Faber and Faber, my publishers at that time, refused to publish the play. I had friends accusing me of "promoting the killing of children." It was not an easy time at all. But I did not write the play with the sole intention of shocking. I have *never* done that.

CJ *How do playwriting and the playwright fit into the digital age of storytelling?*

PR Do you mean will the digital experience "replace" theater in some way?

CJ *Possibly.*

PR Well, I don't think that's the case for an instant. Football matches have been televized for years, and that hasn't stopped matches selling out all over the country every weekend. The thrill of watching something "live" — the *need* for it — is in our DNA. It goes back to sitting round a fire in a cave and listening to someone tell a story. We crave the feel of a congregation around us, all sharing the same atmosphere, all feeling part of something. We need something that has the ritual of truth to it. You know, years ago, when the Mona Lisa was stolen from the Louvre in Paris, its image was suddenly everywhere. On postcards, magazines, posters, tea towels. Everyone, if they wanted it, could have a copy of the Mona Lisa. But a strange thing happened. People started to queue round the block to see the spot where the Mona Lisa had once hung. The "ritual of truth" was that the Mona Lisa was more truly "there" in a place where it had once been, than in a reproduction where it had never been. By queuing to gaze at a bare wall, people were creating their own theatrical experience to help deal with a loss. Humans are social animals. We need to share things with others. We learn things in a congregation that we could never learn alone. For example, using the football analogy again, when 20,000 people start to sing in a stadium, not everyone in that stadium knows that song. At first they begin to hum along. Then as it's repeated they start to learn the words. Eventually, they're singing along as loudly and as energetically as everyone else. They have *learned* how to respond. They have become part of something bigger than them. And that's the experience of theater. You're in the theater and you see something happen and people around you start to laugh. Or they start to cry. Or they start to feel uncomfortable. And you start feeling things with other people. You feel what they feel. When someone else smiles, you feel happy. When they cry, it makes you sad. Other people's problems become our problems. I absolutely *refuse* to say the cringe-making cliché about it teaching us to be human . . . Oh, dear. I think I just have.

Jordan Tannahill*

> **Jordan Tannahill** is a Canadian playwright, director, and film-maker. His work has been presented in theaters, festivals, and galleries across Canada and internationally. His plays include: *Concord Floral; rihannaboi95; Botticelli in the Fire;* and *Sunday in Sodom.* From 2012 to 2016, in collaboration with William Ellis, he ran the alternative art space Videofag out of their home in Toronto's Kensington Market neighborhood. His book *Theatre of the Unimpressed* is published by Coach House Press.

Caridad Svich *What is a playwright?*

Jordan Tannahill A playwright authors action. A playwright is concerned with the fourth dimension: The construction of events in time. And I say "construction" as a nod to the word "playwright" itself, for "wright" is defined by the *OED* as "a worker, especially a construction worker." This feels very apropos. "Wright"-ing a play is labor, it's work; of course it's also a joy, but it involves a great deal more building than simply writing words on a page. As a playwright, I draft the blueprints and then build the play on the construction site of the rehearsal hall and theater.

CS *Does the audience influence your writing?*

JT Yes, they are key collaborators. And there are many kinds of audiences. The actors who read the very first draft of a play aloud are a kind of audience. And then there is the rest of the creative team who might sit in on rehearsals—designers, stage managers, technicians, producers. There are the trusted colleagues who might be invited to a run-through or workshop, the preview audiences, the audiences of the

---

* Interview reproduced with the kind permission of the author and their legal representation.
© Jordan Tannahill 2017.

premiere. I find all these audiences useful, but it's not their opinions I am looking for necessarily. What I require an audience for is proxy spectatorship. I need to see my own play through their eyes. My preference is to sit with an audience, experience a play through their experience of it, and then disappear to make re-writes without too much consultation.

CS   *Can a playwright cross into other artforms?*

JT   Absolutely. It's my hunch that ideas occur to most art-makers that fall outside the disciplinary silos they normally operate within. We often feel beholden to disciplines in ways that ideas do not. Influences, aesthetics, politics—as a playwright I am not solely exposed to these things through the medium of theater, just as I cannot solely respond to these things through the medium of theater.

CS   *Your work in a slightly earlier era would have been categorized as "interdisciplinary," whereas now I think the notion of being a hybrid artist is almost the "norm." You make films—your play* rihannaboi95 *was staged via livestreaming—you co-run Videofag, a storefront/ gallery/performance space, you direct theater, you choreograph dance works, your work has featured non-actors as well as actors. What drives you to make works in different ways, and also, does your playwriting drive your other artistic paths or do you feel that you switch hats, as it were, and sometimes think like a director and at other times like a choreographer?*

JT   As much as possible I try to allow the idea to dictate the form my question/response takes. As a storyteller, I do not feel I become a different self when I am making theater or dance or visual art, perhaps because I feel the division between these forms are mostly superficial or arbitrary. I am drawing on the same lived experience, the same politics, the same set of references and aesthetics. So I treat the label of "playwright" as a kind of endlessly malleable one that I can stretch to encompass and contextualize everything that I do.

To take *rihannaboi95* as an example: A queer teen character named Sunny began taking shape in my head while I was working with a theater company called Project: Humanity facilitating drama workshops in a youth shelter in Toronto's Rexdale neighborhood. When an early draft of the piece was first workshopped in 2011, an actor performed the monologue onstage in a theater as if he was shooting a YouTube confessional video. It felt flat to me—why was this monologue being presented in a theater? Was the only reason because I was a "playwright"? How could I capture both the intimacy of an actual YouTube video while retaining the charge of a live event? I could never figure out the right dramatic container for Sunny, and so I shelved the play.

Then one night, two years later, my friend Jon Davies curated a screening at Videofag called "SissyBoy YouTube Night." The program featured about a dozen videos shot by preteen and teenage boys dancing and lip-synching to the pop songs of female divas. They were gloriously unselfconscious and uncensored expressions of persona, gender, and inner desire. As I watched the screening, Sunny popped back into my mind. Suddenly I knew what his story was, how to tell it, and that the play would be called *rihannaboi95.* In the play, Sunny's world falls apart when a video of him dancing and lip-synching to a Rihanna song goes viral. The play would still take the form of a confessional YouTube video, but it would be performed through YouTube's live-streaming software (which, I think at the time, was a function that had *just* been introduced). By clicking on a link at 8pm EST audiences around the world could watch and even live-chat to Sunny as he told his story. There was something quite extraordinary about holding Sunny on your lap, alone in your bedroom or gathered with a group of friends, as he spoke to you.

For me this is a really clear example of the way in which an idea guided the eventual form it took.

CS *A lot of your work queries identity formation: Queer and otherwise. A colleague of mine said that the self and its remaking/transformation has become a new frontier. Finally. And maybe gender-binary thinking will break down toward a different way of seeing/being in language, thought, and play. How do you see your work within the spectrum of this kind of change?*

JT I love your colleague's assertion. I see my work as operating within a queer paradigm where selfhood exists in a fluid state, as something to be continually questioned and redefined. With my plays I am attempting to craft "open texts" that engender a range of interpretative possibilities; texts which can be sites for inquiry and deconstruction, particularly around questions of gender, sexuality, and socialization.

CS *How has an embrace of failure become part of your own practice and production in the multiple artistic arenas in which you make work?*

JT A lot of the time it's about the editorial process: In allowing oneself to pursue an impulse to its end, even when it feels ridiculous. Not applying conventional definitions of "right" and "wrong," "well-made," and "messy" to something. In allowing an idea or an image to be ugly, if that's what it needs to be. In allowing a text to be uneven, if that's what feels right.

Whether I'm behind the camera, or working on a dance piece, or writing a play, I try to create situations for chance; spaces for the indeterminate. This is where liveness lives. It can be hard sometimes as a writer to do this because the act of writing is so much about fixing meaning to the page. But I am pushing myself to find new ways to cultivate liveness in my writing.

CS *What drives you to make work?*

JT I think all of my plays begin from either a place of anger or incomprehension, and are the process by which I attempt to transform these states into something productive, something I can live with. My plays often center around sublime outcasts and explore the strength of perspective on the status quo offered by the periphery. The theme of collective responsibility is a recurrent one as well. With every play I always seem to be asking: "What are our obligations to one another?"

CS *How do playwriting and the playwright fit into the digital age of storytelling?*

JT Like with most things, the digital age extends our storytelling capacities by presenting us with new questions, tools, aesthetics, and audiences. I am always frustrated by arguments about how *x* advancement is killing theater. The Internet, augmented reality, virtual reality—these are simply new stages for performance. And nothing, not even the digital age, will supplant the human impulse and need for live performance.

Sabrina Mahfouz

Sabrina Mahfouz is an award-winning poet and playwright whose plays include: *With a Little Bit of Luck* (Paines Plough); *Slug* (Nabokov); *The Love I Feel Is Red* (Tobacco Factory); *Chef* (Soho Theatre); and *Clean* (Traverse Theatre). *Chef* won a 2014 Fringe First Award and *Clean,* produced by the Traverse Theatre, transferred to New York in 2014. Her TV short, *Breaking the Code,* was produced by BBC Three and BBC Drama in 2016. Sabrina has been Sky Arts Academy Scholar for Poetry, Leverhulme Playwright-in-Residence, and Associate Artist at Bush Theatre.

Caroline Jester *What is a playwright?*

Sabrina Mahfouz Someone who writes plays for their sins.

CJ *Does the audience influence your writing?*

SM It depends entirely on the project. If it is for a specific group—teens, babies etc.—then of course they are at the forefront of my mind at all times. If there is no target group, then not really; I just write what comes out and what I think I'd quite enjoy listening to.

CJ *Can a playwright cross into other artforms?*

SM Of course. Plays themselves are constantly crossing into other forms: They can contain movement, video, illustrations, digital art, live art, design, fashion, music, poetry, comedy, dance. All artforms seem to me to be cross-artforms in some way, even if it is only that you are telling a short story with a painting or that the beautiful, hand-made costumes are essential to your opera.

There are few playwrights who only write plays. Financially it would be pretty hard going, for one thing, and it's exciting to choose a form because it is the best one for the story you want to tell rather than because it is the only one available. Many playwrights write TV and film scripts, articles, and fiction, and although they are all very different disciplines—TV and film can seem almost scientific in their writing requirements in comparison to theater—there's a fundamental need within all of them to be concerned with the why and how of a story I suppose, usually with a specific character at the center of that story.

CJ   *I saw you say that you are a poet because you "don't like to say anything in normal language." Can you explain what you mean?*

SM   Ha! I'm not sure if I was confused/very young or something, because I definitely do speak in the most normal language possible most of the time! If there's anything I can expand on there it's probably that, when writing about serious, emotive, controversial issues, I find that far easier and more impactful to do with the tools that poetry offers—metaphor, word play, rhythm, surrealism—all helping to create a fiction which has more truth in it than the lies around us.

CJ   *Where or how does poetry and playwriting merge into one artform for you, if it does at all?*

SM   I think there has always been poetry in playwriting. Whether you are asking the audience to "suspend their disbelief" in order that the scene in front of them becomes real, or you're acknowledging their presence and the pretence of it all, the likelihood is that the language being used differs from that on TV or in everyday life, even if only in its abstraction from the whole. It is necessarily heightened and that in itself is a form of poetry. There are also moments of more obvious poetry—from Shakespeare to debbie tucker green. Poetry was originally created to be performed or at least spoken out loud. For me, this makes theater and poetry inextricably linked: They were designed to be heard communally, but this doesn't mean their texts or videos can't be enjoyed in isolation, particularly some forms of poetry, which feel far more satisfying when read in a quiet corner. However, there are many, many playtexts I have far preferred reading in a quiet corner than seeing on stage!

CJ   *You've mentioned that spoken word has a pace and a musicality to it that allows you to delve into subject matter that takes you* *somewhere else. Does playwriting restrict this pace, or do you invent new rhythms because of your ability to transcend mediums?*

SM I'm not really sure of the term "spoken word" and try to not use it, which is difficult because it has become the mainstream definition of non-traditional poetry over the last few years and it is used by others to describe what I do, though I wouldn't use that description myself. I'm sure there is a valid use for it, but I personally am not sure what that is. I think the term "poetry" can be widened to include a huge variety of forms within it, just as the terms "music" or "dance" do. The obsession with separating one form of poetry from another with a more "accessible" term, and then attaching a hierarchical difference to it in critical, media, and academic terms, I often think is just a handy way for the status quo within the white, middle-upper class, male-dominated world of traditional poetry to remain intact and unchallenged.

Anyway, to your question! I think the poetry I write in plays is easily able to retain the pace and musicality it does outside of theater work. It does need to be balanced with variations in rhythm and pace because a play is likely to be far longer than a single poem. But it is often this pace and rhythm which inspires where I go next with the plot or a character's background. For me, it is a driving force of inspiration, almost meditative and hypnotic in its ability to hook me into the heart of what it is I want to say or what I have come to think the character wants to say—as I often write things with a passion that is not shared by me, but is wholly that of the character.

CJ *Performance poetry and spoken word transcend spaces by being performed in small pubs and large opera houses. As a writer and performer, how does this impact on your work?*

SM It makes it exciting, but it can often be difficult working on multiple projects with such huge variances in the space they are being planned for. Some writing works whatever the venue—I've read the same poems in the foyer of Bush Theatre and on stage at The O2 [Arena]—but writing specifically for a school setting does require a different headspace than writing for a public gathering of thousands. However, most of the time, if it is poetry rather than theater, I will write the same regardless and the change may be in performance rather than textual.

CJ *You work for diverse organizations, from museums to building-based theater companies, and you cross over into television to name but a few different homes for your work. Do the ideas for your stories influence where they gravitate toward to be realized?*

SM When I have an idea for a story, it is usually the world of the story which interests me first, then the character, then the actual story. By the time I get to the second point, I usually have a good idea of which medium would suit it best and then I'll chat through it with the relevant people to see if we can get to the third stage together. This is in no way a rule. Plenty of poems have made their way into full plays and I have turned a poem into a TV series and then back into a poetry collection!

CJ *Some of your work begins with workshops with people; I'm thinking of* Chef *as an example where you were inspired by workshops with former inmates of women's prisons. How does this process influence the dramatic structure you select to tell these stories?*

SM I never consciously begin a theater piece with workshops. The workshops I do are usually associated with freelance or voluntary teaching I occasionally do for various groups—poetry, performance poetry, creative writing, playwriting. Every so often, there are members of these groups that lodge themselves in my heart and head and they become part of the inspiration behind a play. Once this decision is made, I will then research further and ask the participants if they're willing to have more discussions around the areas I'm exploring. The process doesn't necessarily affect the dramatic structure, but it makes the act of creating something authentic and impactful that much more pressing, as people have shared painful, private things with you and there is a responsibility and a respect which is attached to that, in my opinion, whilst you also need to be clear with everyone that the end result will be entirely fictional.

CJ *How do playwriting and the playwright fit into the digital age of storytelling?*

SM I'm not sure we *are* in a digital age of storytelling! Live literature and poetry has never been more popular; the theaters are full; people want a connection they aren't getting from their screens and a truth they won't hear from their elected representatives or the mainstream media. I think if playwrights just keep making plays that are important to them and programmers ensure they truly decolonize—not just diversify—their venues and the work they put on, then that is enough. Digitalization is an unavoidable part of everyday life, so I'm sure it works its way into plays without much conscious effort to do so.

Daniel Alexander Jones

Daniel Alexander Jones is an award-winning performer, writer, and director. His work includes plays (*Bel Canto, Earthbirths, Phoenix Fabrik*), performance pieces (*Blood:Shock:Boogie, The Book of Daniel, Cab and Lena*), and devised work (*Qualities of Light, Clayangels*). With composer Bobby Halvorson, Jones has released several recordings, performed at Joe's Pub and Symphony Space, and in the critically acclaimed show *Jomama Jones: Radiate* and *Duat* at Soho Rep. He received the prestigious Alpert Award in the Arts for Theatre in 2006, the Doris Duke Artist Award in 2015, and was named a USA Arts Fellow in 2016.

Caridad Svich   *What is a playwright?*

Daniel Alexander Jones   At best, a playwright is one who activates that occupational suffix "-wright." Wright meant worker, maker, and was associated with carpentry. The playwright crafts both armature and architecture for the play. There is something admirably nimble, even tricksy, about playwrights who make well for others to make well, who learn signs and signifiers, who create deceptively simple shapes, who understand they are making both equations and spells. These playwrights know they are inviting other capacious, dynamic souls to figure their equations and conjure their spells. Like cartographers, they tell us enough to guide us, but not enough to prevent our own delight in discovery. The play, therefore, at best, is the journey we all take, our senses buzzing (map in hand, for a while, then dropped), nudged by signs and signifiers, imbibing the new now, connected to the playwright and their initial vision (a vision we all extend) across time and space.

CS   *How much does the audience influence your writing?*

DAJ   I often say to my students, "there is no such thing as *an* audience." I know I will be in conversation, through the play, through the performance, with a range of people, who possess any number of viewpoints, associations, and opinions. I'm predisposed to polyphony, and so the many voices in the room don't frighten me. Nightly, who gathers to see and be, changes. I strive, as I do in all my communication, to be as clear as I can be about what I intend to share. I do not, for a moment, presume any unanimity of interpretation will meet the work. I think it a fool's errand to craft work based on what you presume about an imagined audience. Strive to accurately perceive the facets of your vision and communicate it with precision and concision. What happens next is beyond your control, but is a tremendous opportunity for your full engagement with the play that's bigger than everybody involved in its making.

I advocate the practice of listening. In more recent work, as I have renewed my interest in structures containing improvised sections and audience interactive passages, deep listening is key to my capacity to "write" extemporaneously and to anchor myself in genuine presence with the people who come to see my work. Even when I was not performing in work I'd written, I would do my best to experience the play as audiences took it in over successive performances to listen to the ways it moved or did not move in the room on a given night. I learned the shifting contours of my plays that way. I suppose if I were following a particular formula, I would use that time to craft the work in response to audiences' responses. But, I'm not following a formula. I'm making an equation. And audience is one of the linchpin variables in that equation.

CS *Can a playwright cross into other artforms?*

DAJ Who made the boxes? Who do the boxes serve? At its most benign, we know that theater as an artform can be spun to mean something about constituency and connectivity, but in fact we know it has a lot to do with branding, selling, and buying. It also has a lot to do with reinscribing the centrality of the unquestioned norm, which is (to use careworn, but nonetheless accurate, terminology) an unnamed but implicit privileged white heteronormativity that picks and chooses its houseguests. I have no truck with that.

Fortunately, just as there were when I was coming up, there remain, and there are increasingly, folks who are committed to making space in their venues, in their festivals, on their stages, and in their developmental processes for work that reflects a complex range of expression and beauty. And, that "where will you fit?" argument is rendered less and less viable when artists aren't knocking at the door for admission, but rather finding ways to make and distribute work on their own; and/or less and less viable with more people who have been occupied these "boxes" smashing down the walls of the traditional spaces (even in the mainstream—*Passing Strange, Fun Home,* and *Hamilton* on Broadway are some recent examples); or, less and less viable by those who simply avoid walls altogether, and serve a banquet all outside.

I have, on occasion, abided with the work of certain playwrights as I might a lover, seeing, reading, and conversing with everything I can access until the scent lingers on my fingers and my tongue. I confess to being liberal with my attentions—I've done the same with the work of singers, painters, dancers, and biographers. I don't segregate my influences. Another early influential artist was Yoko Ono, whose work I first came to know through recordings. Her self-confident expression in all forms further emboldened me. I also tend to be drawn to the work of artists who are deeply invested in the impact of their work upon others and in the resulting conversations and responses.

CS *Where do your theater pieces come from?*

DAJ I am always turning a question about some aspect of the human condition and/or cosmology around in my head. I get my contemplative nature from both sides of my family. But, invariably, the idea for a piece will visit me abruptly. It usually comes, if not whole, in great measure, and I rush to note as many features of it as I can to tease out over time. Sometimes, it will grow more slowly, mostly submerged, out of reach, and I will "feel" it moving in my consciousness until it crests and demands my full attention. When it grabs me, I work like a person possessed. One of my closest friends, also a writer, plans everything out meticulously, with gorgeously detailed storyboards and a rhythmic daily writing process. That is not my method, by a long shot. As a teenager, I drew and painted; art class in my public high school was a site of refuge and inspiration. When an idea for a painting possessed me, I would stay up all night for days in a row, luring that "God's hour" flow, high on the adrenaline from heightened senses and bridged interior and exterior worlds. I have cultivated discipline, and have learned to manage the creative highs and the troughs. I can work in more deliberate ways, but if I'm honest, the plays come with huge gravitational force and demand my attention. They often leave—ahem—a little bit of havoc in their wake. Maybe it's why I'm a bit of a control freak in other aspects of my life. Because I must surrender control to the pieces when they come.

CS *And how does your approach to structure and process differ when building a piece, for instance, for your alter ego Jomama Jones and when you are adapting Baum's Oz book?*

DAJ With *Bright Now Beyond*, the source material of Baum's book and the historical context of its own genesis led me to my initial drafts. He wrote the book in part to provide new material to the two vaudevillian actors who'd made their careers playing the Scarecrow and the Tin Man. So the theater was explicitly in the DNA of the book, and the narrative structure was serrate. Also, the fact that there was something so radical hidden in plain sight (a child protagonist's forced, then willing, transformation of their own gender through magic), a possibility which compelled and delighted me as an early reader, gave me a lot to play with in terms of thinking about the tonal changes in the piece as it unfolded. I had fun sounding out a lesser-known set of stories; *The Wonderful Wizard of Oz* was so dominant and popular that it eclipsed the other books Baum wrote. We had the freedom to play, but also to signify our understanding of the dominance of the original book and its popular cultural impact, particularly through film. But in the end, as always the outside influences ultimately had to fall back, and I had to stay true to the core energetic gesture that revealed itself again and again as I wrote. It was an adaptation in the sense that Patti LaBelle singing "Over the Rainbow" in the 1980s was adaptation. Much of that process ended up being about condensing and cutting, making the most direct shape possible.

With Jomama Jones (not including my early work on her in the 1990s), I began with the songs that became our first album, *Lone Star*. Writing songs was one of the best possible challenges I've ever undertaken. Each song is its own miniature play or performance piece. Then, thinking about the sequence of songs as narrative structure provided another rich compositional invitation. The stories that emerged as the connective tissue for the show *Radiate* did so from the relationships that developed to the songs themselves, which were made and recorded first with Bobby Halvorson. I was encouraged to write a traditional biographical narrative for Jomama and both she and I ultimately balked at that. The real, idiosyncratic story was already present and we just had to wait for it to emerge. The "writing" was in fact a dance between improvisation and some minimal crafting of the transcription of that improvisation. It is an odd thing to describe, but the text of that show was already in the room, already on the stage, and it revealed itself during performance. Any attempt to write it beforehand and impose that on the show was doomed. And this is from someone who delights in the fine-tuning that can happen with phrasing and punctuation, etc. My job was to develop the capacity to see it when it was revealed, and to trust that it would be there every night, until my familiarity with its contours became second nature. It was definitely rooted in theatrical jazz in that specific way. In essence, it was not different than the other writing, except that instead of abiding with the vision and translating that into language on a page, I was immediately moving the vision through my body and into performance, and refining my expression of it through performance. It made clear a specific set of demands for subsequent collaborations. I can handle a script; Jomama, not so much!

CS *How do playwriting and the playwright fit into the digital age of storytelling?*

DAJ Far from signaling the obsolescence of the live, this increasingly mediated time offers playwrights, and theater-makers in general, a heightened opportunity to foreground the inimitable aspects of the live art experience. Live art can be more important than ever—especially work that invites people to set down their devices or use those devices to bring them to somatically rooted, time-based experience. As Erykah Badu sings, "I can make you put your phone down." Playwrights in particular have the chance to practice the ancient new, activating the core social and political power of the live theatrical experience, while also responding creatively to new opportunities for expression and apperception in our shifting cultural landscapes.

I wholly reject the idea that something is impactful only if it is immediately accessible to a large number of people. There is great power in the local, in the limited run, in the intimate encounter, and even in preaching to a choir from time to time. Live art has alchemical force, and the changes that come from a single audience member's encounter with a work can be exponential.

What happens when we rethink the *process* of impact and reimagine the boundaries of the theatrical event by dancing with technology and social media in innovative ways? It is not about grafting live-feed projections onto every production. But it is about understanding that audience members or people who might not consider themselves to be, or might not be able to be, audience members can be involved in the work in meaningful ways that can extend and embolden the core ideas of a given project or a body of work. Considering these possibilities doesn't mean the sacrifice of the playwright's core practice, nor does it mean that the intimate experience of a live play loses its centrality. But, for real, being technophobic or precious won't serve the writer this century. Make work that makes us "put our phones down."

Caridad Svich

Caridad Svich received the 2012 OBIE for Lifetime Achievement and the 2011 American Theatre Critics Association Primus Prize for *The House of the Spirits* (based on Isabel Allende's novel). Key works include: *Alchemy of Desire/Dead-Man's Blues; Iphigenia Crash Land Falls . . .; 12 Ophelias;* and *JARMAN (all this maddening beauty).* She has adapted works by Mario Vargas Llosa, Julia Alvarez, Gabriel García Márquez, and Federico García Lorca. She is published by Intellect UK, Seagull Books, Broadway Play Publishing, and more. She is editor of several books on theater and performance, among them *Innovation in Five Acts* and *Audience Revolution,* both for Theatre Communications Group. She is an alumna of New Dramatists, associate editor of *Contemporary Theatre Review,* and founder of NoPassport theater alliance and press.

Caroline Jester   *What is a playwright?*

Caridad Svich   Sometimes when this question is asked, I think of that ol' Steve Miller song "The Joker." Because it puts me in mind of the fact that playwrights provoke, respond to, and stir up something in space/site of performance and also in the body of the audience, which is the body politic. So, playwrights are jokers and lovers and grinners and mischief-makers, as well as healers (of a kind). And shakers of trees! To riff a little bit on that ol' song.

Other times when people ask me this question I say: A playwright is a text-builder, dreamer, and maker of work for live performance. Or a playwright reflects the trouble and joy in the mind/heart/soul of the times. Sometimes this reflection is mimetic. Sometimes it is not. Sometimes it is a dream of another time or a time to be. A playwright writes for the now, past, and future. One foot in the past, one foot in the now, and with a visionary arrow toward the future.

A playwright engages in civic dialogue.

A playwright stands outside the times they are in as well as within.
A playwright speaks to the ancients and asks them questions.

CJ *Does the audience influence your writing?*

CS Who is the audience? Sometimes the audience is a group of your friends. Sometimes, often, a group of strangers. Sometimes it is one person or two. Sometimes it is the imagined audience in your head while you write. I am my first audience, so I write what I hope moves me and compels me, and that hope then will translate to others. There is the audience of actors that first read the work, and directors and literary managers and the like. All of these people—before the ticketed or free audience walk in. So, by these standards, yes, the audience does influence what I make, in collaboration and also just on my own sitting at the laptop or working longhand. When you work with collaborators for a long time, you think of them as you write. They are part of that imagined audience. Sometimes, too, you think of those whom have passed or with whom you do not have much contact anymore. I recently wrote a piece thinking about a collaborator with whom I worked twenty years ago, a person that impacted me immensely but at the time I was resistant and/or didn't realize the impact that was being made. And then twenty years later, too late indeed, this person walks into my consciousness, and I think, yes, I will make this for you.

CJ *Can a playwright cross into other artforms?*

CS Well, I hope so! We are writers and wrighters. We know a thing or two about building scores for performance and for creative problem-solving. We think like poets and dreamers but are practical beings too. And sometimes we are shamans. So, if we wish to apply our skills, talent, and craft to say, collaborating on a digital storytelling event or a party or the curation of a book or other things, why not? I think "crossing" is demanded of us all in an age especially when disciplines are messy and fluid. When strict "theater" is not really what it may have meant in the nineteenth century (a model that somehow still persists). If you make things as a creative person, then seeking out different ways of making and playing with others is crucial.

CJ *You have translated Lorca's work and adapted novels such as*
Allende's House of the Spirits *for the stage in both Spanish and English.*
How does working on other people's stories inform and challenge your
original work?

CS   Well, I started translating because of Lorca. I minored in translation
in undergraduate school, and really wanted to translate his poetry and
other Spanish-language poets. Of course, Lorca's plays are poems for
the stage. Inevitably, my love of theater and poetry merged and directors
started to ask me if I would translate Lorca's plays for production. With
the Lorca heirs' blessing, I said yes. And it's been a fascinating long
road of living with Lorca's works for a long time. I've translated nearly all
of his plays, including the rural tragedies, but also the impossible plays.
Part of it had to do with a desire to translate his work into American
English rather than British English. Most available English language
translations are British. And actually very few, still, American English
translations are by hybrid Latinx-identified writers. So, there's a double
strand here. Also, unlike perhaps in other countries, Lorca's works are
rarely staged in the US. He's the somewhat "invisible" world dramatist,
even though many of us playwrights, especially Latinx identified
playwrights, cite him as an influence. For me, translating Lorca's works
has been a labor of love and also a way to wake myself up as a dramatist.
One of the things that being inside another writer's brain does for a
translator is open them up to different ways of thinking about space and
time in theater and creative problem-solving. It's a break from your own
stuff and it replenishes you, if the process is fruitful, when you return to
your "own" concerns as a writer.

The novels that I have adapted for the stage—really, they are
response texts, as I do not use any of the text from the novels in the
theatrical pieces—are, thus far (since 2009), Allende's *The House of the*
Spirits, Mario Vargas Llosa's *Aunt Julia and the Scriptwriter*, Julia
Alvarez' *In the Time of the Butterflies,* José León Sánchez' *Island of*
Lost Souls, and Gabriel García Márquez' *Love in the Time of Cholera*.
All of them are, of course, vastly different in form and style and tone, not
to mention content! Each has been a nearly impossible challenge. But I
love challenges. Again, it stirs me out of old habits as a writer and forces
me to think anew. I adapted *The House of the Spirits* first. Imagine
beginning with that novel! Right? It is massive, and labyrinthian, but

also, thankfully, it has an incredible engine in terms of its structure. Very dramatic. Inherently theatrical. Of course Allende started out writing plays! So, she loves the theater. I think it shows in her work. She has dramatic instincts, and an essential playfulness and mischief in her writing. I responded to that.

Writing my version of *The House of the Spirits* took every bit of me, but I was in a great mood when I was writing it. The novel and its characters somehow allowed me to write something of a love letter to theater. There are nods to Chekhov, Brecht, Calderon, Wilde, Shakespeare, and yes, Lorca, in the play, and the kinds of scenes I actually had never given myself permission to write. Big ol' emotional, roaring scenes in the epic style. Making the piece really gave me a new level of confidence somehow as a playwright. It felt as if—if I can tackle this, I can tackle anything! Of course, I'd been rehearsing, as it were, for a while. During the ten years before I wrote my version of *The House of the Spirits*, I had written radical reconfigurations of many of the ancient Greek tragedies, and some Shakespeare, and even Wedekind! So, this whole other side of speaking to the past—conversing with the ancients, giving them my blood, was already in me. And still is. I always say that for me, Euripides and Shakespeare are on one side of my consciousness as a theater-maker, and Lorca and Fornés are on the other.

CJ *You founded NoPassport theater in 2003, which is "an unincorporated artist-driven, grass-roots theater alliance and press devoted to cross-cultural, Pan American performance, theory, action, advocacy and publication." At the time of this interview* After Orlando, an International Theatre Action *in response to the Pulse night club shooting on June 12, 2016, is taking place around the world in the form of new plays written by a collective of international playwrights being read in theater spaces globally. Can you talk about your thinking behind this, and how as well as responding to tragic events through theater you have also created a collective of artists generating work that challenges a "performance" in the more traditional sense of the word and therefore the industry?*

CS NoPassport actually started as a band of twelve theater practitioners that were all, and still are, experimenting with words and music and fluid spaces in between. Among them were Erik Ehn and

Lisa D'Amour. We kept talking about making porous spaces in our works and NoPassport became a hub to sustain a conversation. We collaborated on texts, did word collage, and even performed together on occasion! In late 2003 it grew into a wider band of theater artists that was also making cross-cultural work, often from a Latinx-identified perspective. We staged conferences, symposia, published (and still do) new writing, and kept the network mobile, amoeba-like, and grass-roots in its focus. In 2012, I got it into my head somehow that I was tired of how a lot of new plays get "developed" in the cottage industry of new play development in the US. You may know the kind I mean. A play has a reading and then another and then a workshop and then another reading and so on, from theater to theater, often without an audience, outside of the industry. You're basically talking to each other in the field. And oftentimes the play never gets produced and therefore, seen by an audience, which is the whole point of the thing to begin with! It's kind of a risk-averse model. "If we test drive the play a whole hell of a lot, it will then be ready for an audience and won't scare them away." No rough edges. A "smooth it out" mentality. I was working on a play that was set in the aftermath of the Deepwater Horizon BP oil spill—the largest human-made environmental disaster in US history—and I just thought about how the play's life might be. And I thought, I want to have a conversation with this play *now*. Not tomorrow. Not in five years. Not when twenty theaters decide it's ready. So, I made myself guinea pig for a little experiment. It was the second anniversary of the tragedy and I started calling and emailing colleagues at theaters, colleges, social justice centers, etc. around the world and said, do you want to have a play-conversation about environmental and human rights to mark the anniversary? The "mainstream media" had basically "forgotten" the story. BP's TV and social media ads kept saying "everything is fine in the Gulf," and I knew this was not the case. And still isn't. As of this writing. I thought ten people would say yes, and what happened was that within a two month time frame, fifty venues said yes globally, from as far away as Western Australia to Brazil, Germany, and more. I was rewriting the play as we went along. The work was script in hand. Concert readings. But the flexibility of that meant that this was a lo-fi enterprise. All it took was some time, some actors (amateur or pro), and the promise of a conversation. I partnered with Waterkeeper Alliance and the Earth Institute as emotional sponsors, not fiscal. And on less than a shoestring of no budget, Louisiana Environmental Action Network, Bridge the Gulf, Audubon Society, Platform London, and more were involved. Again, toward theater engagement with a social justice at its core. Ok, I know other people do this. Perhaps it's not so novel. But I don't know. I found myself in the center of something as a practitioner through sheer saying "hello, will you . . .?" Speaking with audiences of all kinds and not waiting to have a "vetted" conversation but speaking through capitalist-structured means. With a play.

CJ *How do playwriting and the playwright fit into the digital age of storytelling?*

CS   There was rock and chisel. There eventually was parchment, and paper and writing instruments. There was the typewriter, and then the computer, and then the tablet and then virtual spaces. There was and is theater, and then also too cinema and the web and more. It doesn't matter what the tools are. One tool of art-making is not better than another. It is just different. It differs in how each deals with the perception of the viewer. It's about ways of seeing. So, how do you want to invite someone into an experience? What are the most appropriate tools to convey what you're trying to convey? Sometimes you want the rock and chisel. Sometimes you want digital film. Sometimes you want a podcast. Form and function. It may seem old-school, but it holds true. Still. The tools are the tools. There are more of them now, which means there are more choices and ways to tell the tale and make the event in space. It's all allowed, to quote the late Adrian Howells.

Tim Etchells

Tim Etchells is an artist, performer, and writer. His work involves the deconstruction of language and the implication of events unfolding in time through installation, improvised text performances, interactive audio experiments, new media, SMS or text messaging performances, and fiction, as well as publicly sited text-works, neon and LED signage. Etchells is currently Artistic Director of Forced Entertainment, the world-renowned performance collective based in Sheffield, UK, whose collaborations began in 1984 and whose works include *Real Magic, Quizoola!, Speak Bitterness, The Notebook*, and *First Night.* The company was awarded the 2016 Ibsen Prize.

Caridad Svich *What is a playwright?*

Tim Etchells I guess I'd think of a playwright in quite a narrow sense, as someone who creates a script or score for a theater event, most likely through the act of writing alone, and most likely in advance of a rehearsal process. So the text is positioned before (and autonomously) from the rest of the making process, and carries some burden or status as primary or originary artefact.

I've only very rarely worked in this way myself, so I don't generally identify myself as a playwright. I tend to identify myself as a performance-maker, as a writer, as a director, and as an artist (the last of which can cover all of the above, I guess).

CS *Does the audience influence your writing?*

TE Not usually in any sense that I'm writing for this audience or that audience, although there have been some projects where that's been the case, specifically a couple of works made for and with children. But for me each project is always about somehow negotiating and testing the relation between performance and audience, so the writing is always a tool with which one's trying to probe and animate that space, that relation. In that sense, audience is always on my mind.

CS   *Can a playwright cross into other artforms?*

TE   Yes, I think it's more than possible for writers and others to cross from one context to another. But perhaps people who have a strict sense of their role—in terms of a job title like "playwright"—don't cross from one place to another so easily or so well. I think of myself as someone that's interested in language, in performance, in making things with other people. I don't have any assumptions about how I'm going to do that or what my role should be, especially in relation to authorship. I'm happy to experiment, to see what happens, to let a project or collaboration find its own shape. If a piece has no text in it at all, that's more than fine by me. Or it can be all text. It can be text that's written by me or it can be text that's improvised, or any kind of mix. More than anything else I'm interested in projects—in the performative propositions they make, in the ways that they reach to audiences, spectators, witnesses.

My work goes from collaborative theater-making with Forced Entertainment and others, to writing texts for and in performance by other people, to writing fiction (novels, short-stories), and writing theoretical texts to working in different ways in the context of visual art (neon signs, text works, videos, installations). I have this sense that I "come from" performance—that my understanding of what art is and how it functions is rooted there somehow . . . but the work crosses very fluidly from discipline to discipline, context to context, For me that seems like a natural way to work because the interests I have, and such understanding as I have, come before any allegiances to form.

CS   *Your company Forced Entertainment has just won the 2016 Ibsen Award. It's the first time it has been given to a company and not a single author. I think this really says something about how ensemble work is being seen and re-evaluated in new writing and theater-making circles that have been predominantly (at least in US and UK models) based on the play to the stage "model." How fluid do you see the movement, when you work at your desk, in the practice hall, in digital mediums (CD-ROMs), and through improvisation? Is it a lateral way of working across* *mediums or do you feel as if you approach the essence of the making differently?*

TE   The form of my works varies a great deal and I'd add that projects determine their own processes—in any situation I just try to figure what's needed, or just to figure a way to start. The specifics of a work or a context might demand particular actions but the stages of the work are probably similar no matter what one's doing. First there is a period of open research, thinking, speculating, perhaps with improvisation, writing roughly, experimenting in different ways; looking for clues. This would be followed by attempts to develop those clues, to expand on them, to link them, to interrogate and critique them; attempts to assemble or clarify materials; the generation of propositions and counter-propositions; the modeling of different scenarios and possible routes to completion. And then the tough part—the final narrowing-down, the working of materials into actual finished forms, the solidifying of the work from a state of potential, a series of alternatives, to a single manifestation; an actual proposition in language or image, time and space. Crudely that's the same process no matter if the form of a work is a novel or a neon sign, a theater performance or a gallery installation. The way you work on those phases is different; the timescales and number/s of people involved vary, but the progression is similar. I'd say the key thing, really, is that shift from potential to actual, the initial opening, and subsequent narrowing of the idea—it's the latter, the act of clarification, that makes the work what it is, determines what you are really saying, what you are really asking people to consider.

CS   *How has your work evolved over the last thirty years in terms of how you think about space, time, and presence in live performance? Have core concerns changed for you over the years or if there has been a sense of constancy?*

TE   One thing that's clear to me looking back over the years of the work is a set of movements toward, and sometimes away from, the audience. The early work in the mid-1980s was quite closed off in a way—cinematic in feel, with a sense that you were looking into another world, often layered with continuous soundtrack, with its own rules and time. From that point we began to discover the pleasures and effects of breaking or rupturing that isolation, so sections of performances where suddenly we were more directly dealing with the audience and their gazes, often without soundtrack, more directly negotiating the presence of audience and performers in the same space. And then over time this space of more direct contact—silent, fragile—became more and more fascinating to me, to us, and we made work that really focused on it, exploring the very raw and live edge between performers and spectators. We used to say that one day we'd make a performance where we were all in a line at the front of the stage, with all the lights on in the auditorium and that we would never leave that line. We didn't quite get to that place yet . . . but near enough, I think!

I'd say that right now we're in a particular phase, a new one perhaps. We've been through a long period where the fact of the performers' presence, as real people, as quotidian actors "doing the job" of performing, has been really important as a kind of base for the pieces—the idea of real time and task, the idea of an event that is being built, boot-strapping itself in front of you—has often been close to the heart of the work in this time. As part of that a certain playfulness of performance itself, an idea of performer-as-author making live decisions has been really key, and it's in that same period that it became more and more common that performers would refer to themselves and each other using their own names during the performances—a kind of underscoring of the real situation, the constructed nature of all that takes place in the work. Now, with *The Notebook*, adapted from the novel by the Hungarian author Ágota Kristóf, and *Real Magic*, a new devised work from the company in 2016, I think we're entering a new phase, or discovering another approach. They're both pieces that know they're in public, but they're also, all the time, deeply private, recessed, as if their contact with the public is through layers, and as though the performers—so much the center of the performances through their playful authorship, subversive impulses, and decisions in that previous long tranche of work—are now more buried, more trapped in something else, a fiction perhaps, or a task that they can't either just step out of, or create a subversive mode from within. I have the sense, as a director, that the performers are moving away from me, moving inside something, that we don't have the need in these works to endlessly underscore the real "here now" situation of the performance. Perhaps that work is done . . . we all know we are here now!

CS *The page is a canvas and also a stage, although its relationship to the reader is different than that of an audience at an event or a live art installation. How do you see the page as a performance space? Or as a score for performance?*

TE In writing I stage myself—to you, Caridad, here, and to other readers. I anticipate the presence of another, and I anticipate the moment of these signs (on computer screen, and then on printed page) being deciphered or unpacked. For me the encounter between reader and page, audience and stage, are analogous. In each of them a proposition is made and an exchange made in relation to it; something happens in the space between art work and its recipient—an encounter, a conversation, a kind of meeting. If dramaturgy is the unfolding or revelation of information over time, it has a corollary in the flow and structure of words on a page, the revelation of sentences and fragments in the two-dimensional space.

Of course there are differences: Performances tend to be socially triangulated between different members of an audience, where readers of texts tend to enter their relation alone. Performances are naturally feedback loop structures in which reactions of spectators can influence the unfolding event, whereas texts in that sense tend to be fixed (free from the real-time influence of social transaction because we read "alone"). But nonetheless, the page and the stage are both structures that allow (or demand) a kind of dynamic activation of the viewer, a relation that is partly as recipient, partly as author/generator/responder.

CS *How do playwriting and the playwright fit into the digital age of storytelling?*

TE In any historical context, a variety of modes and forms of expression or exchange are available and I guess different forms swing in and out of existence (and focus/significance) according to the times. In the twentieth century, radio and then film and then television became prominent forms, defining the kinds of stories that got told, and the ways that they were consumed. In the twenty-first century, those forms persist (along with older forms of course) whilst the dispersed, global space of the Internet has emerged as a new space for storytelling and exchange, demanding new forms, new approaches. You can make certain observations about how this new space has affected our take on narrative, and our relations to constructs like authorship. It's clear that we've moved from the era of the single screen in the corner of the living room to an age of multiple screens and devices, some of which are mobile and which shift location as we shift. We've moved from narratives that are broadcast from a single point to many watchers, to narratives that emerge through interaction and via contributions made and exchanged between many people. Communication in the digital space is many to many, peer to peer, rather than one to many. Authorship is multiple, transformational, viral, never definitive. It's also cross-disciplinary: Text, image, sound, video.

Both the making of texts for use in performance, and the act of performance-making itself right now exist in this context and they draw from the emerging environment, reflecting and refracting it, borrowing tendencies or ideas . . . or else they stay put, stick to the established ground and methodologies of the theatrical form. Either of these routes is fine, I think. My own tendencies have never been very close to conventional theater form or method anyway . . . so I'm a natural vagrant when it comes to approaches and contexts. Other people are more at home in theater "proper"—its definitions of writing and authorship, its approaches to production and meaning-making. I really do think that's fine—any era now supports multiple approaches to art practice.

Willy Russell

Willy Russell is one of the most produced writers of his time. He is a playwright and songwriter. He has written a large number of highly successful plays and musicals for stage and TV, including: *John, Paul, George, Ringo . . . and Bert* (1974); *Breezeblock* (1975); *One for the Road* (1976); *Our Day Out* (television 1977; stage musical version 1983); *Stags and Hens* (1978; filmed as *Dancin' thru the Dark* 1990); *Educating Rita* (1979); *Blood Brothers* (1981; musical version 1983); and *Shirley Valentine* (1986). His novel, *The Wrong Boy*, was published to great acclaim in 2000.

Caroline Jester *What is a playwright?*

Willy Russell The first thing you must have is the *need* to write and not merely the *want* to write. So many people want to be writers, but what I think separates them is that if you are going to be a playwright, and indeed any kind of true writer, then you've got to *need* to do it. Because the journey is going to be that difficult, and I don't mean in terms of success, I mean in terms of realizing the ambition you have for an idea, and turning that into the reality that is a play. But on top of that, it being such a public medium, you're going to need the need to do it because you do operate in a public arena. A play is probably the one work of art that's open to more public scrutiny than any other, and that's even before it gets in front of an audience. Your director will read it, your director will mention it to his barber, his barber will have an opinion on it, his barber will go home and everybody there has an opinion on a play too. And so you have to have the need to do it to propel you through all that, and to follow that ambition. If you don't have that need, if you only *want* to do it, you'll find something else to do—go on holiday, or kick the cat, have a drink. Now, I still haven't told you what a playwright is. He's that terribly cursed and blessed fellow who needs to write in the form of plays. But he must also be a poet, of course.

CJ   *Can a playwright cross into other artforms?*

WR   I think it's implicit that one can work across various forms.

CJ   *What's unique to my knowledge about your work is that your dramas seem to reinvent themselves into other mediums.* Our Day Out, *a television drama, moved to the stage, and* Educating Rita *from stage to film.*

WR   If I'm struggling to write a new play, I don't have the time or the energy to think about anything else other than the Everest that I'm climbing in trying to write that new play. I don't think about whether it will become a film or radio play down the line. The thing you have to get right is the work in its original carnation and you give all to that. The kind of writer I am is strongly narrative driven; I believe in the audience's need to know what will happen next. E. M. Forster called it "the atavistic worm of needing to know what happens next," and I truly believe in that. I've lived and worked in an age where a lot of people have tried to dismiss the plot as being trite and unnecessary, and tried to persuade audiences that a night in theater can be an abstract experience. There's something about being in the theater and making an audience want to know what happens next, which is, I think, absolutely primal in the act of making theater. Now once you do that, it is rather easy to translate the work into another medium because it's story-driven, it's narrative-strong, it's story-strong.

CJ   *And through such strong characters.*

WR   It is character as well. The work is character-strong because I can't write anything until I've got a voice. It can be single voice, as in the case of *Shirley Valentine* and to some extent *Educating Rita*. When Rita first burst onto my page, it was her voice that I heard; it took some time to work out Frank's voice, but Rita's was such a compelling voice I knew she was a play, even before I knew what the play was, because once I have that voice I know. It's because of having been myself a performer, singer-songwriter, and occasional actor, having given a lot of readings of my work, I understand the dynamic of stage performance and I understand the voice that will reach out and grab an audience, engage an audience.

CJ *Does the audience influence your writing?*

WR The audience is crucial because you can't have theater without the audience. It's a rehearsal if the audience isn't present. I'm always conscious of an audience, conscious of a responsibility toward an audience, but I don't think that allows the audience to dictate what I write. My job is to engage that audience, to sweep that audience up in the work so that they come on board and they will then allow themselves to be taken anywhere, to the deepest, darkest recesses of the human soul. If as a playwright your attitude is the audience doesn't matter, I find that an arrogance of such staggering proportion that it disqualifies you from working in theater because an audience is a crucial part of what makes it.

CJ *You wrote and played music before you started to write drama and prose, but within many of your plays and your novel, music either plays a part in the narrative or is there as cultural references. How did that process of being a singer-songwriter influence you as a dramatic writer?*

WR The one way in which music has fed completely into my work as a dramatist is through my involvement for quite a number of years with traditional music, folk music. I hesitate to use the word [folk] because under it so many musical crimes have been committed over the centuries, and one is slightly embarrassed to use it, but what I mean is that great body of work that's usually credited and written by anonymous and is passed down orally rather than transmitted through high art, written music. The "music of the people," it's sometimes called. And I was involved in that music very deeply, as well as writing my own music and parodies and comic stuff, which fit in that particular wider genre. But one of the things that that movement, and don't forget it was a very left-wing movement, it came out of the push for workers' education. Charles Parker and Ewan MacColl made things like the *Radio Ballads* [documentary series], so instead of taking the voices of working people to make documentaries and have them read by actors, which was the common practice up till the 1950s, Parker and MacColl radically went out and recorded fisherwomen, miners, navvies [manual laborers] on the road, and the thing that was being wrestled with was honoring the intrinsic poetry in the ordinary vernacular of these islands. It was something I believed in passionately and when I stumbled into the theater, I came across the work of people like John McGrath and people who were trying to do the same thing in theater and that was a lightbulb moment, because I realized that I was on the same route, on different paths, but going toward that. If you take that forward and you look at something like *Blood Brothers*, which doesn't use folk music, but you can see where my folk DNA is in the music, the whole of the structure of the drama is the structure of a ballad, of a traditional ballad. You could pass it off as a quasi-British ballad if you like; you could sing the story of *Blood Brothers* as a ballad. It begins with a ballad: "Once I had a husband, You know the sort of chap," quasi-folk music. So that fed in enormously.

CJ　*You wrote the music, the book, the lyrics for Blood Brothers, which is unique.*

WR　Well, not unique.

CJ　*Rare.*

WR　Rare, of our times. Noël Coward is the great exemplar.

CJ　*With contemporary playwrights.*

WR　With contemporary playwrights it is.

CJ　*Did the music come and then the lyrics?*

WR　When I first thought of it, I thought of it as sung through. Then I thought of using existing song. I'd written *John, Paul, George, Ringo . . . and Bert*, which is now regarded as the first "jukebox musical"—we didn't even know that term in those days, so I was used to doing that. But once I'd decided I was going to do the music for *Blood Brothers*— that I was going to be the composer, lyricist, librettist—then I just sat down and I literally wrote, "Once I had a husband." I can see where I was sitting when I wrote it. I knew the tune immediately, and I knew the lyric, and when I got to the end of the first verse—"de de dee de dee, like Marilyn Monroe"—I knew that I'd also given myself a rhyming scheme that always had to rhyme with "oh" at the end, you know, "de de de de de, we went dancing," and that kind of thing. So I finished the lyrics and went into the dialogue because I knew that dialogue interrupted this song. But then what I found when I got to "Easy Terms," which is about a third of the way through Act One, I noticed I was so happy working on lyrics that I'm sure I stretched out the amount of time I worked on them. And then once "Easy Terms" is over, bam, back to dialogue, and so I knew the whole thing would happen in a linear way, no matter what was required, hat on, dialogue hat on, lyricist hat on.

CJ *How do playwriting and the playwright fit into the digital age of storytelling?*

WR I'm trying to find out. I mean obviously we're in a state of great flux as we speak, and I've not fully got my head around it because I haven't had to get my head around it other than electronic books, that kind of stuff. I know that if I was a young writer setting out today, I wouldn't half embrace it. I wouldn't be messing about sending, for example, any plays of mine in the hope that I could get a theater to look at them. I'd get my phone out because you've got so much capability in your phones, and make a twenty-minute film. Ricky Gervais, he made a twenty-minute film for *The Office*; nobody would ever have commissioned that work otherwise. I did that initially with a group of actors that were students, and borrowing some bits of set and putting a play on in the college I was in, and then taking it up to Edinburgh. Well, you've got the digital possibility to do that now. I'm sick of writers saying to me, "I've done this, where shall I send this script?" And I go, "it's terribly old-fashioned, get out there and make it, give us an example of the work" and your chances of being discovered are going to be so much enhanced by that kind of thing. I have thought about whether I should podcast some stuff, because I'm a great listener to podcasts when I'm painting, but I'm not at that age where I've got the hunger to do that, or the need to do that. I don't have the need to do that, to bring it full-circle.

J. T. Rogers*

J. T. Rogers' plays include: *Blood and Gifts* (National Theatre, London; Lincoln Center Theater, Drama Desk Award Nominee and Lucille Lortel Award Nominee); *The Overwhelming* (National Theatre; Roundabout Theatre); *White People* (Off Broadway with Starry Night Productions); *Madagascar* (SPF Festival in NYC; Melbourne Theatre Company); and *Oslo* (Lincoln Center Theater). As one of the original playwrights for the Tricycle Theatre of London's *The Great Game: Afghanistan,* he was nominated for a 2009 Olivier Award. His works are published by Faber and Faber and Dramatists Play Service. He was a 2012 Guggenheim Fellow in Playwriting.

Caridad Svich   *What is a playwright?*

J. T. Rogers   A playwright writes for the stage—for bodies in space to tell stories before an assembled group. I'm hard pressed to be more specific than that because the only playwriting rule I know to be unbreakable is that there are no rules.

CS   *Does the audience influence your writing?*

JTR   My experience from going to and writing for the theater in both the US and UK is that we currently live in the age of "the expert." The audience (myself included) enters a theater with a fulsome sense of how much we already know. We sit with arms crossed, waiting to be engaged. We're distracted, often jaded, expecting the storytellers to convince us that they're good, that this is going to be worth my time. So when I'm writing, at some point in the process I actively puzzle over: How am I going to get the audience to uncross their arms and lean forward into the story? I find that the audience is fine with work that isn't

---

like what they've seen or experienced before *if* they believe that by placing their trust in the author they are putting themselves in good hands. (Note that this is not the same as "kind" or "soothing" hands.)

CS *Can a playwright cross into other artforms?*

JTR I resisted writing for film or TV for years because I felt on some inchoate level that by writing in mediums that are almost completely driven by commerce, I would compromise my playwriting voice and never come back to the stage. I was wrong. In fact, I have found the opposite: Writing for film and TV has improved my playwriting. I recently wrote a true-life crime film about the Japanese yakuza; a sprawling movie script about the Murdoch phone-hacking scandal; and created a (not going to be made) TV series for HBO. The shaping of all three required me to become obsessively, almost fanatically, focused on brevity of dialogue and—even more so—terseness of description. When you're writing a film that covers five years in the byzantine history of the British political establishment's comingling with the Murdoch media empire, and you only have 100+ pages to tell said story, every single word gets put to the test. Writing the "stage directions" became a quest: Could I get those five sentences down to three? Two? The result of this was that when I returned after a year or so away to playwrighting, my work in TV and film has led me to a new economy of language and swiftness of storytelling. My latest play, *Oslo,* is three acts, three hours long, and driven by language and ideas. But I really don't think I could have written it without first acquiring the writing tools that I learned through draft after draft of those works in those other mediums.

CS *Many writers talk about history plays and why they write them. Do you ever feel limited by the historical? Do you enjoy the frame of history? Does it allow you to write with an outward as opposed to an inward one?*

JTR As theatergoer and theater-maker, I find that smashing together the personal with the political makes for a good night out. I love writing about and going to see plays that are both vast *and* personal; that tell me things I didn't know and let me see the present better through looking at the past. I never set out to write my "take" on the history or politics a play is set against, just to delve into things that I find fascinating and that usually confound me. I'm often asked in the US, why I don't write more about me. For me, focusing on "me" as the subject of a play stops the writing process cold. I have to slip away from "me" in order *to* write. Perhaps it's because that through writing about others I'm freed from the grip of the need to make my personal statement as a writer. I don't have a statement to make; I'm interested in putting the other—that is, other than me—on stage: Other points of view, other beliefs. The more I can erase myself from my own work the better.

CS *You trained as an actor at North Carolina School of the Arts. While it may seem obvious as a question, in thinking about writing across artforms, often questions that playwrights are not asked have to do with the actor and what it is like to write knowing that you are writing for work to be embodied. How has your training impacted you as a playwright? Have you ever written for a specific actor, or with one in mind? On a technical level, what approach do you have to writing for the voice/ body? As well as the other elements of the stage—plasticity, etc.?*

JTR I went to acting school, which I think was fantastic training for being a theater writer. Almost everything I know about writing comes from being an actor or being in the room with actors. I "act" everything out as I write it, so that it's built, line by line, to be spoken. For me, actors are the smartest dramaturges in the theater. Good actors are thoroughbreds, built to run. Not only are they a joy to watch and listen to, but when they stumble in rehearsal, it's almost always your fault. If the horse is fit and it falls, the problem is the track. So, you, playwright, have to smooth the track—and be grateful for the fact your bumps got exposed in rehearsal and not on press night.

CS *I think of Wally Shawn's work for instance that even on film (in his work with Andre Gregory) and on stage (also with Andre and others, Scott Elliott, etc.) characters either fall into traps—of dreaming, barbarism, racism, etc.—and then those who manage somehow to escape, or think they do. You are very different writers of course, but the willingness to throw your characters straight into moral tangle . . . I feel* *a kinship of sorts between you, even though the dramaturgical strategies you employ are different. [I] Just wonder if you'd speak to this. The question of theater and morality, and what theater throws open when you walk through its door.*

JTR You mention Wally Shawn's work, which I admire very much. What I am taken by in his plays, and what I hope connects my work to his, is his morality as writer. At present, the moral writer I most admire is Chekov. I couldn't stand his plays as a young man; now I think about them constantly. What the Doctor does so wondrously is put people on stage that he clearly loves, or, failing that, admires. In my work, I've come to hold this idea above all others: To only put on stage people I love or admire. God knows I don't have to like them, but to their humanity and intelligence, attention must be paid.

CS *I was chatting with a colleague recently and she said that playwrights should be thought of as other writers (say, novelists and poets) are—as leading thinkers of their times.*

JTR Oh, that's a tricky one. On one hand, trying to be a public intellectual or great thinker through playwriting usually ends in hideous unwatchability. But . . . how many times do you go to the theater and think afterward, "Did this writer *ever* think about what the point of this story is? Do they have *any* ideas to share with me *at all*?" The tension between those two poles keeps me up at night.

CS *How do you see the differences in one form over the other (film and theater), even though they are both within the field of dramatic writing?*

JTR I think we as playwrights often conflate the role of the writer and the role of the director in film/TV. Yes, we have to think visually when writing in those mediums, but paradoxically the one thing we can do that other creative talents can't is create the verbal, structural building blocks of a story.

CS *I chatted with David Greig when The Events played New York Theatre Workshop and he was quite adamant about how all we* *could do now as playwrights was to re-imagine the form. That it was our duty. He said that when he walks into bookshops and looks at the new play shelf, the first thing he does is read the first few pages and if the form is same ol', same ol', he just puts the play down. But if the play, from the get-go, is provoking and challenging the reader/audience, he can't wait to finish the play! In other words, that form itself and how it is played with (toward an end of course and not just for the sake of it) becomes first "waking agent" of consciousness in theater-making. Thoughts?*

JTR   I don't agree with Greig. It's been my experience that in the last twenty years, the love affair with "Form Above All" has cut off much of English-language playwriting from the audience. Many, many, many new plays I go to seem to be written by theater artists for the sole benefit of other theater artists. This is more the case with American playwriting, but in both countries I find that telling a good story has become looked on with suspicion . . . which drives me a bit crazy. But here's the thing: I could be completely wrong. Further, I love the specificity of Greig's thinking about this—and I'm always eager to see everything he writes. There are no rules: That's the only rule.

CS   *How do playwriting and the playwright fit into the digital age of storytelling?*

JTR   Good storytelling is good storytelling, whether it's a revival of Aphra Behn's *The Rover,* or, say, a site-specific podcast play where an audience of one goes through the trash as she's told the history of each item she burrows through. My experience as listener/watcher/writer in the current moment is that the new works that resonate are at their core good stories, well told, using new tools.

Lin Coghlan

Lin Coghlan is from Dublin. She has written widely for theater, including: *Apache Tears* (Clean Break), winner of the Peggy Ramsey Award; *Kingfisher Blue* (Bush Theatre); and *The Miracle* (National Theatre). Her work for screen includes: *First Communion Day* (BBC Films), winner of the Dennis Potter Play of the Year Award; *Electric Frank* (BBC Films), winner of the Leopard of Tomorrow at the Locarno Film Festival; and *Some Dogs Bite* (BBC), winner of the Prix du Public at the Nantes Film Festival and Best Single Drama at Kidscreen New York. She has written for numerous British and Irish television series, and created an original thirteen-part series for the BBC—*Patrick's Planet.* For two years she worked as lead writer on Lionhead Studios/Microsoft's *Project Milo* for XBOX360, creating, storylining, and writing a character-driven gaming experience to complement the emerging and ground breaking "Kinect" technology. Alongside her screenwriting Lin has also written original plays for radios and adapted many classics for BBC Radio 4.

Caroline Jester   *What is a playwright?*

Lin Coghlan   A playwright is a storyteller who specializes in telling stories to live audiences.

CJ   *Does the audience influence your writing?*

LC   The context of the commission influences me. That might mean the audience, that might be a specific audience, or it might be a specific setting. For instance I wrote a play for Red Ladder in Leeds years ago, which was going to be played in the street to the young homeless community. It was called *The Bus Shelter Show* and actually in the end, when I developed the idea, it was about two young people who were homeless and who steal a bus, and we played the play inside the bus for a maximum audience of ten at a time. So a commission like that, yes, you do think about the audience but I don't think it necessarily means you craft the story for that audience. The story could have been played in numerous different situations; it could have been a film, it could have been played in the theater, and in fact it was later on. But the fact that I knew the concerns of the lives of that audience and the issues that that audience was going through in that situation . . . I did think very much about a piece that would resonate with that particular audience. But most commissions don't work like that.

CJ   *Can a playwright cross into other artforms?*

LC   Well, a playwright definitely can and I've benefited enormously from quite consciously deciding to learn how to write in different mediums. I had a very radical, political training at the Rose Bruford College and when I left there in 1982, that training was all about devising and creating new work within a community context. It wasn't expected that any of us would ever do anything else. At the time that we left, there were probably about twenty companies in the country that specialized in TIE [Theatre in Education], in women's theater groups, Clean Break, Red Ladder, Perspectives, and Theatre for Black Women popped up out of the course I was on too, and Gay Sweatshop was already running, so there were places you could go to work if you had a training in devising and you were interested in socially relevant/political theater, taking it into places that didn't have easy access or would not necessarily go to theater. It was all about non-traditional spaces.

After Thatcherism, most of those companies disappeared gradually over a period of about ten years and those people in my peer group who hadn't got one of the rare permanent jobs, an artistic director in a TIE company or in one of those organizations, that generation of people really started either moving over into teaching or retraining, although of course many hung on getting work where they could. I was making ends meet writing plays and running workshops but I felt I wouldn't survive unless I could do other things, but at that stage I was in my late thirties and there wasn't the kind of training available there is now, and the idea of starting all over again in another area of writing where I had no profile and nobody knew me was very daunting. So I began with trying to get into radio and wasn't very successful: I sent a few scripts out and even did a bit of development work on a script, but the producer

I worked with felt that I didn't have an ear for radio—even though now, years later, I've done many, many, many projects for radio—but she just said, "I don't think you've got it," so I just gave up. I was very disappointed. And then I did an MA in Screenwriting at the London Institute, which felt like a really scary thing to do, and that totally changed my life in that I wasn't interested in TV at all but I *was* very interested in film, but the first year was all about TV work and it made me fall in love with television and understand how complicated and interesting it is.

Then over the next ten years I gradually started getting work in television and radio and I made a short film for the BBC, so out of that course I got into the film scene and the TV scene, but it's just like everything else: It's totally hit and miss. The danger about doing lots of things is that you're not concentrating on one career . . . it's swings and roundabouts because I really feel the reason I've managed to stay working for so long is that I can do lots of different things. But the downside of that is you're not driven to get the next job and the next job and the next job in one area, which might motivate you to push through barriers.

CJ *There's another muscle that you've flexed with writing for the gaming industry, and there are few playwrights I've met that have crossed over into the gaming industry thus far. How did your work with Lionhead/Microsoft happen, and why were you attracted to this work?*

LC It happened because games producers are beginning to use writers more. The way the industry works is that up until recently, the writer was originally a coder. Games are becoming much more sophisticated now but they tended to be plot driven—so a series of events that could go a number of different ways—and the person who would have decided on who are the characters and what are the events would have been somebody who was already within the games company and had come up through the ranks, not somebody with a drama or story background. But the games industry was starting to see the value of having people come in from theater and film to bring what they know about story and character.

They had invited a film director to work on the development of the new game and that film director happened to be the actor I'd met at Theatre Centre twenty years before and who I've made a number of short films with for the BBC, and who I then, by chance, ended up working on [the children's TV series] *Grange Hill* with. So we really did both begin together and then overlap a number of different times in different places, and he'd been offered this job and he said, "I think you need a director and a writer at this point, because you're trying to decide upon basic issues of story and character." I interviewed and got the job thinking that it would be for three to six months, but I ended up working there for three years on the piece and in the end we took on another writer supporting me. It was completely unknown territory for all of us because really there's very little crossover in terms of language and understanding of both areas, their side of the craft and our side of the craft. It was very challenging to make a shared language and for us to understand each other, but it was extremely interesting and I think the basics for a writer . . . what you can talk about is what makes a good story, what makes an audience care about a character and how a story can be crafted to help an audience to invest in the story and the characters. I think the main thing that Lionhead were interested in was this whole area of getting an emotional connection between character and player.

When we started working there, we were working on quite a traditional game and the idea was to create a character that would have a particularly strong bond with the player. Microsoft was unveiling this technology called Kinect alongside what we were doing, though, which was very secret, and after we'd been working together for a few months the project changed in that it was going to use this new technology. What happens in gaming is that the game designers—via the actual thing that you can do in the game, how you interact with the game, how the game works, what technology you're using—tend to inform what the story can be. So even if you as a writer go with a great idea for a story, the technology that's being devised and designed around the game may not be able to deliver that story. Whereas the designer might come and say we've developed this amazing interface that allows the screen to dissolve into I don't know—water, say—and they describe some sort of interaction that the player can have with the screen and you can try to develop the story to work within those confines. So the story doesn't always lead; you're often following the design, the technological design. So what happened was this new technology emerged and we needed to follow that and create story and interaction that would be in tune with the technology.

I think what we learned through it was, again, the basics: How do you build a strong relationship with a character? How do you get an audience or a player to care? How does drama work? And how does storytelling work? That doesn't change, whatever medium you're working in. But then the next layer of that is we have, for instance, the ability for a player to view this story now from one point of view, or to experience a part of the journey in a very exciting visual environment. So how can I write to the strengths of that environment but still keep best practice in terms of story and character and drama, jeopardy, all those things that make great stories?

CJ *Do you think this is actually closer to live theater than writing for television then, because there's that interactive experience?*

LC I think that's interesting; I hadn't thought of it like that before, but yes. I mean the big challenge with gaming is the player is in charge, so twenty, thirty years ago, people were getting very excited by novels that could have multiple endings and then stories on the Internet where you could choose how it ends or what happens next. But in order to do that, you have to develop dozens of "what if" scenarios, and there's an element of that in gaming, but the player needs to feel like they're deciding what happens next, but you also need to craft the journey and that's very, very different from theater. But there is that interactivity, there is a shared element, definitely.

CJ *How do playwriting and the playwright fit into the digital age of storytelling?*

LC Well, there will always be a place for stories told to a live audience. There is no other experience like it and we will always gather to have that experience, just like we will always choose to go to the cinema rather than watch movies on our own at home because there's something about being with other people and sharing the emotional experience and the story together that is unique. So I am very positive that there will always be a place for plays and playwrights. What I do feel is that taking those storytelling skills and having fun with them in lots of different situations is very nourishing to writers in my experience, so the digital age just offers more opportunity.

Robert Schenkkan[*]

Robert Schenkkan is a Pulitzer Prize-winning, Tony Award-winning, Writer's Guild Award-winning, two-time Emmy-nominated writer of stage, television, and film. He is the author of fourteen original full-length plays, among them *The Kentucky Cycle* and *All the Way*, two musicals, and a collection of one-act plays. He co-wrote the feature films *The Quiet American* and *Hacksaw Ridge*, and his television credits include *The Pacific*, *The Andromeda Strain*, and *Spartacus*.

Caridad Svich   *What is a playwright?*

Robert Schenkkan   Someone who writes plays. (A triumph of hope over experience.) Someone who writes stories which are performed by actor(s) in front of an audience.

CS   *Does the audience influence your writing?*

RS   I write about what interests me, what I would like to see on stage, not what I think a generic audience wants. However, while writing I think a great deal about the audience and what I want their response to be. Then, during the early performances of that new play, I closely track the audience experience and adjust the text or the performance elements to achieve the response I want.

CS   *Can a playwright cross into other artforms?*

RS   Absolutely. Indeed, I think such crossings are a healthy pursuit for an artist as they expose you to different, sometimes radically different, ways of approaching story and text and performance.

CS *Your career has spanned more than thirty years. During that time, there's been the extraordinary phenomenon of* The Kentucky Cycle—*a landmark work in US theater, and then years later* All the Way *and its sequel,* The Great Society. *You've also sustained a career as an actor for many years, and screenwriter, most recently of the film adaptation of* All the Way *and the film* Hacksaw Ridge *(both 2016). When I think of your work, I do think of the term "history plays," but I also think of the words "epic," and "ambitious." Big panoramas, epic sweep, and a full-hearted embrace of the stage and its possibilities. Can you talk about how you think your dedication to the epic, if we can call it that for now, sits alongside the works you've written and/or adapted for the screen? Similarities, differences? Lessons along the way as a writer?*

RS I do relish the epic sweep of a big complicated story unfolding over time and distance, probably because one can really get "lost" in such an event, swept away. Whether it is poems like *The Iliad*, *The Odyssey*, *The Mahabharata*, or *The Ramayana*, novels like Frank Herbert's *Dune* series, films like David Lean's *Lawrence of Arabia*, I love feeling overwhelmed by this new world and simultaneously being brought into greater and more intimate contact with my own as a result. I think this innate fascination frequently shows up in the kinds of work I have done on film. The big lesson, of course, is not to lose your way in the process. However wild and extravagant the sweep of the story becomes, it is critical never to lose sight of the human heart within.

CS *Most readers of this book will likely know* All the Way, *but not, say, earlier work of yours like* Handler, *and they may not even put two and two together and realize you're also the fellow that wrote the film* The Quiet American, *which starred Michael Caine and was directed by Philip Noyce. I happen to love that film, by the way! Your voice as a writer is supple, assured, but also quiet, if you know what I mean? It has something in it perhaps, and this is my conjecture, of course, of the actor in you. The ability to embody the moment and situation, the bodies of different characters, with sly authority but somehow never getting in the way of the focus of the drama. I wonder how much of how your writing voice has developed has to do with your training and career* *as an actor working in multiple mediums (stage, film, TV)? Or do you see your writing as separate from this side of you?*

RS   There is no question that my training as an actor and the decade of professional work as an actor that followed my studies has influenced my writing. Indeed, since I am "untrained" as a writer, it was by taking part in the new play process as an actor (Sundance, the O'Neill Center, the Public Theater, MTC, etc.) that I actually learned how plays are made. I also think I have a good sense of what an actor needs and am, perhaps, in some ways better equipped to talk to actors as a result.

CS   *A strong sense of compassion and desire to spin a great yarn characterizes your writing, and within that a sustained voice of integrity and morality. Now, we all know, theater is in great part about opening the box to moral ambiguities—the necessary dialectic alive in embodied drama. When you write for film, and not doing "work for hire" but an integral part of the creative team, how do you fight for or focus on keeping the dialectic alive? Like, for example,* Hacksaw Ridge—*the project was in development for fourteen years, before you or Mel Gibson came on board as writer and director, respectively, yet the source material was always the true story of conscientious objector Desmond Doss.*

RS   My relationship with *Hacksaw Ridge* dates to 2006 when I was hired by producer Bill Mechanic to write the screenplay. At that time, the only underlying material available to me was a black-and-white documentary and some research interviews with Desmond and a few of those people who knew him. Desmond died before I could talk to him myself.

CS   *What drew you to the material?*

RS   Story and character. It is an amazing story, a "combat" film unlike any you've ever seen before since the hero is a pacifist and refuses to carry a weapon. Always, what I am drawn to are characters whose inner conflict is at least as great as their external conflicts.

CS   *What was the collaboration with Gibson and the production team like?*

RS Mel and I talked several times but most of my communication was through the producer, Bill Mechanic. This is not ideal from my standpoint, but the relationship between writer and director in Hollywood is more complicated than in the theater and I have long since adjusted to the vagaries. Each film or TV project is different and you have to be flexible. My focus on the Desmond Doss story was always on not "underselling" the inherent challenge of adhering to the stark moral universe that Desmond's faith demanded. In other words, if one believes that Desmond's actions in Okinawa were "pre-ordained," or that his God kept Desmond alive as a divine miracle, well, who wouldn't choose to believe? And how great was Desmond's achievement? But to me, that is not how faith actually works. I think Desmond struggled on that battlefield, and I don't just mean physically. I think there must have been a constant moral struggle as well. How could you not want to pick up a weapon and defend yourself? In the midst of so much cruelty, how could your belief in a compassionate God not be tested? Bringing these struggles to the forefront of the screenplay makes Desmond more human and more accessible to the audience.

CS *What's the great dialectic that you see operating in and through Doss's story?*

RS Sometimes war is necessary, is just. Certainly I would argue that was true of the Second World War. But what if your personal religious beliefs absolutely forbade the taking of human life? How do you square that circle?

CS *And what makes the piece ideally suited to film and not the stage?*

RS Desmond's heroism really only comes alive in the context of the extraordinarily brutal war that was the Okinawa campaign. I think a naturalist approach is almost mandatory and honestly, film does epic complicated action sequences better than theater.

CS *You're also adapting comic books, did I hear that right, for the screen? You have a deal with Marvel Entertainment? That to me seems like a very different universe from the worlds of* All the Way *and* The

Kentucky Cycle. *How do you keep yourself sure-footed as a writer working in such different genres and story tropes?*

RS I have on two occasions adapted comic books for the screen. I adapted the classic Marvel title, *Killraven*, but the project fell afoul of a rights dispute between the then owner of Marvel and Fox and never got made. I also adapted the contemporary comic *Incognito* by my pal, Ed Brubaker, for Peter Chernin's company, where it too, currently languishes in development hell.

In each genre, I am focused on finding the heart of that particular story and allowing that to guide all my subsequent creative choices. I find moving between different genres actually invigorating and keeps me from getting stale.

CS *Has working on a play ever inspired you to make a film or vice versa? In other words, has working on one form impacted upon the other? If so, could you talk about a specific piece? If not, why not?*

RS I wrote a play, a two-hander for two particular actors, called *By the Waters of Babylon*. I am quite fond of the play but it hasn't had the kind of life on stage I would have hoped, for reasons that are not clear to me. As we've discussed, film can do epic, but it can also do intimate, and *Babylon* is a painfully intimate *pas de deux* with strong, almost visceral, surrealistic moments. I became very intrigued by the idea of adapting the play for the screen and we are currently trying to set up the result. Last year, I adapted my play, *All the Way*, for HBO. This was very important to me because I feel that the story of Lyndon Baines Johnson, Martin Luther King Jr., and 1964 speaks to our current political crisis and I wanted that story to have the widest possible audience. From the beginning of that adaptation, I didn't want to just "shoot the play," I wanted to do a full cinematic re-imagining of the story, one which would allow me to get deeper into both character and theme. Because I was both the sole writer and one of only three executive producers (along with Steven Spielberg and Bryan Cranston), I feel like the resulting film truly accomplishes that goal and reflects my aesthetics.

CS *How do playwriting and the playwright fit into the digital age of storytelling?*

RS Stories are stories. Regardless of the evolution of the "delivery system," I think there will always be an audience for a story performed by live actors in real time—two boards and a passion. What the digital age has made possible is the greater/faster distribution of plays, and subsequent expansion of audience awareness of different writers and different styles.

4

I CAN PASS THROUGH ANY BORDER

All of the playwrights in this chapter have had work produced in countries other than the one in which they are currently residing. This is true also for playwrights in other chapters, but we wanted to see if there was something inherent in the type of story that lends itself to international travel in more detail. We asked the playwrights "why do some stories transcend national borders and find audiences in different countries?"

Chantal Bilodeau takes a practical approach when exploring ways of bringing the story of climate stage to global audiences. She collaborates with an artist from a discipline other than theater from the featured nation of each new play she writes about this. It could be seen as modeling on a small scale the international collaborations needed on a much larger scale to address this subject.

Anders Lustgarten, as someone who has been described as the United Kingdom's most international dramatist, doesn't believe you should co-opt another country for your story. You have to always understand the country you are writing about and get under its skin to represent it with truth and accuracy whilst retaining its own spirit.

Frances Ya-Chu Cowhig thinks it's more interesting to think about this from the perspective of human beings. To think about people globally as streams of diasporic migration that transcend national boundaries, and it's the stories that flow from those spaces, not the stories that are already there.

David Hare believes any serious play is going to survive multiple readings, and it is a character within a play that belongs in any culture that gives it the passport to see the world.

Katori Hall's work is a reaction against forgetting. Forgetting is dangerous, for individuals and for nations and for history. All stories can transcend national borders if the storytellers are given the opportunity to transcend them.

Simon Stephens thinks a writer can go to another country but they're ultimately writing about themselves. And his favorite moments in his plays are those without language.

Lucy Prebble has written from the perspective of those who seem very different to her and hasn't shied away from another nation's crisis. But there are many personal resonances within those stories; it is people who tend not to see these because they have an idea of who they think you are and what pattern you fit.

Anne Washburn questions the very premise of this chapter. Has there really been enough of a sample size of plays that have transcended national borders to even have a conversation about it? As a playwright who has had work produced in the US and the UK, she doesn't think there is a shared knowledge of playwrights that cross the Atlantic. Is it that the plays that do make the journey are universal or just that the other work hasn't found a ticket to cross?

Tim Crouch responds to this through his work. He makes his work porous and invites the audience to share an openness within the theater he makes.

But what happens when a play holds a mirror up to a nation's internal battles? **Aizzah Fatima** was asked to change the title of her play when she crossed the Atlantic. Not everywhere in the United Kingdom, but increasingly so. When audiences were given the opportunity to share her story, the issues of being a woman in a society that the play explores transcended religious, ethnic, and cultural boundaries—no matter which country she took her story to.

I hope you've got your passport ready and will be allowed entry into the country of your choice. There seems to be a much wider conversation needed around the opportunities for work to cross national borders and how this can be achieved. The playwrights in this chapter invite us to be a part of this.

Chantal Bilodeau

Chantal Bilodeau is a playwright, translator, and research artist whose work focuses on the intersection of science, policy, culture, and climate change. She is the Artistic Director of The Arctic Cycle, an organization created to support the writing, development, and production of eight plays of the same name that look at the social and environmental changes taking place in the eight countries of the Arctic. She is also the founder of the blog and international network Artists and Climate Change, and a co-organizer of Climate Change Theatre Action. Her translations include nearly twenty plays by contemporary playwrights Sébastien David (Quebec), Mohamed Kacimi (Algeria), Koffi Kwahulé (Côte d'Ivoire), Catherine Léger (Quebec), Étienne Lepage (Quebec), David Paquet (Quebec), and Larry Tremblay (Quebec). She is a member of the Dramatists Guild of America, the Playwrights Guild of Canada, and a core member of Climate Lens.

Caridad Svich   *What is a playwright?*

Chantal Bilodeau   A playwright is a story-maker and a storyteller. S/he is one of the many craftspersons who build, strengthen, question, and challenge culture—and by culture, I mean the complex web of beliefs, values, and customs that shape how we view the world and how we relate to each other.

CS   *Does the audience influence your writing?*

CB   The world I live in influences my writing: What happens, who is affected, who wins, who loses. My work is usually a combination of fact and fiction, so I feel more indebted to the people I'm trying to portray than to the people who experience the finished work because I know the former better than the latter. If I were commissioned to write for a specific theater, it would be different. I would be engaging in a conversation with a specific audience right from the get-go. But most of the time, I don't know where my plays will be produced so it's impossible to write with an audience in mind. That said, I am currently writing a play about Alaska that will premiere in Alaska. It's very exciting because it will be the first time that the subject and the audience are one and the same.

CS *Why do some stories transcend national borders and find audiences in different countries?*

CB Most likely because there's a universality to them that transcends borders, but that's a simplistic answer. Every good story contains a kernel of universal truth, yet every good story doesn't necessarily travel. In reality, I don't think we can predict what stories will find international audiences any more than we can predict what plays will become hits. It has as much to do with the playwright's drive to make it happen as with external circumstances and the story itself. It's often a combination of hard work and luck, a case of being at the right place at the right time, and saying something at the exact moment when people are ready to hear it. It's also about language (wordless stories travel more easily because they don't require translation), cultural accessibility, and the prevalent style and mode of theater production in a given country. The structure of the story—how it is told—can be attractive to another culture or totally incomprehensible regardless of what the story is.

CS *How can plays and their concerns span the globe? This is perhaps more to do with subject matter of works and/or thematic concerns. I think of your Arctic Cycle, for instance.*

CB Intention is the most important ingredient. From the beginning, the *Arctic Cycle* was designed to be circumpolar. (But whether that intention materializes the way I imagine it remains to be seen.) The *Arctic Cycle* consists of a series of eight plays that look at the social and environmental changes taking place in the eight Arctic nations: the US, Canada, Greenland, Iceland, Norway, Sweden, Finland, and Russia. It is both a research project and an artistic project that uses the lenses of science, policy, culture, and climate change to understand how our world is changing and how the communities most affected by this change are adapting (or not). Each play tells the story of one nation, but once the *Cycle* is completed, the eight plays will together tell a bigger story about our evolving relationship with our changing planet.

I made two rules for myself when I started this project: 1) For every play, I collaborate with an artist from a discipline other than theater who is from the featured nation. This is to make sure that my voice is not the only voice in the story, and that the people I'm portraying have a say. It's also a way to model on a small scale the kind of international collaboration that is needed on a much bigger scale. 2) I try to have every play produced in the US *and* in the country where the play is set. Cross-border conversations around this issue are important and the plays provide a great stepping stone to engage people on a somewhat neutral territory. The first two plays of the *Cycle*—*Sila* and *Forward*—are written and have been produced, and so far, I have been able to follow my rules. For *Sila,* set in Canada, I collaborated with the Inuit spoken-word poet Taqralik Partridge. For *Forward,* set in Norway, I collaborated with the Norwegian electropop singer-songwriter Aggie Petersen. *Sila* has not been produced in Canada yet, but *Forward* was developed in the US and Norway, and is currently being translated into Norwegian.

The Arctic is unique because, when it comes to climate change, its stories are both local and global. Climate change is impacting populations locally, at twice the rate as the rest of the world. But it's also impacting the rest of us: When the polar ice cap melts, the sea level rises everywhere. When the permafrost thaws, methane and carbon dioxide are released into the atmosphere, warming the globe for us all and creating more extreme weather events. When the pattern of global ocean currents changes due to an influx of freshwater from melting ice, the climate is affected everywhere. So the stories of the Arctic are our stories. They're what our future will look like. And they're what taking responsibility *should* look like since we, in the developed world, are creating the hardship that people in the Arctic, who emit next to no greenhouse gases, face every day.

CS *What responsibility do you think playwrights should have or not to speaking beyond their localities and local stories?*

CB I think it's a matter of personal choice. We need playwrights who are local and speak to and about their community, and we need playwrights who take a bird's eye view and reach beyond borders. It's the same with scientists. Some scientists do research in the field, and others interpret satellite data. One is not more important than the other because both are needed to get a complete picture. Playwrights who are deeply embedded in, and involved with, their community can capture stories that would otherwise remain untold, stories too often left out of the mainstream. They can strengthen and affirm people's beliefs and values, and provide them with an opportunity to see themselves. This requires a level of familiarity and trust that can only be developed over time. On the flip side, we also need playwrights who can bring the world together by looking at the big picture, playwrights who have the ability to move fluidly between cultures and highlight our commonalities and differences. We have become so interconnected that it is imperative we wrestle with global challenges and learn to make better decisions as a global community. Playwrights who speak beyond their localities provide scope and a context for our local stories.

CS *How do your art and environmental activism come together?*

CB It's funny, the two have been intertwined for so long in my head that I can't think of them as separate anymore. To me, writing about climate change is writing about people. And writing about people is writing about power and oppression and injustice and race and identity—all issues exacerbated by our global crisis. Climate change is like a Russian doll that we have to keep unpacking.

My brand of activism often involves bringing together people who may not otherwise encounter each other, and helping them engage in cross-disciplinary conversations. (We won't solve climate change, or any other problem for that matter, by staying in our knowledge silos.) When my plays are produced, I encourage theaters to partner with local scientists and/or environmental organizations for post-show conversations or specific actions. For example, Cyrano's Theatre Company in Anchorage, who produced *Sila* in 2016, partnered with the local chapter of Citizens' Climate Lobby. Citizens' Climate Lobby provided draft letters and a submission box so that audience members could write to their local legislators about concerns and questions regarding the impact of climate change on the Arctic. (This was very successful.) When the plays are produced at a university, I encourage the theater department to partner with other programs, like the environmental studies program, for example, or departments on campus to offer a more rounded educational experience to students.

CS *Climate change is one of the central issues of our times, and yet I feel that in theater, the subject and its reality is treated as a niche/ boutique topic. It affects us all. Why do you think—if you do agree with this—that in producing circles theatrically, climate change is a sub-sub topic on US stages specifically? If you don't agree, I would love to hear your thoughts too.*

CB I totally agree with you and I ask myself that question all the time. Why isn't the theater responding to the urgency of climate change? Why aren't we seeing plays tackling that challenge on all of our stages? I just attended the American Geophysical Union annual conference, where 24,000 scientists gathered for five days to discuss the latest earth, ocean, and atmospheric science. In a sobering session, Veerabhadran Ramanathan from the University of California, San Diego, said we have fewer than ten years to "bend the curve," meaning we have fewer than ten years to reduce our greenhouse gas emissions if we want to keep global warming below 1.5 degrees Celsius—a safer target than the original 2 degrees. And even at that level, there will be *significant disruption*. Artists take pride in being ahead of the curve and helping society move through major transitions, but on this one, in the theater at least (visual artists took up the challenge years ago), we're desperately behind. In a way, it shouldn't be surprising. The field is acting in the same way as the rest of the population. According to the Yale Program on Climate Change Communication, most Americans (90 percent) are concerned about climate change to some degree. Yet only 17 percent of us are taking individual, consumer, and political action to address it.

Part of the problem may also have to do with the fact that socio-political plays, or what in the field we derogatively call "issue plays," are considered lesser plays. Most theaters don't want them, don't value them, and so there are few incentives to write them. Playwrights are expected to be engaged but not disruptive, and writing about climate *is* disruptive. It challenges some of our most beloved and enduring systems like capitalism, white dominance, and patriarchy—systems within which most of our theatrical institutions are deeply embedded. In certain cases, who is on the board and where the funding comes from might also be a deterrent. I imagine it would be hard to present a play that takes on the fossil fuel industry if that same industry, or the people who represent it, happened to be a major donor.

CS *How do playwriting and the playwright fit into the digital age of storytelling?*

CB Theater is live and digital storytelling is virtual. So the terms of engagement are necessarily different. The stage requires a different kind of theatricality than the screen, and because of the relationship between actors and audiences, theater is more immediate. But I think there is room for cross-over. Telling a story, whether it is acted live on stage or streamed through a website, requires the same skills. That's why we so often see playwrights move into film and television. The story structure may be different, but the storytelling impulse is the same. I suppose we could worry about theater's life expectancy, especially when we can reach more people, faster and possibly for less money, by using technology, but I think there will always be room for the live experience. Even if there comes a day when that live experience doesn't look anything like what we're used to seeing today

Anders Lustgarten

Anders Lustgarten won the inaugural Harold Pinter Playwright's Award for *If You Don't Let Us Dream, We Won't Let You Sleep* at the Royal Court Theatre Downstairs. He is currently under commission to the RSC and the National Theatre among several others, and adapted David Peace's *The Damned United* for the West Yorkshire Playhouse. His play *Lampedusa* had two runs at the Soho Theatre—back by popular demand—and at the HighTide Festival, and toured in 2016. *The Seven Acts of Mercy* opened at the Swan Theatre in Stratford-upon-Avon to critical acclaim in 2016. Anders is also developing original projects for television and radio and is a long-standing political activist who has been arrested on four continents.

Caroline Jester   *What is a playwright?*

Anders Lustgarten   It's a storyteller, obviously, in the same way that any form of fiction or nonfiction is a form of storytelling. There's a human immediacy to playwriting because it's live and it's in the room and it's a collaboration between a group of people, none of whom can do it without the other. What has been written is obviously controlled by you, the playwright, but then there are lots of things that aren't controlled by you, which is more or less everything after that: The interpretation of it, the representation of it, the feeling in the room that is unique to each individual audience. So I would say a playwright is part of a human process of storytelling, in a perhaps less dictatorial or controlling way than a lot of other artforms, a lot of other contemporary storytelling forms, and therefore, if they do it right, is less commodifiable.

The great problem with visual art is that the physical painting is transformed in the contemporary art world into something that has nothing to do with the painting itself, let alone the representations of the world within the painting: It's transformed into a commodity. It becomes a thing that you buy, that rich Americans can say they have and nobody else has, or it's an investment vehicle for stolen Russian wealth that will aggregate in value more rapidly in the art world than it will in other fields. It can be stolen, it can be taken away from the rest of us. It's very hard to take a play away from humanity, though, because it only exists in the performance, there in the room in front of that particular group of people. So of all the artforms it is most resistant to capitalism, which is ironic because people think that theater is just for posh people because of the particular social class that has always tended to dominate and control theater. But in terms of what the theater can be, I think it's quite radical, quite democratic in some ways.

CJ *Does the audience influence your writing?*

AL I think you do have to think in terms of an abstract audience of humans: What will humans get from that particular moment, and what's great textually but just won't land on humans? We tend to be text-based in British theater, which I like (that's one of the reasons I write for British theater, I like interesting and sophisticated texts), but you can forget there are twice as many tools beyond the text which you also have at your disposal, which are the visual and the sensual and all the elements people respond to live in a room. But I also think of the kind of people I would like to come and see my plays, and one of the things that is most satisfying with my plays (and in fact I probably wouldn't do it if they didn't), is that they always seem to reach out beyond the conventional audience that would come to theater.

The very first play I wrote was a play called *A Day at the Racists*, which is about the British National Party (BNP). The protagonists were a black and a white painter and decorator from Barking [East London], and we did it at the Finborough [in Kensington]. And the Finborough office was all terrified we're going to get the BNP coming—I told them the BNP don't travel, the BNP aren't that culturally minded, and they're certainly not going to come all the way from Barking to give us trouble— but they had a hotline to the police and all this. So I'm waiting for the play to start and one of the box office people comes running down the stage and goes "The BNP have arrived, the BNP are here, go up and do something." You want *me* to go up and do something? OK then. So I went up the stairs and there's all these big stocky fellas with leather jackets and shaven heads and three of them are black, so I'm like "OK, unless this is life imitating art, it's not the BNP." So I had a little sit down with them and said, "Alright gents, how are you enjoying the play?" and they're like, "it's fuckin' brilliant." They were painters and decorators from Barking: Somehow they'd heard there was a play about painters and decorators from Barking and they thought they'd come down.

CJ *Why do some stories transcend national borders and find audiences in different countries?*

AL There are some stories that obviously you can say have universal themes—they resonate, the story of a father and son or a mother or a daughter—but I think maybe you're thinking about something more.

I've done another play called *Lampedusa*, which was about the migration crisis and also about austerity and about putting the two of them together because they are exactly the same phenomenon: They trialled austerity in the global South for thirty years under the guise of "structural adjustment." Everything that's being done in Europe as austerity is what's been done by the World Bank and IMF in the global South since the 1970s—so privatization, huge state cutbacks, the reduction of the idea that the state owes you anything, the polarization into the deserving and the undeserving poor. So you want to put these two stories together that are supposed to be completely opposite to one another and maybe the protagonists of which *feel* opposed to one another, i.e., the migrants and the poor people in the West, you want to show their elective affinities when the elite are trying to set them against one another in an age-old, predictable, but deadly effective game of divide and rule. I very often try and write with a little bit of prognosis. I'm slightly on the far shoulder of politics and history; I try to write about where I think things are going and I wrote about migration just before it really hit the mainstream of public awareness. That was quite weird because I wrote it as a consciousness raising thing and then suddenly in the middle of the first run people became aware of these mass drownings in the Mediterranean, and then the reaction to the play became very different.

Lampedusa is now in ten countries this year, and I've been to a few of them and seen the way they respond to the play and the issue differently, and that's very interesting as an experience, both of how the theater is done in lots of countries, but also in terms of seeing how people diagnose the migrant crisis and its origins and how they respond to my representation of it.

CJ *I was looking at which countries and you mention ten countries because you've juxtaposed . . .*

AL . . . the very British thing with the very European thing.

CJ *Yes.*

AL How do they do the British thing?

CJ *It's the brutality of the welfare cuts here in the UK in the story that could or could not have led to the death of one character, so how does that connect to a Maltese audience, to a Swedish audience, to a German audience, to a Catalan audience, and then to New Zealand? Because it's the specificity that's very powerful.*

AL It's interesting. I think people latch onto things that resonate with them even if the specifics are different. That's the fundamental nature of playwriting: You are inherently representing—I believe it's called "metonymy" in literary theory, about which I don't know anything—but you are inevitably representing something much bigger metonymically through an individual character or a couple of characters. If you're quite sociologically driven in your writing, as I am, you try to make your plays accurate but also with room to breathe. My plays are about lots of different places. I probably write more plays set in foreign countries than anybody else as far as I know, and I always try to know what I'm talking about. I've not yet found somebody who comes to those plays and goes, "That isn't an accurate representation of this country," but at the same time you can't get too caught up in an over-academic, sort of footnoted representation of the country. The country has to live and breathe and be infused with the elements of specificity, but it also needs to have a metaphorical resonance.

You never want to come in and take someone's story, that's the thing. If you're going to write about someone's story as a white dude, you've got to come in respectfully and try to write that story from the inside. So you'll see in my plays that, when they're about foreign countries, they're always about that country from the inside. So the play I've written about China, *The Sugar Coated Bullets of the Bourgeoisie*, had eight Chinese actors playing about twenty-five characters and there are no white people in that. The play I did about Zimbabwe is all black Zimbabweans apart from one white Zimbabwean, but no outsider who comes in and says, "I, white person, shall explain this strange foreign country to you!" in a Michelle Pfeiffer in *Dangerous Minds* sort of way. So you want always to understand that country, to get under its skin and represent it truthfully and accurately, but with its own spirit. You don't want to co-opt it.

When a play goes to another country, you really can't control how they're going to take the references to a British society. For a start, the character of Denise of *Lampedusa* is an extremely unlikely character in terms of the sociology of other European countries: A half-Chinese person. They either don't have Chinese people or if they do, they're very much ghettoized and not in wider society, so in Sweden the actress was half-Columbian and I think they kept the whole text and just made her half-Columbian and just maintained the idea of otherness through that. The difficulty is that Denise is the familiar half of the play to a British audience (though in terms of being a poor Northerner not that familiar to a London audience, and London critics in particular really didn't like her because they desperately don't want to know what's being done to poor people outside the London bubble), whereas she's the exotic half of the story to a European audience, so her structural function is different. But like I said before, you can't control everything as a playwright, you have to let certain things go.

CJ You've been described, first for Lampedusa, *as the most internationally minded dramatist working in Britain today, and then more recently Michael Billington wrote a review for* The Sugar Coated Bullets of the Bourgeoisie, *saying that it confirms your status as the United Kingdom's most international dramatist. I know we've touched upon this, but what's your response to that?*

AL I'm glad they noticed! So my degree is in Chinese politics and my post-grad degrees are in political science and comparative politics with a Chinese focus. When I started out, I studied Chinese as an undergrad—I was going to do PPE, which is sort of like the training ground for the future George Osbornes of the world, which is one reason I didn't do it! But also because at that age I was aware that the rhetoric of liberal capitalist democracy being the highest possible state of society was bullshit but I wasn't entirely sure why; I was only seventeen at the time. So I thought what would be interesting is if you studied something that we portray as being really different to us (at the time China was far more different to the West than it is now) and by comparison and by analogy you'd learn about your own society too.

Although since I started studying the Chinese have become vastly more capitalist, they have a long history of understanding the function of society, the function of the individual (which isn't really a particularly strong concept in China), and the function of government and the state from a fundamentally different set of suppositions than we do. So that makes you see that our history and traditions are just one way among many. And it's very difficult to grow up in any environment and not to equate the particular as universal. You think the way we are is the way everybody is. That's why diversity is a good thing: Not just for some box-ticking exercise, but because it helps you understand the true nature of the world, that there are a lot of people who love and breathe and feel quite differently to you. So I find trying to get under the skin of different cultures important; it's very eye opening at least. In my mind there's always a sort of analogical reference back to our own society.

CJ *How do playwriting and the playwright fit into the digital age of storytelling?*

AL It's the analogue corollary to the digital age of storytelling. The more and more we are bombarded with screen-based imagery, the more the digital intermediates our human interactions, the more you email people, you Facebook people, you Facetime people, but you don't actually speak to them in the flesh, the more the irreducible power of a human to human connection in a room becomes important to you. You know, in the same way they now have mindfulness as a billion-dollar industry and leaving the city to "connect with nature" is people's immediate dream. The artistic restoration, the cool draught of water that comes from watching one human cry on the shoulder of another human in front of you when you've been surrounded by screens all week, that becomes more and more needed and powerful.

People need to understand who they are and who *we* are. They need to relate to one another on a human level and they particularly need to be able to do it collectively, because the other thing that's important about the theater experience again (if you can get it out of the hegemonic hands of the pompous rich): In an age where we stay at home more, we just stay at home and stream shit, we're just in our own little box, we desperately need collective experiences where other people are not just a pain in the arse or an impediment but part of the joy. When you're in the theater and collectively you just feel a thousand people around you gasp or laugh, there's something profoundly important in that, I feel.

Frances Ya-Chu Cowhig

Frances Ya-Chu Cowhig's first play *Lidless* won the 2009 Yales Series Drama Award, a Fringe First Award at the Edinburgh Festival in 2010, and was shortlisted for the Meyer Whitworth Award and the 2011 Susan Smith Blackburn Award. Her second play, *The World of Extreme Happiness*, was produced in London by the National Theatre in 2012, at The Goodman Theatre in Chicago during Fall 2014, and The Manhattan Theatre Club in Spring 2015. Her play adaptation, *Snow in Midsummer*, was on at the RSC's Swan Theatre in 2017. Frances is currently an Assistant Professor of Playwriting at the University of California, Santa Barbara.

Caroline Jester *What is a playwright?*

Frances Ya-Chu Cowhig The architect of a dramatic experience. The playwright is the one who creates the blueprint for something intended to exist live in three dimensions in front of an audience. This is often done on paper in solitude before the work is brought to other collaborators, but can also happen in the room, as is the case with a lot of devised or physical theater work.

CJ *Does the audience influence your writing?*

FYC I aim to write in a manner that makes my work accessible and engaging to a multi-ethnic, intergenerational audience. Also, I am always an audience member of my plays at some point and I tend to get bored very easily, so I am always trying to think about what helps me pay attention or maintain focus when I am creating character through lines and writing scenes.

CJ *Why do some stories transcend national borders and find audiences in different countries?*

FYC   That's a tricky question, because if you think about the hegemony of American television shows worldwide, it has to do with ramming a dominant culture down people's throats, and if that is the only thing on, then that is the kind of entertainment one learns to expect.

In terms of theater programming, I don't think it is about a certain type of story or narrative being what works in a certain country. I think it has much more to do with the vision of the theater's artistic producers and marketing team, how they prepare their audiences for their shows, and how much the ticket costs that determine what audience a story finds.

I think it is more interesting to think about people globally as streams of diasporic migration that transcend national boundaries. The ethnically Chinese, Irish, and Latino people are everywhere globally, and have to greater and smaller extents taken their myths and songs with them, and of course these stories change and evolve as people intermarry and make homes in new places. So really it's human beings who are transcending and challenging and interrogating the very notion of borders and boundaries, and the stories flow from these spaces.

CJ   *Around the time of the 2010 UK general election, David Hare wrote in* The Guardian *after watching a performance of* Lidless *at the HighTide Festival: ". . . because the action embodies the consequences of parents' invasive behaviour on their children, it makes for a far more lasting impact than anything offered from politicians in this election on the subject of war or generational damage." This demonstrates your play's ability to bring pertinent political questions and considerations of global significance to individual nations' politics. The play does not achieve this through a replay of traumatic events but by revisiting actions from the past in the present and their continual influence on new generations. Why did you choose Guantanamo as the basis to explore this, or did it choose you?*

FYC   The seed for *Lidless* was planted when I read an article in *The Economist* about female interrogators at Guantanamo and their "advanced interrogation tactics," many of which were sexual in nature— giving detainees lap dances, smearing red paint on them and saying it was menstrual blood. An idea of "depraved" Western femininity was literarily being deployed as a form of psychological warfare, which I found horrifying and fascinating.

The power dynamics at play were interesting to me, because it was a female aggressor and male victim. There is a small canon of dramatic works about reunions between male aggressors and female victims—*Death and the Maiden* and *The Night Porter* are two of them—but there weren't any pieces I was aware of that involved a victimized man confronting his female torturer. So it was this form of reunion—between a former Guantanamo detainee and his female US Army interrogator—that I set out to imagine.

CJ *You've talked about the need for physicality in your plays and not just words, and your work has been described as having a fluidity of form which uses Western and Eastern traditions. Is this a conscious decision to create a new theatrical language?*

FYC In my experience of watching text-driven theater (most regional theater offerings) and physical theater (often found in fringe or international festivals or ensemble companies), it seems like the strength of each is the other's weakness. Text-driven theater is often extremely physically dull—there is often no reason why the play is a "live" event—it might as well be on a television screen. But when the writing is at its most effective, the craft of the story, characters, and dramatic tension can keep me focused and interested and engaged. Conversely, the physical theater world, which often overlaps with dance and new circus, tends to have as its greatest strength in visual spectacle—but is often weak in its narrative storytelling, and usually not by choice.

My aim has always been to try and find the ways the best of narrative text-based storytelling and physical-theater-driven forms of storytelling can intersect in one play. This starts from the way I think about cast and numbers of actors: I often try to create ensemble pieces that require double-casting and a single actor to play very different roles. It also affects how I think about objects on stage and how they need to be treated and woven through a piece in the writing so that they can become visual metaphors, and carry their own narrative weight.

I wouldn't say this is a new language at all—more an attempt to become bilingual and to create works that utilize the strengths of both traditions of theater.

CJ *In a 2011 interview with Caridad Svich, you commented that: "Each of my projects are in part a rejection or violent departure from previous projects." Yet a few years in China has influenced three of your plays. Does this statement still hold true even though there's a common thread with the nationality of the characters?*

FYC   Because it takes me about five years to see a project through from its first inception to its second or third production (at which point it's time for me to let go and stop rewriting), I require all my projects to be distinct and full of enough new challenges that I stay interested and fascinated throughout the development period. Although my mother's family migrated to Taiwan from coastal China many centuries ago, the rhythms and patterns of behavior I notice there do not feel that different from what I have observed in rural China, as we are mostly talking about people of the Han Chinese ethnicity in both places. So you have me going back to Taiwan regularly throughout my life, five years spent living in mainland China, another five years spent visiting my parents while they lived in China, two years spent living in Taipei and two years in Okinawa (which has a very long trade relationship with China, and in many ways feels culturally more similar to China than mainland Japan). And this is all before the age of thirty. So in terms of choosing the "setting" and "characters" in a play, I think it is fair to say that, in fact, rural life in China and Taiwan is, because of family ties, much more intimately familiar to me than any particular regional setting in the United States except that of the Boston Irish, and we certainly aren't lacking for stories about the Irish in America.

Really what I am thinking about when I think about China in terms of the plays I am writing are layers and layers of ideas being exchanged between Asia, Europe, and the Americas, particularly in regards to capitalism and industrialization—in many ways, because China industrialized later than the United States, a lot of what is happening there happened in the United States a century ago—there are so many similarities between what is happening in China now in terms of their ethnic conflicts with their western areas of Xinjiang and Tibet as what happened in the United States in the eighteenth and nineteenth centuries with the Native Americans. We as Americans just find it much easier to wave "Free Tibet" flags and get outraged and morally indignant over coverage of Tibetan Monks setting themselves on fire than focusing, for example, on the tragically high teen suicide rates on Pine Ridge Reservation.

CJ *You seem to be brokering international theatrical dialogues through your work in the UK and the US as your plays have been co-commissioned and produced. Do you see both countries as having similar theatrical sensibilities?*

FYC The differences between the theater landscapes in the US and UK seem to distill down to scale, population density, and arts funding. I usually can't afford to see shows on Broadway, but I can afford West End tickets. In the UK you have the National Lottery funding a lot of arts organizations, which I think is brilliant—I might gamble if I knew that even if I lost, I was supporting theater! There is also superior public transportation infrastructure in the UK—which is much more possible in the US because of scale. So people often come from all over the UK to see shows in London. Then you also have the difference in how plays are engaged by the newspapers—and the sheer number of "mainstream" newspapers in London that are paid attention to. In New York and Chicago, for example, it really is usually one newspaper that makes or breaks ticket sales, while in London you have at least five significant newspapers that are being read, and often these papers have very different things to say about the same play.

I think it really comes down to accessibility and pricing a lot of the time, because when shows are affordable and easy to get to you can have a much more diverse audience than if tickets are expensive. And of course you have the National Theatre, which is an amazing, wonderful, singular place. (And I don't think it's just because they have a full-time nurse and a subsidized staff cafeteria.) There's no equivalent in the US, and I am very, very jealous.

CJ *How do playwriting and the playwright fit into the digital age of storytelling?*

FYC I think they exist in counterpoint to digital storytelling. It seems that at the same time that things are getting flattened onto screens and people are communicating more online, there is a growing desire for its opposite—the tactile, the sensual, the physically, immediately "real." There is something so lonely about staring at a glowing screen, and the liveness and immediacy and ephemerality of theater will always be there as a possible antidote to that.

David Hare

David Hare is a playwright and film-maker. He has written over thirty stage plays, which include: *Plenty*; *Pravda* (with Howard Brenton); *The Secret Rapture*; *Racing Demon*; *Skylight*; *Amy's View*; *The Blue Room*; *Via Dolorosa*; *Stuff Happens*; *South Downs*; *The Absence of War*; *The Judas Kiss*; and *The Moderate Soprano*. For film and television he has written twenty-five screenplays, which include: *Licking Hitler*; *Dreams of Leaving*; *Saigon: Year of the Cat*; *Wetherby*; *Damage*; *The Hours*; *The Reader*; *The Worricker Trilogy: Page Eight, Turks & Caicos*; and *Salting the Battlefield*. He has also written English adaptations of plays by Brecht, Gorky, Chekhov, Pirandello, Ibsen, and Lorca. His first work of memoir, *The Blue Touch Paper*, was published in 2015.

Caroline Jester   *What is a playwright?*

David Hare   A playwright transforms words into action for live performance. It's a definition which fits Aeschylus as well as it fits Peter Handke, even for his play with no dialogue.

CJ   *Does the audience influence your writing?*

DH   Not while I'm writing, no. But the genius of a play is its alchemy with particular audiences. Thus *Hamlet*, presented behind the Iron Curtain in the 1950s and 1960s, was regarded as the most subversive play ever written. Whereas at Stratford-upon-Avon, to a comfortable audience in a democracy, it could sometimes be the most unchallenging. Context is everything.

CJ   *Why do some stories transcend national borders and find audiences in different countries?*

DH   Usually because they have a central character who belongs in any culture. Peter Pan, Medea, Sherlock Holmes, Hedda Gabler, Falstaff,

Jimmy Porter, Antigone, Eliza Doolittle and, yes, Hamilton, are a few of the obvious examples.

CJ *In an interview at The New School for Drama, where you were Writer-in-Residence in 2012, you stated that there is an enormous cultural gulf between the UK and the US. Why do you think your own plays continue to connect with both sides of this cultural gulf?*

DH Joe Papp resisted doing my plays for years. He had put my first play, *Slag*, on in 1971 at the Public Theater, but he only mounted *Plenty* in 1982. He regarded it as an admission of defeat that he had to turn to me and Caryl Churchill to get the kind of political and social theater he loved: He'd hoped to grow it, not to import it. The US response to *Plenty*, *Stuff Happens*, *Skylight*, *Amy's View*, *Via Dolorosa*, *The Vertical Hour*, *Racing Demon*, and *The Judas Kiss* all proved that the American audience is miles ahead of many of its producers.

CJ *Can you describe an experience where audiences in the US reacted differently to your plays than UK audiences, and why do you think that was the case?*

DH Some people at home will not accept what they take to be an implied critique of Britain. When *Plenty* was first shown at the National Theatre in London, it was given a very rough ride. When it arrived in New York, at a distance of 3,000 miles, the play was seen much more clearly. Some people found parallels in it which I had never specifically intended. They were moved, interpreting it as being about the American experience in Vietnam. Later, when I wrote *The Permanent Way*, about the fatal crashes following the privatization of the UK railways, I was really trying to seek out a line between what we must fight against as avoidable and accept as unavoidable suffering. So some American visitors read the play as being about the failure of the US government and New York City to respond to the crisis of AIDS. Any serious play is going to survive multiple readings. A great play, like Brian Friel's *The Faith Healer*, is going to seem almost infinitely open.

CJ   *One of the opening lines in* Via Dolorosa *is "Playwrights are drawn to places—they don't know why." Is this still your belief and if so, why do you think this is the case?*

DH   Yes. We're no different from painters. We don't choose our subject matter. It chooses us. Photographers say something is photogenic, but they can't say why. It's mysterious.

CJ   *In the interview for* The New School for Drama *you said: "I'm not like other playwrights, I can't work without an analysis. I need it to make some coherent political sense to me." Has there been a time or times when the world made no political sense to you and if so, how did that impact on your writing?*

DH   The world makes no political sense to me now. Capitalism had a cardiac arrest in 2008, and even Milton Friedman's closest followers at the University of Chicago used the words "Back to the drawing board." They accepted that the free-market model no longer worked, because there no longer was, in any meaningful sense, any such thing as a free market. In total defiance of theory, the bankers failed and the people were punished. Yet politicians have spent the last eight years re-constructing a perfect simulacrum of a known-to-be-flawed system. Why?
   I don't need to have an analysis of the world. On the contrary, my bewilderment at the world has always been the motor of my work. But I do have to know what my own play is saying. Or rather, intending to say. Some wonderful writers, like Harold Pinter, don't. I do.

CJ   *In the introduction to* The History Plays *you wrote in 1983 that: ". . . more and more I feel writers have little idea of what they are writing. However much they exercise control by will, they remain for years ignorant of the true subject of their own work." Skylight has just won a Tony award for best revival in 2015, after being one of the most internationally successful plays twenty years previously. Did you learn anything new about this play or others that have been revived that you didn't know at the time of writing?*

DH   Neil Armfield's 2013 revival of *The Judas Kiss,* which I wrote in 1998, was a revelation. It was not just the play itself was finally vindicated, but, just as important, its underlying subject was suddenly blindingly clear. Wilde contends that morality is not a matter of telling other people what to do. It's about what you do yourself. That generous proposition sang through to the audience in a way it never had previously. All down to Neil's talent, and Rupert Everett's.

CJ *Your work includes adaptations, monologues performed by the writer, history plays, plays inspired by events and nations, and much more. Do you feel it is your ability to find the structure that fits the narrative which enables you to continue writing with such versatility?*

DH I'm restless with form, and with the conventional expectations of form. I like to experiment, but my heart is in epic. Mind you, I think of my monologues as epics—as much care goes into their structure as in any play of twenty varied scenes.

CJ *How do playwriting and the playwright fit into the digital age?*

DH I think books, newspapers, theater, and cinema are going to survive, because they all have a moral dimension. However sophisticated technology becomes, people are never going to stop asking, "How do I live?" and "How should I live?" Or if they do, they won't be what we call people anymore.

Katori Hall

Katori Hall is a playwright/performer from Memphis, Tennessee. Her plays include: *The Mountaintop* (2010 Olivier Award for Best New Play); *Hurt Village* (2011 Susan Smith Blackburn Prize); *Children of Killers*; *Hoodoo Love*; *Remembrance*; *Saturday Night/Sunday Morning*; *WHADDABLOODCLOT!!!*; *Our Lady of Kibeho;* and *Pussy Valley*. Awards include: the Lark Play Development Center Playwrights of New York (PONY) Fellowship; the ARENA Stage American Voices Play Residency; the Kate Neal Kinley Fellowship; two Lecomte du Nouy Prizes from Lincoln Center; the Fellowship of Southern Writers Bryan Family Award in Drama; a NYFA Fellowship; the Lorraine Hansberry Playwriting Award; and the Otis Guernsey New Voices Playwriting Award. Her journalism has appeared in *The New York Times*, *The Boston Globe*, *The Guardian*, *Essence*, and *The Commercial Appeal*. She is an alumna of the Lark Playwrights' Workshop and graduate of Columbia University, the ART at Harvard University, and the Juilliard School.

Caroline Jester   *What is a playwright?*

Katori Hall   A storyteller who tells stories that demand a witnessing.

CJ   *Does the audience influence your writing?*

KH   Oddly, I do not think too much about audience when I start writing and I don't know if that is a good thing or a bad thing. I think the first audience member I seek to please is myself. Selfish yes, but writing for an audience of one, I think helps you write for an audience of many.

CJ   *Why do some stories transcend national borders and find audiences in different countries?*

KH   I actually think that all stories can transcend national borders, provided there is translation. I just think some storytellers are not given the opportunity to transcend due to obstacles inherent in whatever system they are coming up in. Theater stories are challenging because they are often constrained by time and place—you have to be there in order to experience the story. Musicals can transcend more easily as music is one of our universal languages, like math. Film, due to the dissemination system in place, is a medium by which I see the most stories crossing over to other cultures. Big blockbusters like *Star Wars*, *Jurassic Park*, or the James Bond franchise have *huuuuuge* international audiences. Even with TV, I can't tell you how many times I've walked into a mall in Kampala, Uganda, and seen episodes of *Scandal* (albeit bootlegged) for sale. However, I do find that casting is actually what can help or hinder a story from finding an audience in a different country. There is a Hollywood myth that films and TV shows with black leads do not sell well in other countries. In recent years especially, this myth has mostly been dispelled. However, I think executives' historical hesitancy to greenlight work with people of color at the center is reflective of a deeper bias. I think it has less to do with talent and more to do with the racial empathy gap the world has inherited. Every country is still coming to terms with racist ideologies that have been embedded by generations of slavery, colonialism, warfare, neo-colonialism, etc. Hell, even brown folks in India can often refuse to see the humanity in a character cast in a movie or show that looks more like them than what has usually been deemed the "universal experience" (code for "white experience"). I've heard people getting up in arms about Idris Elba playing a black James Bond or a black Hermione being cast in *Harry Potter*. This is not to say don't cast black or brown actors as leads; on the contrary. This means that every opportunity that arises, casting of people of color should be considered equally to casting someone who is white. It is a tool to fight that racial empathy gap. I long for the day when I see Chinese actor Tony Leung instead of Matt Damon on *The Martian* poster as normal and therefore "universal."

CJ *The Mountaintop seems to have had a unique journey into production. I read that you brought the play to the UK because it couldn't find a home in the US, then it moved quickly to the West End, was the first play by a black woman to win the Olivier for best new play, and then went to Broadway with Samuel L. Jackson and Angela Bassett in the cast. Why do you think it took a production in the UK to connect with US producers?*

KH   The story of *The Mountaintop* not being able to find a US home is actually false. The true story is that the play was still being developed at the Lark Play Development Center in NYC in the spring of 2009 and had not been actually sent out to US theaters to be considered for the upcoming 2009–10 season. However, I got an email from my colleague James Dacre in March of 2009 asking me what I was working on. I sent him my work in progress, which was *The Mountaintop*. A few weeks later he emailed back and said that he had convinced a wonderful theater called Theatre 503 in Battersea, London to produce the play. Even though I wasn't done, I thought, "oh, bloody hell, why not give it a try?" If they hated it, who would know? I re-worked the play those upcoming weeks. My workshop at the Lark ended on May 9, 2009. Two days later I was in the rehearsal room for the play in London. With James Helming and David Harewood and Lorraine Burroughs giving soul-stirring performances, the play received magical reviews even though it lasted for a limited time, closing end of summer 2009. It was not until the play won the Olivier in March of 2010 that my producers (a mix of American and British producers, who had already brought the play to the West End) decided to option it for the Broadway run. It took it two years to get on Broadway post the West-End run. Casting was challenging as Broadway was (and still is) a place where producers wanted a starry cast for box office; however I was blessed to find two class acts in Sam and Angela. They were more than just celebrities; they were true actors with craft and passion, who during our limited run, never missed one damn show. I was one lucky lady.

CJ   *I've read that the play polarized critics and the black community, especially older generations of African-Americans who experienced the civil rights era first hand. As a playwright, were you expecting that and can you explain why you think the subject matter triggered this?*

KH   *The Mountaintop* polarized different communities in different ways for different reasons, which was only slightly surprising. In the play, you have this sanitized myth of Dr. King the Jesus-like martyr being pulled off this proverbial pedestal carved by history. Now older black folks didn't like that he was cussing, drinking, smoking cigarettes, and expressing sexist views and vulnerability in equal measure. He paced his motel room on stinky feet of clay dealing with the pangs of earned anger, and this made some people (black, white, whatever) extremely uncomfortable as it tore at the respectability politics that has created this sanitized, pacifist King everyone likes to say they walked beside. I was told that in attempting to shatter the myth, I had done a disservice to the man and his memory by portraying him as human. Now, the black community is not a monolith—we don't all hold the same views on anything, from King to Obama to the use of the N-word. That being said, many in the black community embraced this humanization project that I had embarked upon. They saw that they too could be kings and that his accomplishments were actually in reach for them. Ordinary people realized that they too could be extraordinary, just like Dr. King.

The critics were another story. While UK-based critics applauded the approach, US critics mostly slammed the portrayal, but not in regards to the humanization of King. They felt that the play continued to perpetuate the myth of King as Jesus verging on the cusp of hagiography because [SPOILER ALERT] Camae, the other character in the two-hander, revealed herself to be an angel sent by God to take King to heaven. They felt that having an angel as a flesh and bone character was a theatrical cop-out that undermined the very experiment I had set out to conduct in regards to exploring King's humanity. What these critics failed to acknowledge is that their white and male Western European aesthetic was clouding their ability to see that as a playwright, I was using Africanistic and African-American spirituality to pitch a different conversation about King—one that created a neo-soul fable in the vein of the many mythical stories that have been passed down through generations. As a black woman who has grown up in the South, I was taught to believe in angels. It is how we have survived the Middle Passage, slavery, the Jim Crow South of the 1960s, and the Jim Crow US of Now. The spirit world lives in the room with us, and spirit is not to be dismissed; it is to be respected, especially when it is not so easily understood. The spiritual landscape that *The Mountaintop* operates within is valid, but most white male Ivy-League educated critics were quick to deem it as not belonging in "their" theatrical tradition. They don't see that Camae is just as much Yemaya as she is a prostitute. And that King is a lamb to be sacrificed for the greater good. Martyrs make movements, this attitudinal black (and proud!) female God demands. Through a different lens and worldview, *The Mountaintop* becomes dream and nightmare, elegy and afro-futuristic parable. It seems as though they were holding up my play against the play they wish they themselves could write or was in their heads and not being able to grasp neither, and therefore deemed mine a lesser exploration compared to something that did not and does not exist. *The Mountaintop* was never going to be a straightforward biographical play because at its core it's more a play about letting go than it is about King. King the character is the vessel of that theme as King the man was of social progress for a small dash of time. I was in a "damned if you do, damned if you don't" place as a writer, as no matter what I wrote, no one camp was going to be unequivocally satisfied. Thank God I wrote the play I wanted to write—unfettered, funny, and undeniably feminist in providing King an equal female protagonist-antagonist to wrestle with in his own Garden of Gethsemane.

CJ *Voices from the past, whether spirits infiltrating the action in the present or characters from the past finding a new way to communicate with an audience today, seem to permeate your work. Is this a conscious decision or part of a creative dialogue between different generations?*

KH I think it goes back to what I said about African and African-American spirituality. My ancestors are always with me. I feel their presence every time I write. And not in a hokey-witchy way, I don't sit down and burn incense and evoke the "gods" every time I sit down to write. It's just factual. It's written in my bones.

I am a firm believer that the past is always present. There are moments we as human beings have moved through—Holocausts, world wars, slavery. We say "never forget," and yet we always do. I think my work is a reaction against forgetting. Forgetting is dangerous for individuals, for nations, for the preservation of history itself. So yes, there is a dialogue I try to create through my bridging of the spiritual world to the real world. Even in *The Mountaintop*, King will always find his way to speak to now. In 2017. In 2020. In 2050 and beyond.

CJ *How do playwriting and theater fit into the digital age?*

KH I do think that in order for theater and playwrights to survive, we will have to come to terms with how the digital world can aid our mission in telling stories that demand a witnessing. Right now, Facebook and other social media have provided a grotesque and gothic frame wherein which we are seeing black and brown bodies executed with impunity by police officers who are supposed to serve and protect. We are literally seeing death in real time. Though it is more documentary, there is still a story being disseminated through the gaze. The narrative of injustice. A powerful story. An American story. The computer has become a proscenium and pulpit where much of our witnessing is happening. I think we should learn how to take advantage of the church of social media that has been created.

There are ways to reach a larger audience, whether by live-streaming online or selling DVDs. I think of someone like playwright Tyler Perry, who tours his shows all across the country and sells DVDs of that show and others through merchandising. He understands that not all of his supporters will be able to make it for the one-time Saturday night show at the Orpheum, and therefore allows for a space where they can receive his story despite those hurdles. I think we are venturing into a time where we need to think about new digital ways that can transport more people to the theater, particularly younger people, who use screens to interact with the world.

Simon Stephens

Simon Stephens began his theatrical career in the literary department of the Royal Court Theatre, where he ran its Young Writers' Programme. His plays for theater include: *Bluebird*; *Herons*; *Port*; *On the Shore of the Wide World*; *Pornography*; *Three Kingdoms*; *Harper Regan*; *Punk Rock*; *Birdland*; *Heisenberg*; *Nuclear War*; and an adaptation of *The Curious Incident of the Dog in the Night-Time*. He has been produced at the Royal Court, Royal Exchange, National Theatre, Traverse Theatre, Deutsches Schauspielhaus, Lyric Hammersmith, and Toneelgroep Amsterdam. Awards include: the Pearson Award for Best New Play, 2001, for *Port*; Olivier Award for Best New Play for *On the Shore of the Wide World*, 2005; and for *Motortown*, German critics in *Theater Heute*'s annual poll voted him Best Foreign Playwright, 2007. His adaptation of *The Curious Incident of the Dog in the Night-Time* won the 2015 Tony Award for Best Play.

Caridad Svich   *What is a playwright?*

Simon Stephens   I think the noun contains the two most important functions of the job. Second part first. We are "wrights," not "writers." We have wrought our plays, not written them, like a shipwright has wrought a ship or a cartwright a cart. Our work is to shape or make a piece of theater, not to write down words. It's also key that we are making *plays*; we are making playthings. Our work is to create play, and the energy and anarchy and disorder and creativity that play incorporates. When children play, they are exorcizing energy, but also making sense of their position in the world through their imaginations. That's what we're allowing our audiences to do too.

CS   *Does the audience influence your writing?*

SS   I do think about the audience, and I oscillate between kind of blanket terror and an absolute sense that they necessarily hate me. It's kind of like affection and respect. I think people work in theater because on some level, they have the kind of faith in humanity. It'd be slightly strange to have that faith in humanity and dislike an audience, you know? I mean, the terrible thing about having faith in humanity is that human beings aren't all necessarily projections of ourselves! They have their own ideas and their own kind of assumptions and attitudes. It's like the Manhattan Theatre Club audience, which everybody's told me is, like, the oldest collection of human beings ever gathered together in one room at one time, but on one hand, it's not completely true. There *are* some tremendously old people in that audience, but there are also some younger people as well. But also, older people are getting younger, aren't they? When I think of a sixty-year old, a seventy-year old now in my head, I'm kind of assuming that someone's born in 1920, but they weren't, they were born in 1950, so their teenager years were spent in the 1960s, not in the 1930s.

When I think of the audience, I do think of myself sitting in an audience as well. I write the plays that I wish other people had written for the theaters I'm writing for so that I can go to those theaters and watch those plays. And they've not written them, so I have to write them. So I can't imagine a play existing without an audience.

CS   Why do some stories transcend national borders and find audiences in different countries?

SS   I don't know. I don't know if there's anything exceptional about my work that lends itself to international travel. Perhaps some of the characters in some of the plays see themselves as being part of stories playing out in an international context—tiny moments in a broader context. I think specificity is universal, and perhaps the tension between specific actions in broad contexts is what resonates. Or perhaps I'm just lucky and have excellent representation and have been fortunate meeting great directors.

CS   In thinking about how you work with structure in, say, Carmen Disruption *(2014),* The Trial of Ubu *(2011),* Pornography *(2007), and* Three Kingdoms *(2011)—because those came out of very specific experiences with director Sebastian Nubling—as opposed to your texts* Harper Reagan, Heisenberg, *or* Birdland, *for instance. Just looking at them side by side is a very different experience. It is clear that the invitation the texts are making for performance are quite distinct, even though there are shared themes that run through the works in and of themselves, and your body of work thus far. Do you consciously set out to subvert structural expectations with each piece?*

SS I think what's important to me is that I write to commission, and the commissions are brought out with different theater cultures. And I find the limitations of commissioning really freeing, actually. I quite like the notion of writing into specific theater architecture. So writing a play for the enormous proscenium of the Deutsches Schauspielhaus in Hamburg, which is the theater that commissioned both *Pornography* and *Carmen Disruption*, or the kind of studio space at the Manhattan Theatre Club, has different dramaturgical demands on the play that comes out of the commission, you know, it's . . . writing into those specific architectures.

CS *So knowing the space—*

SS Knowing the space, knowing the heritage and the history of the culture of the theater. If I'm writing a play for the Royal Court, then that has a particular trajectory and tradition that I cherish and I want to value and respond to, or there's the broader cultural conventions of writing for US or German theater, for example, as well as the broader cultural conventions of writing in a way that are both pragmatic and creative. So, in writing *Heisenberg* for the Manhattan Theatre Club, there's part of me that's aware that the chances of getting a play produced in the US are heightened considerably if you have two actors in it. But actually, in the opposite sense as well: The chance of having a play produced in Germany may have something to do with the fact that the theater company has an ensemble of fifty actors, so they need to offer roles to as many actors as possible, which in turn changes what you make. So, there's a pragmatic element—there's the kind of element of just trying to have the play have some kind of life. In the US, I think that's particularly difficult where plays tend to be read rather than performed, which I think is really, really paralyzing.

CS *David Greig once told me in an interview for Manchester University Press that what freed him up as a writer was the first time he saw a play* *of his staged in a language that he didn't understand. He suddenly went (I am paraphrasing): "That's what it means."*

SS It's really exciting. It's the shape of energy.

CS *Yeah, as opposed to—instead of—it just made him think about making plays altogether differently from then on.*

SS Yeah, exactly. No, I think that's completely right. I shared exactly that experience. With *Herons*, which Nubling directed in Stuttgart in 2003. And *Port*, actually, which I saw later. You know, going and watching those plays and not understanding a word that anybody's saying, apart from the occasional kind of cultural reference to like [UK supermarket chain], Tesco or whatever. But somehow getting the energy of the play, you know, allowing it to be communicated.

CS *Moving figures in a field of play. It's about who's in the foreground, who's in the background, who takes focus, who recedes from focus, and how that can—even if no words are spoken—there's drama in that kind of negotiation with space compositionally across time. Because you're also dealing with time-based art, after all.*

SS My favorite moments in my plays have been moments without language. My favorite moment in *Heisenberg* currently is the moment where Georgie eats the yogurt, which is really nice. It's really nice. In a play where people don't actually really do anything, which is fundamentally linguistic, you know, there's part of me that would quite like the idea of writing a play in which the actors don't actually say anything. You just kind of—

CS *You're already mapping behavior.*

SS —yeah, and you prescribe their internal state for them. Like Kroetz's—what's it called?—Recital Program, is it?
I'd love to do something like that. And then you get into kind of questions about when does theater stop and dance start, performance art. But those are exciting questions.

You know, you're as likely to respond to a suggestion by the designer or the lighting designer or the sound designer as you are by the playwright, and to ignore that seems insulting to those people.

CS *How do you think about language and silence in terms of how you compose your work? But also in terms of how that silence resonates and radiates to the audience and also to a larger community, so thinking maybe hyper-local, local, national, global.*

SS I think, in the actual process of writing, I think silence plays the same role as language. Which, for me, in the actual making of the thing, is fundamentally something of musicality, you know? It's born out of a type of musicality. You're writing a scene, you're writing a line, and just somehow the music of the line, it seems right that people fucking shut up, you know? Normally, because there's something so enormous that they want, the desire is so extraordinary, or the obstacle so profound that it results in them not being able to say anything.

I think what it does theatrically is it creates a beautiful space for interpretation. Audiences love silent moments, because they're just thinking, "What're they thinking?" And if they're doing that, they're not far away from thinking, "What would *I* think?" So it creates a space in which they can imagine themselves, and fundamentally that's what theater's for. I don't think we go to the theater to learn about the world. I think we go to the theater to learn about ourselves. It's why playwrights . . . essayists don't make good playwrights. It's why journalists don't make good playwrights, because they have an impulse to tell the audience about the world, and the theater's not a good space for that. The theater's a good space for telling humans about what it is to be human. And in order to do that properly, you need a kind of investigation of self, investigation of empathy. Dramaturgically, silence is quite a playful space to encourage empathy and recognition of self, and that's a hugely political thing, you know?

It reminds me of this—something that happens in some theaters in London, where plays are commissioned as a rapid response to news events. I think theater's really bad at being rapid, so it shouldn't try to be. It should be—it should try to be slow. People shouldn't commission playwrights to write reactions to the news. They should, you know, get them to write responses to things that happened 500 years ago. The beauty of theater is that you can be slow, you can respond slowly. And if you respond really slowly, then you might end up being prescient. Which is, I think, what Caryl Churchill does again and again. There's no attempt in her work to [be rapid]. She's not going to write a play about fucking FIFA and about the US arresting football. But she might predict the next thing that happens because she's . . . she's working in a space [of consciousness], which is so beautifully slow.

CS *Some writers face the page and they say, "I'm just gonna write about my community, and I'm gonna write about my people," however they identify them. And then other people who face the page and go, "Aw, I wanna think about what's happening in* that *country. Not here."*

SS But the writer who goes to the other country is nevertheless writing about themselves. And the writer who considers themselves to not be affected by the political environment is profoundly defined by the political environment. I don't think of myself as being nationalistic, but it would be idiotic of me not to acknowledge that I'm a 44-year-old white, straight, heterosexual male living in London. I couldn't have racked up the privileges more, you know? It's just like, ding, ding, ding, ding, ding, got 'em all. But I don't try and articulate the perspective of a white, straight English man, father of three, living in London, because that would be incredibly reductive. You know, it'd be really boring; who wants to fucking watch plays about that? But whenever I write about a gay, black, teenage girl, it'd be naïve of me to not acknowledge that my imagination of her is born out of my perspective. I'm not denying my perspective, I'm . . . and you know, it's necessarily an interrogation and a conversation—yeah. And also, recently the plays have been more about the existential emptiness of affluence, actually. *Birdland* and *Carmen Disruption* . . .

CS *How do playwrights and playwriting fit into the digital age of storytelling?*

SS The stage seems like a possible place to have a conversation, which is a very different kind of conversation than the one on screen, because you're live, you're with people. It's about presence . . .
It's really fundamental.

CS *And I think that kind of absolute presence feels harder to achieve now, in terms of culture, in terms of—*

SS Sitting still in the same space as somebody for a long time, looking in the same direction as a stranger.

Lucy Prebble

Lucy Prebble's plays include *The Effect*, which won best new play at the Critic's Circle Awards and was a finalist for the 2013–14 Susan Smith Blackburn Prize. *ENRON* transferred to the West End and Broadway, and Lucy is adapting it for Sony Pictures. *ENRON* won the award for Best New Play at the TMA Theatre Awards and was shortlisted for the *Evening Standard* and Olivier Award for Best New Play. *The Sugar Syndrome* won the George Devine Award in 2004 and TMA Award for Best New Play. Lucy created the TV series *Secret Diary of a Call Girl* and was Head Scene Writer for Bungie's video game, *Destiny*. In 2015 she wrote and shot a pilot for HBO with Sarah Silverman.

Caroline Jester   *What is a playwright?*

Lucy Prebble   A playwright is the person responsible for having the idea, creating the world, and forming the action and characters on stage in a piece of theater.

CJ   *Does the audience influence your writing?*

LP   Very much. I find there are three acts of writing: Before rehearsal, during rehearsal, and during previews. Though each shortens drastically in length, each is as vital and thorough as the one before. The third act (previews) is defined entirely by the presence of an audience. There is a strange circularity to it. As you sit in an auditorium with an audience for the first time you are closest to the state in which you sat down to write the first draft. You are keenly aware of the lack of knowledge about what is about to happen, newly appreciative of how information is given, how realizations are made. You become the audience again, which is what you were to begin with, when since then you have become closer to the characters, begun to know too much, become all onstage.

CJ *Why do some stories transcend national borders and find audiences in different countries?*

LP   I can't tell. It is normally related to basic needs that everyone can relate to. I think most people like to laugh. And I think most people recognize and fear death. I think between those things, love, jealousy, hope, rage, and fear all play central parts that we all weave around.

CJ *Writers often start off by writing about what they know and not by tackling Texan energy firms. Can you explain why you were drawn to this subject matter that became* ENRON *and was this a conscious decision to find a story outside of your immediate comfort zone? I'm making an assumption here that this is outside of your immediate comfort zone, so my apologies if this isn't the case. It might also be that you started off writing a number of plays before* The Sugar Syndrome *and* ENRON *came to the public's attention, so the question could be about this transition.*

LP   I appreciate the phrasing of the question. There is something to be said for taking on an idea that seems to be outside your personal experience. It is curiously freeing. In the way that if you want to see who a man truly is, you give him a mask—writing from the perspective of those who *seem* very different from you allows a brutality, honesty, and color to emerge from yourself that society normally mocks or disallows. It is an extension of the drive to write in the first place. To be seen by hiding. To hide in the words you'd like to say.

Privately, there are actually many personal resonances for me in *ENRON*. People tend not to see them because they have an idea of who they think you are, what pattern you fit. I'm a young, British woman. They equate me with the woman in the play, if at all. But I am very close in many ways to other male characters. The play certainly has resonances with me about work, belonging, friendships and their inequality, about being a child to a father, about abuse by those in power, from the political to the familial, and about the fury of intelligence and the loneliness of mendacity. All of these are private wounds I was squeezing to bleed.

CJ *After successful runs in the UK,* ENRON *transferred to the US This generated a debate about the US theater scene and questions* *were asked as to why American theater couldn't produce its own ENRON, why was the story told from a playwright from the UK, and so on. What was your experience of this, and do you think this physical distance from the origins of the story gave you more creative freedom?*

LP   Probably, but I think America is a sort of cultural center since the last century. Even I was raised on mostly American music, film, and TV. So I have been inundated with it, but I also write from a particularly British, outsider's point of view. I think it seems broad and simplistic to Americans. And that's probably right. It's written from a particular place for a particular audience.

I think the US cultural scene does have an understandable animosity toward some UK artists co-opting or lecturing them on their own news and country. We did oppress and rule them not long ago and some artists still get an unearned respect and deference out there simply from having accents and a subsidized CV, which must be tiresome. It's not clear-cut.

CJ   *One US critic felt it was the case that some American critics hadn't got the aesthetic sophistication to process postmodern dramaturgy or ideological ambiguity. Do you think there is such an aesthetic divide across the pond?*

LP   I did notice at the time how completely tied to naturalism all the plays on Broadway were at the time—one-set affairs. But that's not illustrative of New York theater more generally and has changed now.

I think if there is any difference, it's more that American art is dominated culturally by the idea of family. All the great American art, from the *Sopranos* to the *Simpsons*, to Tennessee Williams and Arthur Miller live there, and that's not a subject my work seems to be interested in. I also think, probably for a related reason, I lack a central sentiment that I have seen US audiences respond to. Occasionally, I find myself dry-eyed and with toothache at something brilliant on Broadway that's just too sweet for me. But I guess there's not much I can do about my cold dead heart except be true to it!

CJ   *You've been quoted as saying there's nowhere a writer can't go, particularly a woman writer. You've taken your audiences to* *uncomfortable places, including chatroom fantasies of paedophiles, and in your television writing in* The Secret Diary of a Call Girl *there's the suggestion that prostitution is a career choice and not necessarily seen as victimhood. Could you talk more about this and where your ideas come from and find their way into these dramatic worlds?*

LP I think I'm motivated to write when I feel an itchy sense that something is not being said, often something quite big and dangerous.

Work-wise, I remember feeling very confused, pre-2008, that corporate finance seemed to take up so much space politically, financially, and even personally with so many people I met working in relation to it, but was never spoken about, understood, or framed in any way publicly. Equally, though *Secret Diary of a Call Girl* was not artistically successful in my opinion, I felt something about women's sexuality was being hidden or rewritten in most public life. And the blog the show was based on captured something of that secret.

Always there is an elephant and a room. That's where I start. Picking the elephant and designing the room around it.

CJ The Effect *is opening in the US now and is a co-production between UK and US producers. Your writing stands out in my opinion because of your ability to transcend borders on many levels but in such distinct ways.* The Effect *is an intense piece, with four characters mainly in one location, yet it has found its way across the Atlantic and takes the audience into an exploration of love and feeling, what do I feel, how long will it last. Could you talk about the responses to this play in both countries? Was there such a divide in opinion to this piece like there was to* ENRON *and if not, why do you think this was/is?*

LP I have been interested that there has been more animosity generally toward the more intellectual explorations and debates in the play in the US. Many Americans I know seem much more comfortable framing things personally, whereas some of my more repressed British friends are uncomfortable with that and like to talk about ideas more. Both are valid ways of expressing yourself, but I feel the audiences in America tire more quickly of bald explorations of ideas, while UK audiences will get fidgety if a play stays locked in a writer's personal grievances too much. But those are appalling generalizations, I guess.

From a clinical point of view, it was interesting to me that questioning the efficacy and morality of psychopharmaceuticals felt a much more extreme and aggressive thing to do in NYC than in London. There was a lot of hostility toward the ideas in the play (which I even toned down), which explored the use of drugs for depression as mercenary or even ineffective. In the UK back in 2012, that felt like the more mainstream position.

CJ   *I've read that you love gaming and that it's an artform just like theater. Has this influenced you as a storyteller and if so how, when, and why?*

LP   I got into gaming at about the same time as I really got into reading, back in the mid-1980s with the first text games. I think there's a similarity to the experience. They are both about entering new worlds to obliterate the real one and they are private, intimate experiences. As a storyteller, it's made me more aware how much a player likes to be at the center of the piece and to experience it themselves. There's something very special about that. The memories I have of playing games as a child are much more visceral and strongly painted in my mind than books as I felt the story was happening to *me*, not a separate, well-drawn protagonist.

I also think games have taught me a lot about making a world interesting. I always start with the world. What world am I looking at entering? What do I want that to feel like? And then I work inwards from there.

CJ   *Are there stories from around the globe that are calling out to you at the moment? If so can you tell us what they are? If you can't reveal what they are, can you reveal why you're drawn to them? What's calling you? When do you know that there's an idea that you will be able to realize?*

LP   Right now I'm working on a play I've been thinking about for years about the golden age of magic. It is about the loss of liveness in art, as well as in a marriage. Hopefully it has something to say about now too, but I cannot explain why I need to write it, only that if I don't, no one else will, and it's very rare that I think that would be a shame.

CJ   *How do playwriting and the playwright fit into the digital age of storytelling?*

LP   I don't know yet. I suspect very well. Theater and game are by far the most similar of the artforms. Far more similar than film and game for example. They both let the player/audience look where they like. There's no control of POV. It's only the shared experience of the screen that makes us think that film and game are very similar: They really aren't.

Anne Washburn

Anne Washburn is from the West and Northwest US and as a result prefers her foliage and landscapes a little on the drastic side. Her plays include: *The Internationalist*; *Apparition*; *The Communist Dracula Pageant*; *Mr. Burns*; and a transadaptation of Euripides' *Orestes*. Her work has been produced by 13P, American Repertory Theater, Soho Rep, Playwrights Horizons, Vineyard, Almeida, and Gate Theatre (London), among others. Support includes residencies at MacDowell, Yaddo, and the Guggenheim.

Caridad Svich   *What is a playwright?*

Anne Washburn   A playwright used to be the most exciting and technologically up-to-date popular storyteller. Now, a playwright is someone who isn't writing film, or TV, or a pop song, but is instead writing plays.

A play is a place where an idea can be more than three sentences long, where language can be a visual or emotional medium and/or contain multiple points of meaning, and where the content can be specific enough to be of interest to no more than, oh, thirty to 10,000 people.

A playwright disburses words on the fly, in a time-based medium.

A playwright is someone who is willing to traffic with non-permanence on every level.

CS   *Does the audience influence your writing?*

AW   An imagined perfect audience (curious, alert, loving, demanding, and fierce) influences the writing of the first draft. After that . . . I do have a weather eye out, during rehearsal and previews, for clarity and engagement but, the more you listen to what audiences are taking away from plays—yours, others'—the more it becomes clear that attention is a very mysterious process. Chatting with people after shows, fielding talk-backs, just listening to conversations afterwards; I went to a revival, on Broadway, of *Who's Afraid of Virginia Woolf* and afterwards heard a group of what seemed to be perfectly intelligent and sophisticated people discussing whether or not the child was real. So I think you can only go so far when thinking about how people are making sense of your play. And as far as interest and enjoyment and affection go . . . *Mr. Burns* was a real flashpoint in this way but all of my plays, some people seem to really respond and others it's absolutely not their cup of tea. I just throw up my hands, really, and write the play I myself would like to see, and know that some number of other people will come along and I can't anticipate who it will be or why.

CS *Why do some stories transcend national borders and find audiences in different countries?*

AW I'm very curious about that . . . but has there really been enough of a sample size to know? I talk with theater people in the UK and they don't know and have never seen any work by at least half of the US playwrights I'm most excited by—and the reverse is true as well. Is the affection for some work from another nation because that work is in some way universal, or just because there hasn't been exposure to the rest, or because the exposure hasn't been framed or contextualized in an effective way? Also, how important is the framing of a work when it crosses national boundaries? And translations into English are generally, I think, made in a slightly haphazard way, often not by playwrights, or often by playwrights who aren't given the resources to do it super thoughtfully . . . so I think that if you say—and I think it's an important thing to say—that a play is about the way language is used as well as narrative, that we aren't so exposed in the English-speaking theater to work from other languages . . .

I can imagine there are some plays which are, joyfully, so wrapped up in a particular language or in a particular national concern or set of circumstances that perhaps they can't translate, not linguistically or culturally, even if they are framed carefully (and it's precisely the work which people say can't be translated which most intrigues me), but I don't know that we've really tried hard enough to know.

CS *Theater, among many things, is a space for reflecting on moral ambiguities, not certainties. How do you go about doing so in your work?*

AW I suppose I assume that the degree to which I am a moral person—which is to say a troubled and perhaps troubling person, although I wouldn't describe my moral compass as an awesomely powerful or accurate one—is the degree to which those questions will occur in my work inevitably, if erratically.

I do feel like it's my job to never write (reprovingly) about a person I feel is less moral than myself. Although I can't say my life is without stain or shame, it's true that the Ceausescus, Madame Mao, Eva Perón, Imelda Marcos, the entire Bush administration, and the nuclear industry are, technically, *yards* guiltier than I am of pretty much every sort of sin, but I feel like I have to (and largely do) regard that primarily as a question of circumstance.

I feel like it's the job of playwrights to address moral questions instinctively and irrationally, because in doing so you can more comprehensively straddle the quasi-rational discussions the culture/society claims to be having, and the fully irrational discussions it is having at the same time. I don't think it's the playwright's job to articulate viewpoints, so much as it is to elucidate the spirit and appetite which constellate around viewpoints.

CS *For a while, at a certain time in downtown NY-based US new writing, there was this kind of electric, unique circle of artists who were tearing apart how we see and re-see poetics for the stage. This unofficial "school," which came to be discussed critically by Elinor Fuchs and Una Chaudhri as one of landscape drama, gave way to, if you will, deliberately flattened linguistic affect in writing for live performance also based in NYC's "downtown scene." I am not asking you to position yourself within a critical apparatus, but rather to articulate, if you will, your own approach/es to language(s) for the stage, and whether you feel kinship with prior historical streams in US new writing.*

AW I feel like I would actually start that with Shepard and Mamet, 1970s and 1980s, who were not the first to use language in a nonutilitarian manner, but the first successful American writers to make a big hairy deal out of it. I started writing plays in the early 1990s, in the Northwest, and we didn't know New York writing really. My first playwriting was very influenced by Sam Shepard, who to me was wild and loggeriac and driving and mildly surreal, and also by Mamet, who was rhythm and percussion and aggression, and created a great illusion of verisimilitudinousness. I feel that Mac Wellman and Len Jenkin and Erik Ehn, who I came to know a bit later, were a further liberation and a big shift not only in the sheer word "joy" and in the continuing exploration of a language which was very specifically American—but also hugely in terms of topic—they would just quite madly and gleefully write about *anything*; they opened up huge terrain for what could function as a dramatic event.

At the same time, although there's something more than fantastical about the work of Wellman, Jenkin, Ehn (and Suzan Lori Parks was part of that same scene at that time, as were Jeff Jones and Connie Congdon), I think their work also comes from a place of real observation, close observation of language and also close observation of the stories we actually tell ourselves about our own lives; the works are actually very acute observations of the irrational sections of our brains; their work is often at the same time both highly linguistic and acutely pre-linguistic.

Similarly, I feel like Rich Maxwell's works come from a place of both acute observation and real artificiality. The super deliberately super simplicity of his language, and the extremely measured way in which it's presented, give it the valance of poetry. And throw into this writer-performer David Greenspan, who is his own thing really, but who creates work which is hyper-intimate and naturalistic and at the very same moment hyper-theatrical and charged. So, yes, I feel that's all much of where I come from, much of the challenge I struggle with.

I feel like many of those writers are also influenced by performance as much as by the traditional theater: Isn't that what defines Downtown theater, ultimately, that it's theater made for an art audience rather than a traditional theater audience? And I do feel like many US playwrights of more or less my generation, including myself, have been working to unite some of the particular joys of performance-based work to the narrative pleasures of traditional playmaking.

CS *How do playwriting and the playwright fit into the digital age of storytelling?*

AW The digital world is intoxicating, but after hours spent with a screen, no matter how engaged, you generally feel sort of fried and spent and mildly dissatisfied with your existence. After hours in a room with other humans, watching a story together—if you like, the thing you're all partaking of—you feel rather more geared up and alive (watching a movie in a theater splits a difference on this). So theater has a biological edge up. In theater the audience creates the experience along with the actors, and is absolutely integral, and people like to feel useful, so theater has a social-emotional edge up. I'm going to go ahead and say it has a spiritual edge up without quite troubling to work out why.

The fact that theater is yards less convenient is a curse, which is also a blessing. You can easily turn off a screen or leave a movie theater, but there's no greater torture than being wedged in the middle of a row during a play you dislike. Weirdly, there's no way of mental escape (I had a teacher once who said that he would count and study the lighting instruments and I've tried that, but it really gives you only five minutes' worth of respite). So the theater presents hardships which screens do not. And people enjoy conditions of hardship (in retrospect) if it all works out at the end, because people like to feel challenged. So there's that.

Tim Crouch

Tim Crouch is a UK theater artist based in Brighton, on England's south coast. He writes plays, performs in them, and takes responsibility for their productions. His plays include: *My Arm* (Traverse Theatre 2003 and UK and international tours, Prix Italia 2004); *An Oak Tree* (Herald Angel 2005, OBIE 2007); *ENGLAND: A Play for Galleries* (Edinburgh Fringe 2007 and UK and international tours, Fringe First, Total Theatre Award, and Herald Angel 2007); *The Author* (Royal Court Theatre Upstairs 2009 and UK and international tours, Total Theatre Award and John Whiting Award 2010); *what happens to the hope at the end of the evening* (with Andy Smith, Almeida Festival); and *Adler and Gibb* (Royal Court). Oberon Books publishes all of Tim's plays: *I, Shakespeare* (a collection of Tim's hugely successful *I, Caliban, I, Peaseblossom, I, Banquo, I, Cinna (the poet)* and *I, Malvolio*); and *Tim Crouch: Plays One.* He has also written a body of work for younger people including *Kaspar the Wild* and *Shopping for Shoes* (Brian Way Award 2007).

Caroline Jester   *What is a playwright?*

Tim Crouch   I'm slowly becoming more accepting of the definition of myself as a playwright. I've often described myself as a theater-maker. I don't necessarily think I'm a writer but I might be a "wrighter," in terms of structuring time and space and live relationships. I don't think playwrights should be studied as literary figures; they are people who organize time and space in front of an audience in a live environment.

CJ   *A description of you reads: "Tim Crouch is a U.K. theater artist. He writes plays, performs in them and takes responsibility for their production." I find the words "takes responsibility for their production" interesting.*

TC   When I am writing, I am very aware of the three-dimensional live space and I'm structuring thoughts, words, and narrative around that space. I would find it very strange to then relinquish responsibility. I come from a practical background as an actor, so I'm thinking very practically about every aspect of the plays. When we did *The Author* at the Royal Court, we spent a lot of time working with the ushers because they are also part of the play. The entrance to the theater is also part of the play and how the audience is lit is also part of the play. The price of the tickets is also part of the play. To want to think about all of those things speaks to the idea of what a playwright is to me, because they are all connected. I can't see a visual artist making a piece of work and then not bothering about how it is placed in the gallery.

CJ   *Does the audience influence your writing?*

TC   All my plays have an empty seat in them which is a seat marked "the audience." It is the most important seat in the theater, metaphorically and literally. Leaving a space for them to be at the table of the show informs how I write, how I think, how I direct, and how I produce.

The play *ENGLAND* wouldn't exist without an audience. The audience in *ENGLAND* is a grieving, veiled widow who speaks in the play. Everything she says is heard through the voice of an interpreter, who is the second actor in the show, so without an audience I'd be looking into an empty space. It's a symbiotic thing; I think about the audience a lot and the audience influences how I think about the audience. *Adler and Gibb* is a classic example. There is a very active scene where two young people break into the property of an artist. The scene is played vocally and it is played textually, but it is not played physically. So I need the audience to see that scene in their heads. I'm interested in what the ears see. It's an audience, it's not a spectator. It comes to them as much through their ears as through their eyes and I'm very interested in when there is a contradiction with what their eye sees and their ear sees. All of these things are geared to try and engage an audience in feeling needed and of being co-authors of the experience.

CJ   *Do you feel some stories transcend national borders and find audiences in different countries?*

TC That's really hard to speak about from the inside. My play *ENGLAND* was written as a response to having started to do foreign touring with my work. I did my play *My Arm* in Romania in 2004, and I felt very peculiar, because the work was being touted as emblematic of a certain kind of theater, or should I say of representing a certain kind of theater, when it's just my work, and it's not representing Britain or British theater, etc.

In *My Arm*, the central character, through an artless gesture of placing an arm above his head and refusing to lower it, becomes a cultural icon. His gesture is read as art. When I perform the play, I ask the audience to share their everyday objects with me. In the course of the performance, these objects "become" figures in the story of the play. For instance, a pencil handed to me by an audience member, turns into—in their mind's eye—the central character's mother in the story. The piece in performance plays with ideas of substitution and how an audience perceives visual signs and creates associations with what they see. Thus, the play explores, in part, the idea of one thing being inside another. In *ENGLAND,* this notion is taken to another level. The idea of one culture inside another is one of the triggers of the play. And then, narratively, that's picked up by the idea of a central Asian heart inside an English body. In *ENGLAND,* one character's heart is transplanted into another person's body. In this case, an English body. So, where is the integrity of Englishness? Where is the heart of Englishness? I'm delighted by its pluralism but I know that that's a big issue in this country. It has to be an English heart beating inside an English body, and what the hell does that mean?

ENGLAND came after *An Oak Tree*. I did a lot of foreign touring with *An Oak Tree* where I would be standing on a stage opposite a Russian actor or standing on stage opposite an Italian, and that was always a fascination for me. I'm bringing the play from my culture and you are a different actor from your culture. What happens with *An Oak Tree* when these two things come together? *ENGLAND* explores that narratively as well as formally.

ENGLAND has toured over two hundred times around the world. Originally I wanted to call it "a work of art from England." There's a line in the play where the protagonist offers a valuable artwork to the widow of the man whose heart is now inside them. The protagonist says, "it's a work of art from England." They then say, "it's worth a lot of money, you can do what you like with it, for your village." This exchange is fizzing with complications around internationalism and the idea of Western value and Western art.

CJ   *Do you feel the United Kingdom's decision to leave the European Union will impact on your work?*

TC   The big word for me is "open." To make work that is open, work that is porous in the writing, in the producing, in the forming. So it lets things in as well as it lets things out. I don't think the Brexit vote was a decision of openness and the work that I make tries to be as open as possible. Open and accepting of anything. In *An Oak Tree*, the second actor in each performance can never get it right, because the premise of the play in production is that the second actor steps into their role that night without ever having rehearsed or seen the script beforehand. I don't want them to get it right because there is no "right" in art. The Brexit vote was predicated on an idea of homogeneity around the idea of Englishness. It became a closed decision on June 23, 2016 and the work that I make attempts to keep all positions open.

It's all in the story. Not in how it is told. I want the audience to think about the story. We don't know if the protagonist in *ENGLAND* is male or female, and that's openness. Some reviewers said it's about a man and some said it's about a woman. The play isn't about gender politics. I think the fluidity of the play's protagonist, in the mind's eye of the audience, is a deeply important thing.

CJ   *How do playwriting and the playwright fit into the digital age of storytelling?*

TC   I did a performance of *I, Malvolio* last night, one of my pieces that explore Shakespearean characters that are not at the center of the plays in which they appear. In my play, Malvolio says at one moment: "This is analogue." He's putting on a shirt and it takes quite a long time, and just to fill the time whilst he's doing that, he says: "This is analogue." It thrills me that that can be named. The form that I am excited about is the analogue form. Now it's possible perhaps to make that analogue form and supply it digitally, but I think the analogue result is what I'm looking for. I am quite old fashioned about the idea of transformation in theater. We can and will transform the space we're in into another space. We can and will transform ourselves into other selves. I'm excited that that can happen through analogue means.

I want to expand the definition of what a play can be. I call my work "theater." Andy Smith and I will one day write a book and the title of the book is called "Theatreness." What is the thing that is theater? What is the theaterness of theater? And I think it is very much about being corporeally, physically, temporally in the same place, and transformed as well. To be me and also not be. To not be in Illyria but also to *not* not be in Illyria. Those things happen most excitingly in our brains and in the body of an audience. They can happen very excitedly digitally as well but that's probably for other people to explore.

Aizzah Fatima

Aizzah Fatima is an actress and writer from New York City by way of Mississippi. After training as a microbiologist and working as an ads engineer at Google, she traded in her Google perks for the arts, and hasn't looked back. She is a graduate of the conservatory at The American Academy of Dramatic Arts. She is the writer and performer of the comedy one-woman play *Dirty Paki Lingerie*, which was developed with Matt Hoverman and Wynn Handman. The play had sold-out performances and rave reviews at the Edinburgh Fringe Festival, in NYC (The Flea Theater, 59E59, Abington Theatre Company), in Toronto (Harbourfront Centre), and during a tour in Pakistan sponsored by the US Department of State as well as a US college tour. It is the first play to be invited to represent the United States at the International Theater Festival of Turkmenistan.

Caroline Jester   *What is a playwright?*

Aizzah Fatima   We're storytellers first of all, and we hold a mirror to the societies that we live in. We try to convey their truths and their realities and share them with the general public.

CJ   *Does the audience influence your writing?*

AF   When I first read that question I thought, "no, the audience doesn't influence my writing, I just write what I want to write." But that's not really true because if you are a woman, a minority, a person of color, if you fall into any of those categories, then by default any art that you make becomes political.

Dirty Paki Lingerie was the first play I wrote and my intent was not to be political, but it has become this political piece. I was thinking of my audience because I wanted to create a piece that educates people about American Muslims. There was a lot of misunderstanding in my world, even here in New York, on a daily basis, and this was six years ago and sadly it's only gotten worse. So in some way the audience definitely does influence the writing.

CJ *Why do some stories transcend national borders and find audiences in different countries?*

AF I know it's true of *Dirty Paki Lingerie* and I know it's true of other stories as well, and the common thread in the stories that transcend boundaries is that they are very specific stories. When you tell a specific story, it appeals to the masses and becomes universal.

CJ *Is there a moment when you see that in action?*

AF I know that largely the play is an immigrant woman's story. Here in the US everyone's an immigrant, because somebody's grandparents came here or their great-grandparents, so the immigrant story really resonates. I had a Japanese-American couple who said, "Oh that's our story," and then I had a Jewish guy write and tell me one of the characters reminded him of his mom. I had a black woman in the Bronx tell me that one of the characters was just like her aunt.

The things that really resonate with a lot of people, men and women, is this pressure to assimilate. Where do you come from? A new culture? So which things of this new culture do you take with you, and which things of the old culture do you keep with you? I think the pressures of marriage on both men and women is something else people tell me that resonates with them a lot. Also, these are women's stories, and they don't necessarily belong to a specific culture. Women in Pakistan, Canada, the US, the UK, and Turkmenistan have all told me these stories resonate with them.

CJ *The title was changed to* Dirty Pakistani Lingerie *when it came to the UK; how did you feel about that?*

AF The first time I came to Edinburgh we didn't change it. Then I took the play to London and we weren't asked to change the title. Then the third time, it was a five-city tour, we had a lot of trouble with the title.

There was a theater in Bradford that I'd been talking with for months and they were saying, "we'll programme you," and then they said, "no, we can't programme you; our board doesn't feel comfortable with the title, we can't do it right now." There's a Bradford Literary Festival that happens every year and those ladies wanted the show and they were saying, "we're gonna do it," and then nothing happened. They didn't even give an explanation. I'm positive it was the title.

So in Bradford there's an organization called JUST Yorkshire, and they sponsored the show, and local activist and journalist Sabbiyah Pervez really championed it. We had a long conversation about how Bradford is known as "Bradistan" among the British Pakistani community because there are so many Pakistanis there. They really wanted to involve the community, and have a dialogue around the various issues discussed in the play around sexuality, racial profiling, family, religion vs. culture, and bullying. We had a talk-back after the show with Sabbiyah, and a local imam. The majority of the people who came to see that show wouldn't usually go to the theater, and they certainly wouldn't see their stories being depicted on stage. So we ended up doing a show for free in a community center: We turned it into a proper theater and I kept the title. We started with just 100 seats, and they kept having to up the capacity because more people kept wanting to attend. Eventually we had to get a bigger hall to accommodate 200 people. It was a majority British Pakistani audience. In Birmingham we had a similar situation where a theater dropped the show after months of back and forth about programming due to the title.

CJ *What you've just described there is so relevant to the recent referendum in the UK to leave the EU. The difference within, say, London and Scotland where there was a strong vote to remain, and then different responses in different areas within the UK.*

AF It does relate to what just happened. So this round, when we did the fifteen cities, our fourth time in the UK, including Edinburgh, what I found really fascinating was in Scotland nobody asked us to change the title. All five of the theaters in Scotland said: "Bring it, it's art, it's your art, it's not our job to tell you how to do it or what to say, you tell us as the artist what you want to call your play." Then in the rest of Britain people insisted that we change the title.

CJ *So there was a difference . . . as this is over a couple of years, the different tours . . . you saw a difference in responses?*

AF Oh definitely, because I think the play was never as relevant as it was this time around during our 2016 tour in the UK. The whole refugee crisis . . . the immigration debate that's going on in the UK made it really current.

CJ *The tour to Pakistan was sponsored by the US Department of State. How do you see your connection between your work and international political dialogues?*

AF It's interesting just to be able to use this one piece to go to all these different countries and relate to people at that level with what's going on politically in their country. I think the issues of being a woman in a society that the play explores, they definitely transcend all religious, ethnic, and cultural boundaries, no matter what country you're in. The limitations put on women, and the suffering of women, are universal issues. That happens in the United States as well as in Pakistan. It doesn't matter what country or what ethnic background you're from.

CJ *A line from your play is: "If women here really had the right to choose, then that Congresswoman in Michigan wouldn't have gotten thrown out of the state house for saying the word 'vagina.' The Republicans are like the Taliban. And the Taliban don't practice true Islam, Islam gave women the right to own property while women in Europe were still being treated like cattle."*

AF It's so true. I wrote that line three years ago, and it's so true even today.

CJ *There is actually now the possibility that Republican Presidential candidate Trump could become President.*

AF Right, and put us in camps.

CJ *He's made comments about wanting to ban Muslims from the US. As an artist, as a playwright, what role do you feel playwriting has to play here?*

AF I think it's an important time right now for us as people of conscience to stand up and say, "hey, this is wrong, and we should do something about it." It's interesting that when I came back from the UK, I met up with a mentor of mine, an older gentleman. We were talking about what's going on politically, and Trump, and the fact that I'm Muslim, and he said, "Aizzah, what are you going to do about it?" What am I going to do about it? What can I do about Trump? But I think again the only thing to do is use my art to entertain and educate people in the process. That's where the work that we do becomes something of importance, because when you educate people while entertaining them, the message stays with them. You're conveying an important message and it allows the audience to let down their guard, see themselves in the characters. It's hard to think negatively of an entire population once you start to see them as human beings just like you.

CJ *How do playwriting and the playwright fit into the digital age of storytelling?*

AF I know more and more playwrights who are doing digital storytelling in one form or another, and I think that's just become the nature of our work right now and because of the times we live in, where digital media is so easily accessible.

CJ *So where does theater fit in?*

AF I think technology and the digital age are making things better for theater because I can live broadcast theater. I can do something here in New York and broadcast it to Turkmenistan if I want. There have been some really interesting pieces where an actor in Italy is interacting with somebody in Bulgaria and it's been live broadcast here in New York. I think the possibilities are endless and it's a good thing.

5

WHAT ARE YOU RESPONSIBLE FOR?

When a playwright has finished a script and pressed "send" to the theater who commissioned it, they can then sit back and wait for the awards that are sure to follow the production. Well, we've already heard that the days of sending a play to a producer and sitting back isn't the way most plays find their way in front of an audience, so it might be a long wait. Playwrights are mavericks but are they also responsible for everything that happens before, during and after a production? We asked all of the following writers, "do you consider the role of the playwright as having to take responsibility for anything other than the writing of the play?" And yes, you've guessed it, there is not one definitive answer . . .

Gurpreet Kaur Bhatti challenges the word "responsibility" in the question. For her, this implies culpability and she sees herself as someone who takes charge. She sees, however, a wider need for the industry to be educated in freedom of expression.

David Henry Hwang sees diversity within the field as his main concern: In terms of gender, race, and class. As well as how to ensure the vitality and relevance of this artform in a country where people of color will constitute the majority by around 2040.

David Edgar doesn't think anybody should be taken to the stake for not thinking they have a responsibility beyond the play, but he does think theater has a particular role in holding a mirror to society, and to the profession and the role of the writer within the industry.

Saviana Stanescu often feels like director, dramaturg, critic, performance artist, actor, designer, and musician when she's writing a play. She feels this interdisciplinarity and multiculturalism will thrive despite newly emerging nationalisms and attacks on globalization.

Tena Štivičić would hate to write issue plays, even though her plays contain issues. She's just trying to make sense of some of the core things about existence, creating order out of the chaos of life.

Janice Connolly always writes plays that are based on research and her talking to the people who are at the heart of the subject matter. And we mustn't think that theater is only for a certain type of person: It is fundamental to everybody and everybody can get it.

Neil LaBute has a responsibility to himself as a writer and to the plays and the characters he is creating. He has a responsibility to his characters to tell their stories truthfully. He thinks there's a vanity in thinking you can change the opinion of an audience or audience member but there is a possibility they could see things from a new perspective.

Erik Ehn doesn't find the attraction lies with writers themselves, but they can help create a field of fascination. An impulse to make art might lead you on a lonely path, but have faith in the assembly. Know your heart and share it with others.

And in **Christopher Shinn's** own words: "Art is not about imposing a point of view in an authoritarian way on another. It's about being open, communicating openly and holding this openness, which entails deep respect and consideration of the other."

It may be impossible to answer the questions, but they must keep being asked, and these playwrights are brave and not afraid to do just that.

Gurpreet Kaur Bhatti

Gurpreet Kaur Bhatti has written extensively for stage, screen, and radio. Her work includes *Behzti* (Birmingham Repertory Theatre), which won the Susan Smith Blackburn Prize; *Khandan* (Royal Court); and the feature film *Everywhere and Nowhere*. Her first collection of plays, *Gurpreet Kaur Bhatti: PLAYS ONE*, is published by Oberon Books. She writes regularly for the long-running UK radio series, *The Archers*.

Caroline Jester *What is a playwright?*

Gurpreet Kaur Bhatti For me, it's somebody who has something to say about the world and chooses to present that in a dramatic form, or indeed a comedic form.

CJ *Why do you make the distinction between dramatic and comedic?*

GKB I didn't want "dramatic" to restrict plays that are funny or are silly or farcical or absurd. I say "dramatic form" meaning that it's in an environment, not necessarily a theater but usually a theater, so somebody who has something to say about our world by creating an artificial world.

CJ *Does the audience influence your writing?*

GKB When I write, I'm not really thinking about pleasing anybody and I'm not wondering "are they going to like this, are they going to get this?" But I am very aware that I'm not writing a novel; I am writing something that is going to be made. There is going to be a set, there is going to be a design, there are going to be actors. I'm very aware that I'm going to take the audience on a journey and I think about them from the point of view of the nature of that journey—what I would like them to feel, where I would like them to feel empathy or joy or sadness, where I would like them to be unsettled, where I'd like to shake them up.

The audience is not a homogenous lump, either. It is made up of different people with different life experiences, different everything. I have *my* idea of what this journey is, but I don't know how they're going to experience it. I don't actually know until the first preview or press night. And that's quite exciting. What I saw in the question was the audience influencing what I'm writing and I'm very anti that.

CK *Do you consider the role of the playwright as having to take responsibility for anything other than the writing of the play?*

GKB Instinctively I felt, "no, move on to the next question." But actually I think there are two elements. Theater is a collaborative form, hopefully when your play is on, you are going to be working with a creative team, so you have to communicate your intention, you have to communicate your creative universe as well as what is in the play. The other element, and this does come back to my experience, and having written *Behzti* and the response and the huge furore, the international and national furore that occurred, I choose to say something. I put myself in the firing line and I think that I was prepared to face what came my way. Now that doesn't mean that it was OK for people to threaten me, or it was OK for the play to be closed down, that any of that was OK, but I chose to say something and stand by it wholeheartedly. "Responsibility" is such a weird word because it implies culpability in some way. I took charge, I put myself in the firing line, and I was prepared to stand in the firing line and vigorously defend what I believed and what I wrote.

CJ *Behzti has had readings and productions outside of the UK and it has led the way in discussions around censorship and freedom of speech within art. Why do you feel, if you do, that there has been a resistance in the UK and not in other countries?*

GKB Obviously it was a big event here and it did become something that people had knowledge of internationally. Why do I feel there's been resistance here? I don't know if I feel there's been resistance. It could be because I'm not sure that conversation has really moved on, how to put on difficult work, how to put work on about people from different cultures that is not comfortable, that is not entertainment, that is challenging, that is provocative. I think that's still quite difficult. And I think the other thing is people might not like it. I mean, it was my second play. People might not think it was very good, which is a valid reason not to put something on. I honestly don't know; I think it's probably more about that conversation not moving on and it's become a watchword for work that's dangerous or is going to be problematic.

I think we look at how work is commissioned and how work is produced in this country. We have a feudal system. Theaters are almost like little kingdoms and you have a kind of monarch at the top. That is the system and there will be some places that really like your work, that really get your work and want to put it on, and there will be some places that don't. So I think you have to be honest about the landscape as it is; it's not just about having a conversation between artists and producers; you have to be honest about how work is commissioned and how work actually gets on. And I think we are still in a time of austerity where the arts have been cut to the bone. How can that not influence people and the decisions they have to make in terms of making the math add up?

I think artists need to align themselves with producers and directors who understand and are passionate about their work and not everybody is going to do that. Before you have solidarity you must have trust between artists and institutions. And I think that institutions like theaters and producers need to be educated in freedom of expression because a lot of them don't have a clue of what their rights are, what it means, what to do if there's a difficult situation. Certainly after *Behud*, Index on Censorship held a conference and created an information pack, and one of the recommendations was that artistic institutions should have a freedom of expression policy. Unless these things are inbuilt into the institution, nothing really changes and I think otherwise we're talking in vague, well-meaning, liberal terms about showing solidarity and being brave. Everybody would agree with that in principle, but when it comes down to it, people don't know how to respond and so edge toward cowardice.

CJ Behud *is a completely different style and imagination triumphs in the end in that piece. How important was it for you as a writer to share your experience using this dramatic—but you might challenge that word—format? Did it allow you to voice things you couldn't in other formats? How could the artform facilitate your process?*

GKB I think it was really important. I'd written various articles, I'd given a speech at the Cambridge Union, and I'd gone to different countries to speak about my experience, but I think the way it's been best articulated for me is in the dramatic form. It's not that it was just important or necessary to use my form, to use the theater, which is the writer's temple to challenge, to express, to tell this story. It was simply the best way of communicating what happened.

CJ *If you were starting out now, what advice would you give yourself?*

GKB I would say be brave. I would say know what you will not let go of and know what's worth discussing as regards what you're creating. Align yourself with other creative people who understand, or who at least try to understand, what you're trying to say. Be grateful for the opportunities that you get, but don't be too grateful. Hold onto the thing. Listen by all means to what people say, but hold onto it in your heart, because you in your heart know what it is. I think there's also something in the industry of new writing, which I think is particular to the UK, where sometimes imperfection is not valued. And work hard!

CJ *How do playwriting and the playwright fit into the digital age of storytelling?*

GKB I have no idea. I'm not on Twitter, I'm not on Facebook, I just about manage on email. But I find the whole thing exciting because I like new things and I'm intrigued. I think it's just storytelling. I had a show on at Rich Mix a couple of years ago, a play called *Londonee.* The guy who was directing it was extolling the virtues of plays and he was saying plays are much more important than novels. I asked him why he thought that. He said because in 2,000 years, somebody will be sitting here discussing how to do your play, but they won't be talking about novels from the same period. I'm not sure I agree with him, having just reread *Madame Bovary*, but I get what he means. A play is a malleable form because there is always scope for interpretation. And the human need for drama and live performance is as basic as the need for food and water.

David Henry Hwang

David Henry Hwang's work includes the plays *M. Butterfly, Chinglish, Golden Child, Yellow Face, The Dance and the Railroad,* and *FOB*, as well as the Broadway musicals *Aida* (co-author), *Flower Drum Song* (2002 revival), and *Disney's Tarzan*. He is also America's most-produced living opera librettist, who has worked with composers Philip Glass, Osvaldo Golijov, Bright Sheng, Unsuk Chin, Huang Ruo, and Howard Shore. Hwang is a Tony Award-winner and three-time nominee, a three-time OBIE Award-winner, and a two-time Finalist for the Pulitzer Prize in Drama. He serves on the boards of the Lark Play Development Center, American Theatre Wing, and the Actors Fund, and as the President of Young Playwrights Inc. David Henry Hwang was recently a Residency One Playwright at New York's Signature Theatre, which produced a season of his plays, including the premiere of his piece *Kung Fu*. He is Associate Professor of Playwriting at Columbia University.

Caridad Svich   *What is a playwright?*

David Henry Hwang   Strictly speaking, a playwright is someone who writes plays, though I would broaden that definition to an artist who creates stories for live theatrical events, which would include everyone from composers, book-writers for musicals, and librettists, to those who shape narrative for Cirque-like spectaculars.

CS   *How much does the role of the playwright influence your writing? Is responsibility connected to audience? In your case, I know this question opens up many other questions—whether you are working as librettist on a musical or opera, or as a screenwriter, etc.*

DHH   I agree that the question of "audience" depends largely on how the work is to be produced. I divide my work into two categories: Pieces which are completely self-initiated (usually, plays), and those where I serve as a craftsperson to help another artist realize their vision (operas, Disney, staff writing on TV, etc.). I consider audience in the latter category, but not the former. Going into *Yellow Face*, for instance, I thought I was writing that play for a primarily Asian-American audience, and that it would premiere at Los Angeles' East West Players. Instead, it ended up attracting a much wider national, international, and digital audience. Conversely, a Disney musical for Broadway is intended for the largest possible audience, and I do keep that in mind as we create it.

CS   *Art and trouble, or what I like to call "necessary art," usually stems from awakening an audience and culture to what troubles us all. How do you wrestle with trouble, if at all?*

DHH   I feel that, for better or worse, social and political impulses have always motivated my personal work, and are therefore inherently embedded in the artmaking. My best pieces have been fueled by anger, the sense that I'm doing something "naughty," which will upset or rile at least some people. In both *M. Butterfly* and *Chinglish*, for instance, I'm trying to challenge tropes of Western—particularly, Western male—social and sexual superiority. *M. Butterfly* reflects the power dynamic of the time in which it was written, with the West still dominant; *Chinglish*, our more contemporary era with China clearly in ascendance. In *Yellow Face*, I am to a large extent reacting against the forms of racism which Asians still face in America, through incidents from the *Miss Saigon* protest to my father's persecution in the late 1990s, and how I believe there is a connection between those two public events. *FOB* reflects a young assimilated Asian-American's early discovery of ethnic identity; honestly, I'm happily surprised that this 35-year-old play (with references to the Bee Gees and John Travolta) still gets produced with some regularity on college campuses today.

CS   *You are in a mentorship position as head of playwriting at Columbia University. So, you have a direct relationship to what it is like to be a mentor, but I am also curious as to experiences you have had as a theater-maker where you have felt a strong sense of mentorship, too.*

DHH In the thirty-five years I've been working, the theater has "professionalized" considerably—which has both advantages and disadvantages. The field used to be smaller, with fewer theaters both in NYC and across the country, programming decisions were made more impulsively, and play "development" was little known (though many dramatists certainly did rewrite). *FOB* went from a dorm play to a production at the Public Theater in a mere fourteen months, which is hard to imagine happening today (though the success of Ruby Rae Spiegel's *Dry Land* proves it's not impossible). Mentorship was similarly more informal and scattershot. I was fortunate to have a number of great mentors, though most were not playwrights: John L'Heureux, Martin Esslin, Joe Papp, and Lloyd Richards, to name a few. Nowadays, the larger and more formalized nature of our field has put greater importance on MFA programs as gateways to the profession. Even before I joined the faculty at Columbia, I always believed it was my duty to mentor younger dramatists. Writing a play is one of those rare practices which hasn't changed radically in the past few centuries. So I think we're like cobblers, passing down the trade of making shoes.

One interesting production shift I've noticed recently is the emergence of alternatives to not-for-profit models. The benefit of a theater company having non-profit 501(c)3 [charitable] tax status has diminished in an age of little to no government funding. Moreover, fiscal sponsors like Fractured Atlas have helped push the disadvantages of running a not for profit to outweigh the advantages.

CS *How do you consider the circle, not only in terms of immediate community, but also in the creation of reference points for your work(s) and how you make it?*

DHH I've written earlier about how the work of other artists almost always serves as a model for my own. I therefore believe in a sort of artistic zeitgeist, where our work influences each other, usually less deliberately than I personally experience. I feel that playwrights form a particularly generous community—not that we don't have our petty rivalries or feel competitive, but a surprising amount of genuine appreciation exists for each other's work, considering that on any objective level, we're all fighting over a very small pie. Still, I think we all realize how hard this is to do, and most of us feel genuinely excited about works which advance the form we love.

CS   *How to sustain a life in playwriting?*

DHH   Financial advisors tell clients to diversify their portfolios. I believe playwrights must also diversify their artistic portfolios. In other words, learn to do as many things as you can, and be open to finding work in many arenas. When I was coming up, the common wisdom among dramatists was that writing for other forms weakened one's playwriting. I happen to believe the opposite is true: Any form of dramatic writing only puts more tools in one's toolbox. Furthermore, I believe that in order to do our work, we first have to survive. There's no shame—in fact, there's a kind of honor—in being a good craftsperson as well as a good artist.

CS   *Might you chat about works and/or moments when you felt the work was turning/moving toward something else/in ripe evolution, and how it affected what you made after those moments/points of turning, and why?*

DHH   Generally, I feel my turning points have been my failures. When I first started writing plays in my spare time in college, and a professor told me they were bad (which was true; he later became an important mentor), I kept writing. My first Off-Broadway flop, *Rich Relations*, gave me the experience of creating non-Asian characters, which I applied to my next play, *M. Butterfly*. The very public and humiliating failure of *Face Value*, which closed in previews on Broadway, eventually gave birth to *Yellow Face*. I guess the central principle here is my desire to continue learning and growing as an artist. Generally, hits are more enjoyable, but flops have more to teach you.

The failure of *Face Value* is a useful case study. I wanted to write a farce of mistaken racial identity, and tried to create a physical, Feydeau-like show, which I wasn't skilled enough to pull off successfully. But I continued to think the concept was exciting, and experimented over the next twelve years with short plays, which took varied approaches to a comedy of racial identity. Eventually, this led to *Yellow Face*, which now feels like the culmination of a project which lasted over a decade.

CS *What are your chief concerns now in the field?*

DHH My main concern with our field is diversity: In terms of gender, race, and class. How do we lower ticket prices? How do we deal with the fact that actors hired in New York theater (in terms of Broadway and the major not for profits) are 80 percent white (70 percent in 2014–15, which hopefully represents some long-term progress)? How do we increase the number of female playwrights produced? In short, how do we ensure the vitality and relevance of our artform in a country where people of color will constitute the majority by around 2040?

CS *Now that you have a considerable body of work, how do you see yourself examining and/or reflecting upon matters of identity?*

DHH Nowadays, I believe in the concept of reciprocal assimilation. In the 1970s and 1980s, "assimilation" was a dirty word, because it connoted an individual of color pathetically trying to ape the majority culture. However, I now feel that a personal identity which is static, which never grows and evolves, is equally stunted. Of course, the culture in which we live is going to affect us—and should! The imperative is to make sure we affect the culture as well. This is what I hope I'm able to do—leave my mark upon the identity of this society, as it has certainly left its mark on mine.

CS *How do playwriting and the playwright fit into the digital age of storytelling?*

DHH I don't feel the digital age has much impact on storytelling. If anything, the proliferation of platforms has made all forms of live entertainment (from concerts to sporting events to theater) more valuable, because as humans we continue to appreciate real social contact and connections. I have had one work adapted for YouTube, which while taking advantage of a digital platform, does not feel conceptually different from adapting a play for a movie or television.

David Edgar

David Edgar was born into a theater family and took up writing full time in 1972. In 1989 he founded Britain's first graduate playwriting course at the University of Birmingham, of which he was director for ten years. Original plays for the RSC include: *Destiny*; *Maydays*; *Pentecost*; *The Prisoner's Dilemma*; and *Written on the Heart*. Original plays for the Royal National Theatre include *The Shape of the Table* and *Playing with Fire*. Other plays include: *If Only* (Chichester Minerva); *Daughters of the Revolution*; *Mothers Against* (Oregon Shakespeare Festival and Berkeley Repertory Theatre); and *Testing the Echo* (Out of Joint). His stage adaptations include: Albie Sach's *Jail Diary*, Charles Dickens' *Nicholas Nickleby* and *A Christmas Carol*, all for the Royal Shakespeare Theatre); Gitta Sereny's biography of *Albert Speer* (National Theatre); and Julian Barnes' *Arthur & George* (Birmingham Repertory Theatre), as well as a version of Henrik Ibsen's *The Master Builder* (Chichester Festival theater). He has written two community plays for Dorchester: *Entertaining Strangers* and *A Time to Keep* (with Stephanie Dale). He is the recipient of numerous awards and the author of *How Plays Work* published by Nick Hern Books.

Caroline Jester   *What is a playwright?*

David Edgar   A playwright is a writer who writes for live performance, also often for publication. A traditional play is something that aspires to be repeated. It's written with the possibility of an additional production in mind, and thus aspires to enter a canon, to be done in other productions by other companies, possibly in other countries and other languages. A play starts life as a draft or a series of drafts. It then goes through a developmental and rehearsal process, which will change it. If it's done by a major company, it will be published, and then it may reappear in productions overseas; it may go into another medium, it may go into radio, or television, or film, and all of those mediations will change it again. Finally, a play is a copyrightable piece of work that is owned by the writer.

Obviously there are other ways of ending up with text for plays which are also writing. They include various forms of devising processes.

CJ *Publication was your second thought. Are you conscious of that in the initial creation?*

DE No, I don't think so. There's usually a little note in the play, "this version was printed before the end of rehearsals so it may differ slightly from the play in performance." I've had plays that have differed very substantially from the play in performance and on occasions I've done a pre-deal, particularly with a play at the RSC, where you know it'll be done in Stratford and then it transfers. I have agreed with my publisher that, if there are substantial changes after the first published draft, they'll publish a revised version when the play transfers. Then there are plays like *Pentecost* that have been done so often, particularly in America, that the script has changed very substantially, but it isn't republished. The playwright who thought about publication most seriously was probably Shaw. His stage directions are not really stage directions for actors: His trick of not naming the characters until they're named in the play was intended to give the *reader* what the audience experiences, to make reading the play as like seeing it as possible. Now the fashion is to give as little information as possible, even not attributing lines to characters, making it a completely different experience to seeing the play.

I tend to publish in a rather Shavian way. I tend to write a preface or an afterword because a lot of my work is fact-based. I tend to put in chronologies. I tend to put in the kind of quotations you might have in the programmes. It should contribute to a deepening experience of seeing the play.

CJ *Does the audience influence your writing?*

DE The answer clearly is yes, in a number of ways. It's a big question, so a big answer: I think one of the big things which happened in the last twenty-five years of the twentieth century in theater, the arts, and every other aspect of life was a shift of power from the producer to the consumer. In whatever form, socialism is a producer-oriented way of organizing society, and both social democracy and communism were called into great question in the last quarter of the last century. That represented a shift of power from the people who produce things to the people who buy them and consume them. In the arts, the first victim of that was the high avant-garde. When I was growing up in the 1960s and beginning to work in the 1970s, the presumption was that if you didn't understand a piece of contemporary music or an avant-garde play, it was your fault. I think that disappeared in the 1980s. Before that, in the rehearsal rooms of the major subsidized theaters, you didn't talk about audience response (even if you were thinking about it). You were talking about what the play was communicating; you were talking about it from the supply side, not the demand side.

I have a theory that when a number of great subsidized directors did their big musicals in the 1980s, and then returned to Chekhov and Shakespeare, and new plays, they brought back a much stronger sense of the audience. It was permissible to talk about how the audience would respond, and indeed to a point where I think a lot of playwrights found it tiresome to be constantly asked, "will they get this?" for that to be the only topic of conversation. But I think the turn toward audiences was not before its time.

CJ *Do you consider the role of the playwright as having to take responsibility for anything other than the writing of the play?*

DE Are you saying that they should only take responsibility for the play? There are a number of contexts for answering that question. There's the sort of "art for art's sake" debate: Is the sole purpose of the play to entertain and to amuse or divert, or to be an artistic expression of some sort or another? But also, does the playwright have the responsibility not to offend, or is it his or her responsibility to offend? Does the playwright in the strange medium that has this tiny audience but this huge amount of attention devoted to it, actually have a responsibility to be radical and experimental? Does that give us the responsibility to do things that can't be done in much more expensive mediums like television and film? I don't think anybody should be taken to the stake for not thinking they have a responsibility beyond the work, but I do think theater has had a particular role since 1956, and arguably before, in holding up a mirror to society.

CJ *I have read that you stated that your ambition was to "be a secretary for the times through which I'm living." If that is the statement that you made, who then are you working for?*

DE I can't remember when I said that. I do think that if you were to look at the subjects that I have written about since 1971, when I started writing professionally, it's a pretty good selection of current issues of the times. I wrote about the impact of the late 1960s counter-culture, I wrote about the rise of racism, I wrote about the move to the right, I wrote about the consequences of the fall of communism, I wrote about multiculturalism, and I'm now writing about the new fault lines of politics. And I wrote a play about feminism, and I like to think the work has been touched by that in particular. I also was one of the first white playwrights to put non-white characters in contemporary plays onto the stage. That said, I'm also who I am with my history, and there are various things that my canon leaves out. The Balzac phrase, "being secretary for the times," is probably a bit grandiose and probably easier to say half-way through my career when there was a larger number of plays again to come. That was easier to say than it is now.

What I do think is true is that there were some certain key decisions that I took. You can exaggerate the intentionality of your career. When people ask, "why did you write *Nicholas Nickleby*?" I have to catch myself half-way through this long answer by saying: "I wrote *Nicholas Nickleby* because the Royal Shakespeare Company wanted to adapt it and they asked me to do it." However, you do take some decisions and I think the decision to write about the right in the 1970s and 1980s was significant. I think in the mid 1970s it was by no means obvious that the next fifteen years were going to be dominated by the right: We thought the opposite, actually, so that was a prescient decision. And I think another good decision was to stop writing about this country in 1989 and write a series of plays, actually an astonishing number of plays, set abroad: There are the three Eastern European plays, but also *Albert Speer*, set in Germany, and *Continental Divide* is set in America. So I was for a long period trying to be an English-speaking global playwright, and it was a decision that meant I wasn't writing about certain other domestic things that were going on.

CJ   *You've been a leading force, if not the leading force, in supporting the professional writer and their rights. You founded the Theatre Writers' Union and you've been President of the Writers' Guild of Great Britain. Why have you spent your time doing this? Do you feel it's the playwright's role to look after the profession as well as their individual artistic pursuits?*

DE   I come from a political generation which believed you should join your union, and I and some other playwrights set up the Theatre Writers' Union, which later on joined the Writers' Guild. I do think it's important to defend playwrights. Playwrights are under attack from two wings. It's particularly threatening, because while you do have to employ actors, you do have to have a designer, you usually have to have a director, and with music you have to have musicians, but you don't have to have a writer. You can either use a dead one or you can make the play in a different way. And the very moment when the amount of revivals was going down in the 1990s was the moment when the amount of devised work was on the increase. I think I certainly felt I'd fought for the Arts Council to encourage all these new plays to be presented, and at last it was coming to fruition really dramatically, and at that very moment there were lots of companies popping up that were doing new work but not using writers. I felt that somebody had to speak out about that and say, "hang on a minute," and made myself unpopular thereby, but I think it's important. And I believe that if we didn't have the union agreements we negotiated in the 1980s and 1990s, many, many more playwrights, including playwrights who don't join the union, would not be writing stage plays.

CJ   *How do playwriting and the playwright fit into the digital age of storytelling?*

DE   In the same way as the great dramatic subject in the 2000s was the perils of Western intervention, the sort of generic play in which Westerners went into a foreign country, didn't understand it and fucked it up, similarly it seems to me that people's acceptance of the amount

Google and Yahoo and everybody knows about us, the surveillance economy and the surveillance state, is one of the great subjects of the noughts.

But there's a counter to that, which is to ask, what are the great, new forms of activity which have emerged over the last five or six years, which are clearly very important to people, and to note that among them are book-reading groups and choirs. And they are both about people coming together to do things that you could do perfectly well privately. You could sing in the bath, and books are designed to be read on their own. It's people creating collective experiences, which have to be undertaken together, i.e., non-digitally by their very nature. People want to come together and do real things in real time together, face to face, and that's what theater is. There's a bit of me that says theater should not be the enemy of the digital age, should not oppose it, but that it should be an alternative to it, and be about the direct experience.

Saviana Stanescu*

Saviana Stanescu is a Romanian-born playwright, poet, educator, and editor. Her works include: *Ants*, *Aliens with Extraordinary Skills*, *Useless*, *Waxing West*, *Bechnya*, *Lenin's Shoe*, *White Embers*, and *Polanski Polanski*. She co-edited the anthologies *Global Foreigners* and *roMANIA after 2000*. She is member of Ensemble Studio Theatre and a Usual Suspect with New York Theatre Workshop. She was a Playwriting Fellow at the Lark in New York City. She teaches playwriting at Ithaca College.

Caridad Svich *What is a playwright?*

Saviana Stanescu A writer of plays, someone who plays right, and who is right about considering herself a playwright!

The Romanian word for "playwright" is "dramaturg," so basically we can't make the distinction between the two professions in Romanian. I am a Romanian-American writer with Balkan roots, and am constantly living on the bridge of *inbetweenness:* Negotiating between two cultures, two continents, two cities (NYC and Ithaca, where I teach), between the West and the East, between being an artist and a teacher. I am used to hyphenating identities and integrating dichotomies. As an author of dramatic texts for the stage, I often think like a director, a dramaturg, a critic, a performance artist, an actor, a designer, a musician, when writing a play. This is probably the new normal in the age of interdisciplinarity and multiculturalism, and it's going to thrive despite newly emerging nationalisms and attacks on globalization. However, at the end of the day/night, I consider myself mainly a writer, aka someone who puts together word after word in meaningful sentences and structures.

I started as a poet, writing in Romanian, publishing three books of poetry. In the late 1990s, a Romanian critic labeled me "the tough

* Interview reproduced with the kind permission of the author and their legal representation.

poetess-playwright at the border between millennia"—another *inbetween* that defines me. When my dramatic poem "The Outcast" was performed in Paris at Théâtre Gérard-Philipe in 1998, I was considering myself a poet, but people were calling me a playwright. So I started to believe it. I went to Germany to study Playwriting in English with David Harrower and Phyllis Nagy at the Ruhr International Theatre Academy. Then I went back to Romania and won The Best Play of The Year UNITER (Theatre Guild) Award for my new play *The Inflatable Apocalypse*. I officially became an award-winning playwright. And back to your question: A playwright is someone who identifies as a playwright and, hopefully, is recognized by others as a playwright. Do we need to go to school to learn how to be a playwright? It can certainly help hone one's craft through a rigorous process of learning and doing, tight deadlines, useful feedback, and industry connections, but it is not absolutely necessary.

CS *Does the audience influence your writing?*

SS It was one thing to write in Romanian for Romanian audiences who had specific social, cultural, and political references, and it is a completely different thing to write in English for US audiences. My writing has changed. In Romania I used to write absurdist plays with feminist, sexual, revolutionary, and anti-consumerism undertones.

In the US, I am more concerned—like everyone else—with identity politics, particularly issues of immigration and being a global foreigner, an "alien" (my US visa for "aliens with extraordinary abilities in the arts" wouldn't let me forget that). I lived in NYC for fifteen years, and I thought that audiences in the Big Apple were different than the ones that attend regional theaters. Now I teach in upstate New York, in Ithaca, and I realize that, although I write for NYC audiences mainly, the work speaks to regional America as well; they love to see plays that premiered in NYC and were a hit there. When my play *Aliens with Extraordinary Skills* got produced in Mexico City at Teatro La Capilla (after successful runs off-Broadway at Women's Project and regionally) in Spanish, under the title *Inmigrantes con Habilidades Extraordinarias*, I noticed different things that were relevant and impactful for Mexican audiences. When the play was produced at Odeon Theatre in Bucharest, under the title *Clown Visa*, Romanian audiences resonated with other aspects of the characters and storyline. They responded in a more emotional way than the intellectual reactions to my dark absurdist comedies written in Romanian, before I left for the US, on August 23, 2001. (FYI: August 23 used to be the national day of Romania during the totalitarian system, the day when we had to march and sing propagandistic songs, and now is the day I completely changed my life crossing the ocean and challenging my hi/story . . .)

CS *Do you consider the role of the playwright as having to take responsibility for anything other than the writing of the play?*

SS Yes, I think that the role of the playwright in the contemporary society is to respond to the spirit and the issues of our time, to question the unquestionable, to address the difficult topics, to challenge the taboos, to subvert the mainstream power, never to retreat in an ivory penthouse and provide easy answers to stereotypical questions . . . Maybe because I was in the streets, as an idealist college student, during the Romanian revolution in December 1989, and then I worked as a journalist in the newly created free press, I still believe in the revolutionary writer—the writer who's always on the barricades, fighting for the underdogs, pushing the borders of human knowledge and the understanding of The Others.

My first assignment as a journalist in the early 1990s, in Bucharest, was to write about the pulling down of Lenin's statue from its pedestal. Then I had to interview the first woman prime minister of Turkey. Those experiences informed my playwriting much later. In 2006, in NYC, I wrote *Lenin's Shoe*, a play about a trauma of the Past "pulling you down" from the reality of the Present. It seems that I needed time and distance (personal, political, cultural) to better understand my own past and hi/story, and explore them in my writing. In *Waxing West*, which won the 2017 New York Innovative Theatre Award for Outstanding Play, I was finally able to have a character, Daniela, who deals with the memories of the 1989 Revolution, as she is trying to make a life for herself in NYC. I dramatized Daniela's inner conflict: She is haunted by dictator Ceausescu and his wife Elena, who appear to her as vaudevillian vampires. In *Aliens with Extraordinary Skills*, Nadia, the protagonist from Moldova, is harassed by imaginary immigration officers, symbolizing her fears due to her undocumented status. I always try to find a theatrical way to explore concepts that go beyond psychological realism. I guess this is happening not only because of my Eastern European heritage but also because, as a Writer-in-Residence for Richard Schechner (*YokastaS Redux*, *Timbuktu*) in my first years in the USA, I learned to write in English with an enhanced sense of the performative possibilities of a theater piece.

CS *How do you see the role of the playwright in culture, particularly differences between Eastern Europe and in the US?*

SS I think that a playwright needs to respond to the hot issues of the society, to have an impactful voice, and play an active role in triggering social change. When I left Romania in 2001, writers were still public intellectuals; their opinions mattered on a political and cultural level. We were interviewed by TV channels and asked for our perspectives on various matters, we wrote columns in the main newspapers. We had a voice as individuals and citizen-artists. To a certain extent, that is still the case in Eastern Europe, although I think that the role of the writer in the society has diminished compared with the 1980s and the 1990s, when intellectuals were stars, celebrities. In the US, of course, this is not the case. US theater is focused on the playwright and new play development/ production, but the playwrights here don't seem to have a strong voice in the society as public intellectuals. Celebrities are Hollywood actors, politicians, and, unfortunately, certain reality TV stars who can capitalize on their fame to gain political clout . . . and even become presidents. US playwrights struggle to make ends meet, they have to teach or write for TV in order to pay the bills. It's hard to have any public clout in those circumstances. Your focus is on survival as an artist; you still need to write what you have to write, and tell the stories you need to tell. Luckily there are a few significant grants, awards, and fellowships that help some playwrights to continue doing their work, so for folks who get enough mainstream recognition, life gets a little easier materially. But they still don't have visibility and public clout in the society, they are not well known public intellectuals like the Eastern European counterparts.

CS *Have you seen a shift in Romanian new writing for the stage in the last few years? And if so, why and how? And your own position within Eastern European/global context?*

SS Yes, the most interesting and impactful young(er) theater-makers are director-writers, auteurs who develop the dramatic text with an ensemble of actors and tackle significant social issues: (post)communist political dossiers, economic migration, refugees, education, the gap between generations, women issues, youth crisis, small town inertia, etc.

I am considered an American playwright over there, in Eastern Europe, and—ironically—an Eastern European writer here, in America. So I am probably doomed to live somewhere in between, in the sky, above the ocean! Joking aside, this is the reality for immigrant writers: We have one foot in each country and a brain that is trying to make sense of that *inbetweenness,* while dreaming to find a place to call "home" . . .

In most of my plays I explore the ways in which the American Dream can turn into a nightmare at any given moment, but also strategies for survival through love, friendship, and human connection. George Bernard Shaw is credited with saying: "If you tell people the truth, you better make them laugh, otherwise they'll kill you." I am trying to do that: Spice things up with humor and playfulness, employ a theatricality that comes from the Romanian folkloric saying, "one eye laughs and one eye cries."

CS *In times of austerity, Brexit, and Trump and the rise of nationalist populist movements globally, how does an "international" artist survive? Define oneself? What strategies do you think are possible?*

SS This is a big question indeed. I was thinking about writing a book, *The International Artist's Survival Guide in New York.* Your survival depends on so many things if you are a foreigner, an alien, a global citizen, an international writer—you need a few of the following basic "items": A strong community who supports you, a family, good friends, money, branding oneself well, writing in a second language or having a good translator, the relevance of your home country in the public eye, etc. It was one thing to come from Romania during the Cold War or in the early 1990s, after the fall of Soviet communism, and it's a completely different thing to be a Romanian in the US now. At that time, stories from Eastern Europe were exciting and powerful and sexy, people wanted to know more, to understand what was happening there. Not so much now, although with Putin's new ambitions, Eastern Europe might become "hot" again, and not in a good way . . .

On the other hand, I resist the idea that—as a Romanian writer—I should only write about Romanians or Eastern Europeans. I like to be able to write about whatever I feel like writing. I'm concerned with issues in the contemporary society that affect all people, not just Romanians; I care about the inequality gap, racial injustice, poverty, underdogs, outcasts, Others.

I don't like to be put in the "Romanian" box. I believe in intersections, in expansion, in a global humanism. It's very limiting to reduce a writer to her biography, no matter how rich and meaningful that is.

Brexit, Trump, and the rise of nationalist populist movements globally are scary on many levels. They put us in boxes, they pit us against each other, they encourage hate and violence, they make us *the Others*. It's the old *Divide et Impera* imposed by/for the rich one percent . . .

The only strategy I see for us, artists, is to support each other and raise our voices through our work. To be more revolutionary than ever.

CS *How do playwriting and the playwright fit into the digital age of storytelling?*

SS We need to incorporate the new forms of communication and socializing in our writing, of course. To speak to our times. In my American plays, I have scenes or choruses that take place in chatrooms, on Craiglist, Facebook, etc. I use spoken emojis sometimes and they are lots of fun for audiences and actors. In all my devised theater pieces, there is some Internet forum or cyber-chorus of text messages and emails: *E-dating*, *Riots*, *Back to Ithaca—A contemporary Odyssey* (based on interviews with Ithaca veterans), *Trust* (about the relationship between the police and the civilians), *The Others* (about microaggressions on college campuses), *Dream Acts* (co-written with Chiori Miyagawa, Jessical Litwak, Andrea Thome, and Mia Chung). In my Romanian play, *The Inflatable Apocalypse*, I had "commercial breaks" and a postmodern non-linear structure that intersected different narratives. I actually think that my writing style has become more traditional here in the US, although it's still somewhat "experimental" compared to mainstream dramas.

Tena Štivičić

Tena Štivičić was awarded the Susan Blackburn-Smith Prize for her most recent play, *3 Winters,* which opened at the National Theatre to five-star reviews. Other plays include: *Can't Escape Sundays; At Deathbed; The Two of Us; Fragile!; Fireflies; Invisible; Europa,* and plays for children, *Perceval—the Quest for the Grail,* and *Psst.* Her plays have been performed in a number of European countries and translated and published in ten languages. They have won numerous awards, including the European Author's Award and the Innovation Award at Heidelberg Stückemarkt for *Fragile!* She is a columnist for *Zaposlena* magazine in Croatia and has published two books of her columns. A feature film adapted from her play *Invisible* is in pre-production.

Caroline Jester *What is a playwright?*

Tena Štivičić For me, playwriting is much like any writing, creating order out of the chaos of life. I don't know whether there's anything more specific to it in terms of playwriting but I tend to try and look at every argument from every possible point of view, which I think is something that is particular, specific to theater. I'm not really sure I chose playwriting because that's how I look at things, or whether I tend to look at things like that because I'm a playwright and have to give each character equal weight.

CJ *Does the audience influence your writing?*

TS I certainly have a lot of respect for the audience. I think about the fact that what I'm writing relies on people coming out and paying sometimes huge amounts of money and giving over their time to what I've written. I find that sometimes quite a daunting responsibility, but certainly something that inspires respect. I don't believe we write for ourselves and I don't believe it when people say they don't care about what the audience thinks. Mamet once said that an audience can consist of individual idiots but collectively they're always smarter than you. That is absolutely true. You can always feel it when you're watching a performance, that sense of the energy in the room, how taut it is when things are right and how it starts to sag when they aren't, when they're dull, flat, boring. You can just feel that the audience is dying away from it. I take that into consideration when writing. The desire is to perfect writing skills so that there isn't a moment where the audience won't be wondering what comes next.

CJ *Do you consider the role of the playwright as having to take responsibility for anything other than the writing of the play?*

TS Such as?

CJ *Let's take it on the mechanics of the production first.*

TS Once you're finished writing, I don't think the playwright needs to assume any other responsibility. That assumes a certain amount of willingness to give yourself over to interpretation and allow for a margin of error. Maybe it's not error but it will differ, it will invariably differ from how you see it in your head. You can only ever really influence the productions that you're invited to take part in and even then only to a degree. It's also a joyful process to be part of the play coming to life and it's one of the rare opportunities that you get as a playwright when you're not entirely alone. But ultimately you can't go around the world following your plays wherever they are produced, making sure that even in different languages and different cultures every note is right, every meaning is correct. Inherently in plays there is a factor of interpretation that we have to allow for. Having said that, the rehearsal process is a great test for what works and what doesn't, so I often do a last draft in the rehearsals of the first production.

CJ 3 Winters *is a piece about Croatian history from the Second World War to the present through the perspective of women in one house. It found its first production at the National Theatre in the UK, a story that's very specific about another country's history.*

TS   I never thought of the play as a play about Croatian history and I never pitched it like that. I really wanted to write about women, women in one family throughout a hundred years and look at what happened to them, to their position in life, to their voices, to their sense of self, to their self-awareness, how each generation impacted on the next, particularly with the background, the backdrop of the terrifically turbulent events of Croatian history. So the fact that each generation lived in a different country, and under a very different regime, I figured must have done something to influence how those female voices developed. That was the kernel of the story. Because it's so rare to see a big family saga unapologetically set in a different country and dealing with a lot of that country's historical events on a major British stage, the discussion was moved to it being about *Croatian* history. But that was not the intention of the play. It would be a dauntingly ambitious idea to write about Croatia's very complicated history. I think the theater and the audiences responded to the play because politics and history are woven into domesticity and intimacy, and are instrumental in shaping the lives of the characters.

CJ   *You're talking about stories that connect with everybody; stories about women, migration, and migration is a theme that seems to run through your work and that is our story of now.*

TS   It really is, but I'm not really an issue writer. I would hate to be forced to write issue plays. So even though the plays contain issues in them, I'm just trying to make sense of core things about existence. It's astonishing that migration, one of the core experiences of humankind, is continually such a contentious issue. That's worth exploring over and over.

CJ   *Do you often feel that you're asked to be a spokesperson for your country, as opposed to being an artist?*

TS   That kind of happened with *3 Winters*, in that Croatia really did get a lot of exposure through that play. The thing with small countries and their writers is that they're destined to only get a spotlight on them in the international arena if something atrocious is happening in their country. As unfamiliar parts of the world flare up on CNN maps, we see writers from those parts coming into prominence. Some of them survive in the international world and some of them fade back to obscurity as things in their countries settle down. The fact that the National Theatre put on that play even though Croatia really isn't on anybody's radar at the moment, except maybe when it comes to its beaches . . . that, I think, is a testament to both the play and the broadminded vision of the National Theatre.

I'm not trying to be an ambassador for my country. By virtue of being a Croat I promote it with my work, but I don't think I have a responsibility to do so. Playwrights only have a responsibility to tell their truth. But we live in a world, I think because of the migratory nature of it, where it's increasingly becoming more important where you're from and if you're not from here, it's something that follows you around. I don't think I'm ever allowed to forget that I'm the Other, in a polite and sometimes even jovial way, but the label is there.

CJ *To your work, to you as an artist, or to you as a human being?*

TS Maybe all of it. I'm not sure how much that is to do with this culture. To a degree it's simply to do with the magnitude of a place like London, the sheer volume of the people involved in the industry. There's a need for shorthand and reference frames.

CJ *For me* 3 Winters *is a story about Europe, a story of the European Union, and you've talked about being interested in writing about being on the brink of great change. So as a Croatian you've experienced Croatia going through great change and you explore some of this in the play. You arrived in the UK from a country that wasn't part of the EU but which is now, and now we in the UK may not be part of the EU soon. Are we on the brink of a great change, and is this exciting you as a writer?*

TS Every time is exciting for a writer. The world is changing immensely and I think we're intellectually able to understand that the map of our world is clearly changing because hundreds of thousands of refugees won't stop coming. That's one thing. The other thing is climate change, which is soon also going to cause mass migration. We have all the information that how we live now is unsustainable. Probably within our lifetimes, our lives are going to change quite dramatically. But I think we're emotionally incapable of understanding that change because otherwise I don't think we'd just keep going as if nothing is happening; it's virtually keep calm and carry on. In terms of Europe, I do think that the repercussions of leaving Europe are completely unforeseen and it will have a lot of very long-term effects on this country. The likelihood of this country falling apart if we leave Europe is considerable. What scares me the most is a future Europe broken up into separate, isolated little countries run by conservative, right-wing governments, which is what it seems we're heading toward.

CJ *How do playwriting and the playwright fit into the digital age of storytelling?*

TS   I'm a bit of a dinosaur. I'm not on Twitter and I'm not on Facebook; I am addicted to my phone and emails but I find Twitter and Facebook quite irritating and unnerving, actually. I have great confidence in the tenaciousness of theater and playwriting. All our experience, all our wisdom, is in stories that we tell, that playwrights and writers have been telling for thousands of years. But if we start to compete with the digital age, try to make the work somehow digital-friendly and edgier in that sense, I fear that's a losing battle. However much it may seem that playwriting is old-fashioned, I don't think there's anything more powerful than live people on stage in a real-time performance. I think we have more to fear from a political agenda that cuts the funding to the arts and reserves it for the elites.

Janice Connolly

Janice Connolly is a founder member of Women and Theatre and has been its Artistic Director for the past twenty years. She has written, directed, and performed in many projects for the company. Janice is a trained teacher and has worked both in mainstream education and as an education project worker for the children's charity Barnardo's. In 2017 Janice was awarded the British Empire Medal for services to Community Arts in the West Midlands. She is also a successful performer in her own right and has featured in series such as Peter Kay's *Phoenix Nights* (Channel 4), *Dead Man Weds* (ITV), and *Thin Ice* (BBC2) as well as appearing twice in *Coronation Street*. Her theater roles include *White Open Spaces* (Pentabus), *A Taste of Honey* (New Vic Theatre, Stoke), and *Tartuffe* (The Rep, Birmingham). Her alter-ego, Mrs. Barbara Nice, is a well-loved comedy circuit headliner as well as a Birmingham icon.

Caroline Jester   *What is a playwright?*

Janice Connolly   It's what it says on the tin; it's somebody who writes plays. I personally think it means someone who writes plays that are going to be performed, because that's my experience. I don't think I've ever written anything on spec without knowing that it was going to be performed. I know that other people's experience is different, and that you might see yourself as a playwright because you write plays. But to me it's connected to performance: You write a play and it gets performed and the two go together.

CJ   *You've never written a play without knowing that it is going to be performed. Is that because of your company? You're Artistic Director of Women and Theatre and the company has been going for over thirty years.*

JC And [I am] one of the founder members. I have written or been involved with devising I should imagine at least three plays a year over thirty-three years, so that's ninety-nine plays.

CJ *Ninety-nine plays.*

JC At least.

CJ *And they've all been performed?*

JC Yes. But what's the definition of a "play"? I've been involved with writing stuff that gets performed in theatrical ways.

CJ *Does the audience influence your writing?*

JC There has always been a purpose in mind, with the writing that I've been involved in. It's always been based on research and talking to people who are directly at the heart of the subject matter. So the people who it's about, they influence it, very much so. I care very much about audiences and you want to make it accessible so of course you think about the audience when you're writing. But the first port of call is thinking about the people who are at the heart of the subject matter that I'm trying to explore. They come first in the process.

CJ *Do you consider the role of the playwright as having to take responsibility for anything other than the writing of the play?*

JC The whole thing, because I'm part of a company. The whole of the story, the whole of the set-up, the casting, the marketing, the reason behind why we're doing it. Thinking of the idea in the first place, [and] what areas do we want to look at next? It's a total of coming up with all the aspects.

CJ *I've read that your aim is to "reflect the language and lives of ordinary people giving voices to those not usually heard." How do you identify voices that aren't usually heard? And the use of the word "language" is really interesting.*

JC   The language, it's just brilliant, it's beautiful. One of the many, many projects we do are seasonal shows. This came from an idea that if people are institutionalized, maybe for mental health reasons or age reasons, they're not as able to feel the seasons as much. It was an idea of trying to bring seasons into institutions. We've done one show about Spring and we've done a Winter, Christmassy, one, and I'm just doing an Autumn one now. And the way that we're doing that is going to talk to older people in institutions about Autumn. Writing down all the things people say, and then going back with actors and work-shopping some of those ideas and then I write from all of that. One of the things this fantastic woman—who is in a mental health ward—was saying was that she'd never had bonfires or fireworks or anything like that because her father was a drunkard and they had a terrible childhood. This other woman said to her, "you have risen from the ashes of your childhood." It was so beautiful, such a great phrase, and I think people say the most amazing things. I don't think playwrights necessarily have the best turn of phrase.

I'm particularly interested in class. I'm absolutely proud to be working class by culture and by values, and I want that language represented. I want the terms and phrases and the way people express themselves represented because it's so eloquent and beautiful. I want it to be listened to, to be shown. We mustn't think that theater and language are only for a certain type of person. It's fundamental to everybody and everybody can get it. I was brought up watching *Play for Today* on the television and the Wednesday play with my mum, who is a housewife. We watched some of the most wonderful plays together and she got every single nuance. Theater is for everybody and the language of the streets, of families.

CJ   I think that word, "voices," is often used when people mean working class. I'm fed up of using that word "voices"; let's talk about it in terms of . . .

JC   Class.

CJ   Yes, that word.

JC   I think class is extremely important, and I do think the language of the working class and of all those communities really is so fantastically beautiful. I've certainly learned my craft through having to do it. Not sitting in a room and going, "I'm going to be a playwright." We wanted to make this work and the way you did it was by becoming a writer. I was initially a performer, but I've become a writer.

CJ *You also cross artforms. You've got your wonderful character Mrs. Barbara Nice, who you perform on the comedy circuit and you are adapting for a new sitcom for the BBC. She's very politically active.*

JC Yes, she is.

CJ *When I watch you as Mrs. Barbara Nice, it must be like a play that never ends because you're constantly putting her in new situations. How does that connect with your craft as a writer?*

JC The time when it feels most like writing craft is when I do shows for the Edinburgh Festival. That is like gathering, thinking what's this going to be about? I wrote a show several years ago for the Festival called "Squirrel Proof." At the heart of it is the way we try and keep nature at bay. If you look now we can't see any animals outside here—if you're lucky, you might see a bird. We want nature to go away and not to be around us. It was about Barbara finding some squirrels in her attic, trying to get rid of them, and realizing they'd gone of their own accord and then missing them; that was the story. Within that, you have to make it funny and I do a lot of audience interaction, but you've got to really script the audience interaction. People might think it's lazy to do audience interaction, but it's really complicated because you've got to get it in the right stages so that they trust you. You give out signifiers that this might happen in a minute. You do a lot of callbacks in comedy; it's very, very detailed. In terms of performing, the rest of the times when I'm doing sets in comedy clubs, you're adding to it all the time. But once I've written an Edinburgh show, then I can take bits out of that and put it into my set.

CJ *How do playwriting and the playwright fit into the digital age of storytelling?*

JC I think we've got to be careful in that we don't think digital is what everybody wants. I've just been doing some work, which is basically talking to people as Barbara about what they treasure. I went up to this lad and he had his phone and I said, "Do you treasure your phone?" He said, "No. I hate my phone, I'm just doing it because there's nothing else to do." I think we mustn't fall into the trap of thinking that's what everybody wants, things to be digital.

There's no replacement for live performance and the witness of people sitting together, watching something together, because you can feel each other's response. I know digital doesn't necessarily mean on your own, though.

I performed last night as Barbara and this woman who had just come out of hospital said to me, "this has made me feel so great, it's much better than watching Netflix." It's about witnessing together and breathing the same air as the performers. However, I think digital stuff can be great in performance. You do a lot of great audience interaction by getting people to use phones but it must be for purpose not just for fashion. It's great that we've got another tool and I'd never say I'd never use it, because I think I probably will actually: It's good to be seen to be *au fait* with stuff, and I don't want people to put Barbara in a box. If it fits in stylistically—if the theme of it is correct, and it fits in—then that's brilliant, but I don't think everything should be digital. It's another color in our palette. It's something to use, but only if it really serves the central purpose of what that piece of theater is about.

Neil LaBute

Neil LaBute is a film director, screenwriter, playwright, and actor. His plays and films include: *In the Company of Men*, *The Shape of Things*, *bash*, *reasons to be pretty*, *The Mercy Seat*, *Fat Pig*, *Autobahn*, and *wrecks*. He has written and directed many films, among them *Possession* (based on the A. S. Byatt novel), *Some Velvet Morning*, and *Dirty Weekend*. He created the TV series *Billy & Billie*, also directing or writing several of its episodes.

Caridad Svich   *What is a playwright?*

Neil LaBute   That's a good question and one that seems to be ever-changing. The good news is probably that, more and more, it can be whatever you want it to mean and you're still at least partially correct. Is "playwright" just a "writer of plays?" Yes, I suppose that's true and as there are nearly all kinds of plays and many genres and forms, it's nearly impossible to really find an adequate absolute for the term. These days, however, plays are built in many ways and that makes the task even that much more difficult. Groups write plays together but also fashion them out of gathered information and dialogue, use bits of news articles, create fairy tales, and/or take classic texts and mash them about into something akin to "stone soup" to create their work for the stage. That's all good and I'm happy to let anybody experiment on the stage and call it what they like. To me, though, a playwright is still that craftsperson who slowly and deliberately creates a work for the stage that entertains and educates and challenges its audience. All dialogue or virtually none, what matters is that clarity of purpose—an honest and straightforward effort to create a story that is best served by being on a stage in front of a live audience. The rest is glitter and artifice.

CS   *Does the audience influence your writing?*

NLB   The audience definitely influences my writing but in ways different than you might imagine. I don't think about them in terms of "will they like this play?" or "will they enjoy this character?" as much as I care about connecting with them in a visceral way with the material I present (both story and character). I want to get close to them and make them feel the events in a real way—to break the fourth wall, to look them squarely in the eye, and challenge them to leave, but force them to stay (by making the work compelling, not by having guards at the doors). I care more about being true to my characters than I do to the audience, but I want to do such good work that the audience finds that they have no choice but to continue watching.

CS *How much does the role of the playwright influence your writing? Is responsibility connected to audience?*

NLB I have an immense responsibility to myself as a writer and to the plays that I write and to those characters. I respect that bond far more than I do my bond with the audience. The one contract I have with the audience is to try and tell them a story, one that they haven't heard before or at least haven't heard in this particular way before. Outside of that, all bets are off. I can say whatever I want or go wherever I need to in search of that story and this is the very place that I should be raising the questions that I raise: In the theater. We are on the safest and yet most treacherous ground imaginable when we're in the theater. It's a place of magic and possibility. I don't go there (as an audience member) to be told things I already know or believe in. I go to be surprised and challenged or confronted with and that's the same way I want to serve it up as an artist. I am responsible to my characters, to truthfully tell their stories, and to begin and end their stories as they're meant to begin and end. Not in some false way that might make an audience feel better. That's just pandering bullshit.

CS *How does playwriting help a global dialogue?*

NLB Each new play gives us a lens by which we can see one more little portion of the world, whether that lens comes from the US, UK, Turkey, or Korea. Everyone has a story and/or a new take on an old story or form. It's hugely important that we nurture new artists and venues that support new artists—but also reiterate to new artists that a "stage" can be almost anything and anywhere and for them to not worry about playing on Broadway or at the National Theatre in their respective countries, but spending their time writing and then getting that work in front of an audience, of whatever size and in whatever space they can. That's what "theater" is: There is no one-size theater or audience that is more important than an author hearing their work in front of *an* audience. Be happy when your work is on its feet. Be glad to see your work and the work of your peers in reading and performance: It means that even after thousands of years, the recipe still holds, and the spell that good theater casts over an audience still exists. It's a bit of magic. It's a bit of religion and it's a lot of hard work that creates the magic that I still believe in, nearly thirty years into my career.

CS *So, gotta ask, especially given how your works are often reviewed: Morality and theater. Thoughts?*

NLB This is a tough one to answer, since I've so often been accused of not possessing a moral compass! Of course, I disagree and think that I have created a fairly large series of plays that are asking honest and moral questions, although again I do not feel a responsibility to do it. I think it's fairly vain of us to believe that we'll change the opinions of an audience (or even one audience member), but we do have the ability to have them see things from a new perspective, to hear a question raised that might not have been asked in that particular way before, or deal with an issue that, up until now, has not been on their radar for whatever reason. Will ninety minutes of my work turn their attentions around 180 degrees? I doubt it, but who knows? Anything is possible. Theater lives in the realm of possibility and not probability, and that's what I love about it.

CS *How do you approach telling stories about the human spirit?*

NLB The human spirit is one of the rare things that I believe to be most similar in people everywhere. We all have a certain set of desires— to live and love and endure—that gets captured in a specific way by writers as diverse as Chekhov, Churchill, and Congreve, and yet we understand that all they have to say (or most of it, anyway), regardless of language or time period, because there are eternal truths that authors somehow touch upon that are correct now and tomorrow and forever.

That happens in the US and the UK, and on various stages in countries throughout the world. That's the way it has always been and I hope that it will always be so. That's the real power of what we do. Sometimes, despite all the other dialogue and jokes and insights, we say something right and important and worth saying. Something of great and lasting and universal power. The chance to try and do that makes it worth getting up in the morning and putting pen to paper, time and time again.

CS *What has changed in the field, as you see it, in terms of mentorship, opportunities for artists, modes and means of production, and intergenerational dialogue about craft?*

NLB I think the fact that someone has been brave enough to put their voice down on paper and allowed it to be played out in front of an audience (whatever the size of that audience) is already a sign of their grace and strength. That voice might not make the most noise or be heard from all ends of the earth, but it doesn't make it any less valid or important or vital to our artform and to the greater dialogue of mankind. I think every day people or companies or theaters all over the world are working to create new programs that help writers and artists find their footing in some way. Some programs are surely lost, too, so the job is unending, but that is the way of the world. I think the opportunities are boundless for the zealous artist, from monetary help to newer and more numerous avenues in which to make their work visible to the world (things like YouTube and the like), so I think we're in a very healthy place. Do we still have places to go? Without question, female artists and artists of color still don't get as much work in major venues as their male counterparts, and hopefully that will continue to be rectified. If we all do our part, though, even in the smallest way, we cannot help but make progress. From workshops to teaching to internships, I try to "send the elevator back down," as Jack Lemmon memorably put it.

CS *How do playwriting and the playwright fit into the digital age of storytelling?*

NLB I don't want to believe that it has anything to do with the digital age—an age that I am less than interested in or comfortable with—but that there is something in that particular story that resonates with our shared human experiences, be they lived out in New York or New Delhi or Johannesburg. Stories from the theater have been experienced and appreciated across the world long before any sort of "digital age" existed and I think the same thing will be true years from now when we are in the middle of some other new-fangled age. *Oedipus* and *Woyzeck* and *Death of a Salesman* have worked their magic across the ages because they work as both literature and stories, which when lifted from their literary roots, move us in the telling of their individual tales. It's not magic but sometimes it appears to be—why one story moves people and another one doesn't.

Erik Ehn

Erik Ehn's work includes: *Maria Kizito; Heavenly Shades of Night Are Falling, Yermedea; Drunk Still Drinking; The Saint Plays,* and a series of seventeen plays, *Soulographie,* on the history of the US in the twentieth century from the point of view of its genocides. His works have been produced in San Francisco (Intersection, Thick Description, Yugen), Seattle (Annex, Empty Space), Austin (Frontera), New York (BACA, Whitney Museum), Atlanta (7 Stages), and Los Angeles (Cal Rep, Museum of Jurassic Technology), and Belgrade (Dah), to name but a few. He conducts annual trips to Rwanda/Uganda, bringing teams to study the history there, and explore the ways art is participating in recovery from violence. He is Professor of Theatre Arts and Performance at Brown University and a former Dean of CalArts.

Caridad Svich   *What is a playwright?*

Erik Ehn   An energy toward and a bending from contact; an electromagnetic field that purifies anxiety to yearning—around and about the thing itself. Writers are not attractive in themselves but help create a field of fascination, charging space by rushing-to and refraining-from.

CS   *Does the audience influence your writing?*

EE   An audience is defined as those who have influence on your work. Audience are your co-makers—those you can depend on from the first moment of fear when you fall out of your head and toward an idea. An audience equals the excitement of your first idea.

CS   *Do you consider the role of the playwright as having to take responsibility for anything other than the writing of the play?*

EE   A play is a sound trying to get silence right, and action trying to get stillness right. As humans, for a while, we're gifted with sound and action, and charged with giving these gifts away (the best gift turns the receiver into a giver). The purpose of a record is not to locate a fact but to establish a pattern, a rhythm, a music. A record should in itself be invisible and empty-headed; a play should disappear, and represent nothing—a mirror, especially a confused or confusing one, that does not allow for the fetish of the image (Borges?).

CS *Be wary of the big idea, I tell some of my students. There is a tendency to want to write to the big idea but it can actually get in the way of the work. Plays can come from anywhere. Where do yours come from?*

EE As much as possible, I try not to have ideas. I don't know what ideas *are*—their content or reality. Mostly I'm looking for an excuse to hang out with people I love (love being complex and ultimately indifferent to me, as an individual). Structures and tasks are appealing—barn raisings or razings; the challenge of knotting or unknotting poetry is often a nice activity (drawing ensemble around finding an original sound—or constructing a resonator to attract and translate a sound heard early . . .).

CS *But what about form, then? How should we think about it?*

EE Does a form live? Or does it attract (and frustrate) life?
   I go with poetics the way I rely on a standard measure for the height of a step . . . Conventions allow me to locomote faster, even thoughtlessly. Or there are other conventions that help me move slowly, thoughtfully. Pre-existence is an aspect of rhythm . . .

CS *But the shape of the thing. Of where it takes place. Does this shape the shape? Shape you?*

EE Again, I avoid consideration; I try and both make and respond to invitation—which implies the use of attractive emptiness. Where space is empty, spare, neglected . . . or prosperous and needs to be emptied: That's where I want to go. The resource is hospitality . . . which relates to host, which relates to guest, which relates to ghost. I want to be empty in the way I want my hospitable spaces wide-empty; I want to be a stage for the Holy Ghost.

When a space is full of too much expectation, especially expectation of outcome, I back out. This frequently makes me rude.

CS *How do you negotiate the process, then, of locating a moral compass for the audience in the work?*

EE Writing and performance are caught up in learning and teaching seeing. Teaching teaches learning, and comes from learning. A play (for example) that isn't learning is incapable of addressing its responsibilities to teach. So a play needs uncertainty, dependence, ignorance, and thirst. These things, mainly, and first. Then we take time with experiments (play equals taking time, taking time with experiments)—earnest effort to find direction by stumbling down this path, then this path. A play is a set of mistakes forgiven by the promise that the play will somehow quit at a point deeper into the maze or forest or conundrum. A play is what we do, experimentally, so we don't need to do it again, so that we are ready to do and to be in a way that's closer to our secret or closer to our revelation. *Maria Kizito*, *Heavenly Shades*, and *Soulographie* are failures loaded with meaning for me, and the infinite, following process of finding forgiveness is the stuff of community-formation. These plays and projects are starting, in the degree to which they are disappearing.

CS *The point of vanishing. Yes. Where all art is connected. And in performance, constant negotiation of the vanishing element. Phantom traces. But you're head of playwriting at Brown University. You are mentoring and that work is not one of vanishing.*

EE A mentor, like Pi, keeps you bending, holds you in perpetual irresolution, in a shapely and specific way. Laurie Carlos and Mac Wellman are great mentors to me; I don't see them that much, but the sense of them in my life is my math—the principle by which I turn; make script. I don't always hold my plays out to *them*, but I always write in the shadow of their math.

Nothing has changed in terms of mentorship; back to ghosts, it is a kind of haunting, and haunting has been the same since we first invented longing and invisibility (math is notation for invisibility, script sought by visibility, in longing). Mentors are hosts, ghosts, invisible guests—the ethic by which we give and receive courtesy.

CS *I think of mentors as guides, pointing paths, possible ones. Or impossible ones. But to ways of being in the world, conducting a life in the arts or in life!*

EE Find art by moving into the world, as we find Christ. An impulse in art-making may lead us to loneliness, but always and ultimately has faith in assembly. Know your heart, and make it public—be willing to share it. You're in for a lifetime of frustration if there is any sense of private property in your process.

Partnership isn't a bad idea—somebody who can help you a) know your heart and b) pay rent.

CS *Truth and power. Root cause of much writing. Speaking truth to . . . or the desire. Negotiating the balance of ego. We show our best behavior and our worst in plays sometimes. We show who we are, and who we might be. The voice of the one silenced need speak. Not just the one with megaphone.*

EE Two dimensions to bringing your light out from under a bushel— allowing your light out, and allowing the gaze in. We *show* ourselves as who we are, and (sometimes a separate courage) we *allow ourselves to be seen* as who we are. "Radiance" is equitable distribution.

Gather to speak, gather to listen; the craft celebrates neither the light nor its reception but the lifting of the bushel. Gather and gather and gather—with one other, with many others; with spirit, with matter—if with spirit, then spirit in the world. If material, then matter as icon—as path.

Find that principle that in itself is absolutely enough—even in your hunger, even when you're shamed, you know that this faithful idea or audience (material, immaterial) or lover or word is enough . . . [It is] Likely not always enough to make you happy, but the sources of your misery are oppression and misery, not insufficiency. And likewise, find a geography or geometry that casts you into a space (the "there" in your *Dasein*) that is ample enough so that you and all you carry are themselves carried—or at least floating, contingent, not all-you. Find the Not You that holds you in suspense. We make nothing, acquire nothing, leave nothing, and this is an absolute freedom.

But to get real for a minute, our society (including government) needs to take better care of our living cultural treasures and intangible cultural assets . . . God bless Michelle Memran and all she's doing for Irene Fornès.

CS *Indeed. Fornès taught us all. And is still teaching us. Through the work we keep discovering. Through the lessons we remember. Irene sometimes talked about career when we were at the Lab (Hispanic Playwrights-in-Residence Laboratory at INTAR Theatre in New York City). She spoke about how if she had "branded" herself like Sam Shepard had done, her career might have really taken off, but she was too restless an artist. She didn't want to "fix" her terrain. She wanted open terrain from which to write. Follow curiosity. Desire. Passion. Invitation. But she did understand that the word career mattered more and more to those coming up in the field.*

EE My career is not significant. I am not in motion when I am most myself—I'm still, and being created. The imitative acts of creation that I perform are there to preserve me in time, so that I may be operated on (life is durational performance, a show; I show as I am shown). When, just a few times, passing times, no longer retrievable, I have been able to tell the truth . . . then I've been most enlivened by the energy of praise. Praise is the restoration of words to their source—words abandoning language. I make nothing; I am made; what I do means to praise this making, means to fail my language.

I personally have nothing, and am not interested in claiming a career. The Good is held in common; I write just enough to hang out with people who have actual talent, and we're any of us worth something at the mathematical center that is in the midst of us all, and in no one of us. Converge, convene, gather. The work is a way to get there—to the common ground—an excuse, not a destination. Time is, definitionally, temporary. Art is an impulse in pattern (longing without resolve; no end-in-time). Art objects are accidents and intentions; art itself is more.

CS *How do playwriting and playwrights fit in the digital age?*

EE To paraphrase Brecht: "In the digital age, will there also be singing? Yes, there will also be singing about the digital age."

Christopher Shinn

Christopher Shinn made his playwriting debut in 1998 with *Four* at the Royal Court Theatre. His other plays include: *Against*; *Other People*; *The Coming World*; *What Didn't Happen*; *On the Mountain*; *Where Do We Live*; *Dying City*; *Now or Later*; *Picked*; *Teddy Ferrara*; and *An Opening in Time*. His work has been produced at the Almeida, Royal Court, Donmar Warehouse, Lincoln Center Theater, and Manhattan Theatre Club, among others. His adaptation of *Hedda Gabler* for the Roundabout premiered on Broadway in 2009. His plays are published in the US by TCG, in the UK by Methuen Drama, and in acting editions from Dramatists Play Service and Playscripts. In 2005, Shinn received an Obie in Playwriting and a Guggenheim Fellowship. He was a finalist for the Pulitzer Prize in Drama in 2008 and shortlisted for the *Evening Standard* Theatre Award for Best Play in 2009. He teaches playwriting at the New School in New York City.

Caridad Svich   *What is a playwright?*

Christopher Shinn   A playwright searches for truth and for clear and open communication. I can try to convey my soul, my truth through a play; I don't think I should work too hard to control how audiences respond to them. Art is not about imposing a point of view in an authoritarian way on another. It's about being open, communicating openly, and hoping this openness, which entails deep respect and consideration of the other, will allow a dialogue to truly begin.

CS   *Does the audience influence your writing?*

CShinn   Because I can only know myself then my job is simply to do that—my sense of truth is based on my self-scrutiny. My sense of what's true may resonate with some; others may think I'm wrong based on their own self-scrutiny. Some may not like my sense of what's true because it threatens their psychic equilibrium for one reason or another.

Difference is traumatizing and one reason I resist representing myself is I am afraid that the ways I am different will lead others to reject me. Hopefully, being aware of this gives me the courage to tell the truth as I see it, regardless of the possibility that I will be inviting punishment, rejection, or other forms of negation.

CS *Do you consider the role of the playwright as having to take responsibility for anything other than the writing of the play?*

CShinn I think a writer has a responsibility to tell the truth and to communicate effectively. So I spend my time trying to locate the truth in myself and then find a way to communicate it that feels successful— clear and alive. I probably spend the most time worrying that what I am representing is not true enough, does not have enough truth in it. How can I convey more truth without overburdening the text? That is the work of revision.

CS *Related to the responsibility of the playwright/text-builder, is the moral compass of the artist. How do you wrestle with or position your moral compass vis a vis artmaking when you work on a piece?*

CShinn Because I live in the world I think about the world, but mostly I think about myself. Even when my play is dramatizing something or investigating something happening in the world, I hope the audience will fundamentally receive the work as a single psyche scrutinizing itself as honestly as it can. Because we perceive everything through our psyches, I want the exploration of the psyche to be foremost. I want my plays to say something about me, not the world.

With *Dying City* I was thinking about why violent pornography excited me, and I tried to link that to Abu Ghraib and war in general as that was happening at the time. With *Now or Later* I was thinking about my rage at my psychoanalyst, and that became an exploration of how the intellect can be used to rationalize all kinds of primitive emotions and actions, in a time of ongoing conflicts, aggression, and terrorism. In *Teddy Ferrara* I was going through a rough period personally and found myself remembering that in my late teens and early twenties I had trouble telling the difference between desire and love, and between genuine suffering and emotional manipulation. This turned into a play about how sexuality and trauma exist in and at universities today, in an age of increasing awareness of interpersonal abuse and bullying and dominant culture oppression.

Because social reality is real, my plays have social reality in them. I don't think I could write a "pure psyche" play because I don't believe the psyche is untouched by society. But many writers I admire, like Ibsen and Beckett, do have such stripped-down plays toward the end of their writing careers, and I often wonder what a "more psyche, less society" play would look like from me.

CS *You mention Ibsen and Beckett. I am not being facetious when I ask why do you admire them? What stirs you about their works? Are there specific pieces that you call upon or look to and why?*

CShinn   I admire any writer that I feel really puts her own psyche onstage and manages to look at it critically. I think this is very rare! I think most writers project their psyches into their plays one way or another, but it feels rare to me that a writer self-scrutinizes meaningfully. Shakespeare will always be a model in this regard because the tragedies in particular seem to scrutinize motive at the deepest level. Ibsen's entire journey as a writer with each play is less examination of the world and more examination of himself. The plays move in a profound inward direction. Beckett's work is almost painfully internal, charting the psychosis of everyday life in a world rent with violence and meaninglessness. More recently, I think Caryl Churchill manages a focus on the intimate even in the context of highly political work. I feel her psyche dismantling itself in order to take a frank look at all of it. Sarah Kane's best work I think is essentially self-scrutinizing. What all these writers seem to find in themselves is violence. These plays are not an interrogation of violence "out there" but of violence "in here"—again, which doesn't mean they are apolitical. But the fundamental exploration is the self. Kushner does this in *Intelligent Homosexual*, Mamet in *The Cryptogram*—both plays are profound explorations of narcissism, arrogance, denial, emotional withdrawal. This is the kind of drama I admire and aspire toward.

CS *Do you consider yourself part of a circle of artists?*

CShinn   I have been in psychoanalysis with the same person for over a decade. That's made an impact on who I am and how I write. I have a few very close friendships that have affected my writing. With these friends I've developed a common vocabulary that has helped me think more clearly about my life and what I believe about reality, as well as how to communicate what I think and feel to others more successfully. Beyond that there is not a really big circle. Because I think art is about communication, I focus on really deep, intimate, even intense communication with just a few people rather than seek a broader circle of folks to share with. I'm not a lone wolf but I'm probably not too far off.

CS   The ecology of theater/performance is strong but it is also fragile. I am deeply interested in the idea that the "small" or what may be perceived as a "weak" voice in society actually can radiate out with the power of its own truth and integrity.

CShinn   I always find it amusing when a playwright thinks of themselves as famous. There are maybe three playwrights in America who could correctly perceive themselves to be famous—and even that is pushing it. To be a playwright means to be in the margins. But the margins are the center now in a way—or rather, there is no center anymore. Because there is so much content out there, not only via the arts with the spread of new technologies and modes of distribution, but also self-created through social media, I think fame doesn't exist today the way it once did. Even famous people aren't really that famous. Theater people certainly aren't. So I think to be in the margins now is really to be where everyone is, more or less. Of course some people are more influential than others but I don't think fame is that big a deal anymore, and people who think it is are holding onto an old form of society, an antiquated way of being. I think lots of people want to believe the center still exists, and so there is a kind of shared delusion that it's there, and that has an impact. But really it's a mirage.

But when I'm tempted to set up strength and weakness against each other and fantasize that weakness will last longer because it is deeper and truer than the bluster of strength—then I try to stop myself. Because I don't think it's good to imagine some idealized future where justice is realized and the values I hold most dear are ascendant. We live in a time when it is not foolish, in fact it is important, to consider the possibility of apocalypse, suffering beyond what human beings have yet had to endure on this earth. Imagining a just future seems like a way of avoiding thinking about the overwhelming problems of today.

I confess that every once in a while I get cynical and think I should just "go big." It seems more appealing to people and maybe I could get more fame and money that way. And when I get anxious about my students' suffering financially, I think I should teach them to be strong and big so they can make lots of money and be safe in a scary world.

But I know all that is essentially perverse—favoring trickery over truth. I think the truth is always partial, evolving, complex if not contradictory—and so will always be most at home alongside the "weak" and not the "strong." And if that means the truth will lose out in the end, so be it. At the end of the day you have to pick a side, and I have chosen truth over power.

CS *How do playwriting and the playwright fit into the digital age?*

CShinn I think digital culture both has and hasn't changed us. People use technology for three reasons: To get information; to communicate; and to distract themselves. These were achievable options in other ways before digital culture took off. I am sure the ease and ubiquity of technology mean that our notion of time and distance from others have changed, in a way I can't fully understand because I came of age before the technology explosion and so smoothly transitioned between the two eras. What it's like to be twenty-five now and never have known anything else I can't say. But I have young friends and manage to connect with them even as I feel they are different from me in some fundamental ways—there is enough overlap for relationship to occur. As technology becomes more and more integrated with our moment-to-moment living and functioning, we'll see if it alters human subjectivity even more. I expect it will. Narcissism has been a human problem from the start but technology may make it a likelier outcome for people, and harder to undo through culture. How capitalism and technology intersect is obviously crucial here. They go together, and together they appear unstoppable by anything but catastrophe.

Great drama has always articulated that human truth will forever exceed our capacity to understand and grasp it. I think that this tragic structure of human life will therefore be with us forever, and will unite people despite generational and cultural differences. Tragedy may have different era-dependent forms but its deep structures will remain the same no matter how much we "advance." I'm not usually an essentialist, but I do believe that the structure of the human psyche is tragic—that tragedy is the representation of what happens when we try to, or believe we can, flee this truth. I don't think much else in our culture agrees with this view of the psyche save for certain strains of religion, spiritual practice, and psychoanalysis.

My play *Teddy Ferrara* is a test of my theory since the play is set now but I based the action on my experiences in my late teens, when no one had cell phones and email was still pretty exotic. Hopefully the play feels truthful to those both younger and older than I am.